Praise for
Rachel Maddow's *Drift*

"Maddow's distinctive voice in *Drift* is highly intelligent, often incredulous, and intermittently humorously profane."
—*Washington Post*

"Provocative . . . asks fundamental questions about the process by which the U.S. now goes to war that pretty much never get asked by the media."
—Wired.com

"Lively but serious . . . her cheerfully snarky voice is instantly recognizable . . . a thought-provoking and timely book."
—*New York Times Book Review*

"Crosses partisan lines . . . a compelling, intelligent read filled with Maddow's trademark wit."
—*Chicago Sun-Times*

"Engaging but sobering . . . sometimes it takes a gutsy, determined woman—a Nellie Bly, Rachel Carson, Ida Tarbell, Elizabeth Neuffer, Molly Ivins, or Rachel Maddow—to hang a literary lantern on a revolting situation."
—*Austin American-Statesman*

THE #1 NEW YORK TIMES BESTSELLER

MORE PRAISE FOR

Drift

"Thank Ms. Maddow for picking this and every other fight that *Drift* provokes. It will be a smarter public debate than the kinds we're used to."
—**Janet Maslin,** *New York Times*

"Witty and worthwhile."
—*Military Times*

"Thoroughly researched . . . written in her signature broadcast style—provocative, satirical, passionate-bordering-on-outrage . . . Progressive fans of her show may already know what to expect. Yet the book still surprises."
—**Joseph Williams,** *Minneapolis Star Tribune*

"Full of head-smacking stories about America's military meddling and muddling . . . Maddow sounds an alarm this country needs to hear more than almost any other."
—**Catherine Lutz,** *San Francisco Chronicle*

"*Drift* is infused with Maddow's sharp wit and her vast political knowledge. She dexterously reveals how we became the nation that spends more money on militarism than all other nations combined . . . 'The path to American amnesia is worth recalling on this Memorial Day,' wrote Tom Engelhardt. If you want to jog your memory, I encourage you to dive into Maddow's brilliant testament to remembering."
—**Natalie Wilson, MsMagazine.com**

"Recommended reading . . . There's a deadly serious argument here that deserves way more attention than it gets."
—**Kevin Drum, MotherJones.com**

"A biting, bracing tour of the rise of American military bloat . . . Rachel, if you can get those ideas a serious hearing, you will be much more than TV's funniest wonk."
  —**Emily Bazelon, Slate.com**

"Even though she's an ideological broadcaster, Maddow doesn't resort to demonization and hyperbole. It makes her case much stronger."
  —**Conor Friedersdorf, TheAtlantic.com**

"[Maddow's] observations are sharp and something Americans need to hear, particularly as the U.S. military beat the drums to preserve their XL budgets while the wars in Iraq and Afghanistan go away."
  —**Dan Simpson, *Pittsburgh Post-Gazette***

"In her hard-hitting debut, popular MSNBC host Maddow examines how the country has lost control of its national security policy . . . [Written with] humor and verve."
  —***Kirkus Reviews* (starred review)**

"In *Drift*, people who love Rachel Maddow will discover that her gift for finding amazing anecdotes and funny, revealing details totally translates to the page."
  —**Ira Glass, host of public radio's *This American Life***

"An insightful look at the cost of military vigilance to ideals of democracy."
  —***Booklist* (starred review)**

"Maddow wears her expertise lightly, counterbalancing hard details with phrases (e.g., 'the lemons-into-lemonade-moment' or 'the sliding-off-the-aircraft-carrier-thing') that keep her narrative invigorating . . . Highly recommended to all readers engaged in the world today and with how we got here."
  —***Library Journal* (starred review)**

"Rachel Maddow brings her passion, wit, cool common sense, and intellectual firepower to the epic and darkly farcical story of how America has declined into an overfunded and unchecked national security state . . . Could not be more timely."
  —Frank Rich, writer-at-large, *New York* magazine

"*Drift* is a provocative, important book that displays all the qualities of its author: intelligence, humor, depth, and originality. America's most charismatic liberal has crafted here an argument for skepticism about our military-industrial complex that will persuade many conservatives—a remarkable achievement."
  —Steve Coll, author of *Ghost Wars*

"Here's this conservative's assessment of Rachel Maddow's *Drift*: It's scathingly funny, deeply insightful, and informed throughout by a deep and abiding sense of patriotism. Bravo, Rachel!"
  —Andrew J. Bacevich, author of *Washington Rules:
    America's Path to Permanent War*

"Scathing . . . The author presents sharp, well-supported analyses . . . spicing them with a caustic wit . . . incisive."
  —*Publishers Weekly*

"Startlingly insightful and well-written . . . One of those rare political books that can transform Americans' understanding of what their government is actually doing."
  —Glenn Greenwald, author of *With Liberty and Justice for Some*

"*Drift* never makes the case that war might be necessary. America would be weakened dramatically if we had underreacted to 9/11. However, Rachel Maddow makes valid arguments that our country has been drifting towards questionable wars, draining our resources without sufficient input and time. People who like Rachel will love the book. People who don't will get angry, but aggressive debate is good for America. *Drift* is a book worth reading."
  —Roger Ailes, Chairman and CEO, FOX News

"Maddow revives a radically old-fashioned idea: waging war should be wrenchingly difficult for a nation, for that is what prevents unnecessary battles from being waged. This courageous book deserves to spark a national debate about the purpose of war."
   —**Naomi Klein, author of** ***The Shock Doctrine***

"Brilliant book. *Drift* will stun Americans with its portrait of a hyperventilating United States that has produced too many real live Dr. Strangelove moments . . . Every page informs and angers at the same time."
   —**Steve Clemons, Washington editor at large,** ***The Atlantic***

"Written with the flair for scintillating satire that has endeared Rachel Maddow to liberals and moderates alike—and infuriated neo-conservatives, evangelicals, and some tea partiers—*Drift* is funny, rich, and right. But at its end, when you put it down, you will be troubled. We are losing our republic and Ms. Maddow tells you why."
   —**Lawrence Wilkerson, professor of government and public policy at the College of William and Mary and former chief of staff to Secretary of State Colin Powell**

"*Drift* is a serious and carefully conceived piece of investigative reporting, illuminating a subject—the vast and mostly secret militarization of our society—that most Americans have no idea of, thanks in large part to the failure of many high-profile journalists to discuss it . . . Written in the same bright, clear, engaging style she brings to broadcast television."
   —**Matt Taibbi, author of** ***Griftopia***

"Rachel Maddow's *Drift* is a long-overdue and provocative examination of the abuses, excesses, and just plain foolish elements in our national security systems. These are issues that deserve our attention."
   —**Tom Brokaw, NBC News special correspondent and bestselling author of** ***The Greatest Generation***

Drift

The Unmooring of American
Military Power

Rachel
Maddow

BROADWAY PAPERBACKS

New York

BROADWAY

Copyright © 2012 by Rachel Maddow

All rights reserved.

Published in the United States by Broadway Paperbacks, an imprint of the Crown Publishing Group, a division of Random House, Inc., New York.

www.crownpublishing.com

Broadway Paperbacks and its logo, a letter B bisected on the diagonal, are trademarks of Random House, Inc.

Originally published in hardcover in the United States by Crown Publishers, an imprint of the Crown Publishing Group, a division of Random House, Inc., New York, in 2012.

Library of Congress Cataloging-in-Publication Data

Maddow, Rachel.
Drift: the unmooring of American military power/Rachel Maddow.—1st ed.
  p. cm.
Includes bibliographical references and index.
1. National security—United States. 2. United States—Military policy.
3. United States—Armed Forces—Appropriation and expenditures.
4. Militarism—United States. 5. Political culture—United States.
6. United States—Foreign relations—1989– 7. United States—Politics and government—1989– I. Title.
  UA23.M17 2012

  306.2'70973—dc23   2012000998

Printed in the United States of America

ISBN 978-0-307-46099-8

eISBN 978-0-307-46100-1

Book design by Ralph Fowler

Cover design by Christopher Brand

Cover photography and interior illustration by Kevin Van Aelst

10   9   8   7   6   5   4

First Paperback Edition

To former vice president Dick Cheney.

Oh, please let me interview you.

Of all the enemies to public liberty, war is, perhaps, the most to be dreaded, because it comprises and develops the germ of every other. War is the parent of armies; from these proceed debts and taxes; and armies, and debts, and taxes are the known instruments for bringing the many under the domination of the few. In war, too, the discretionary power of the Executive is extended; its influence in dealing out offices, honors, and emoluments is multiplied; and all the means of seducing the minds are added to those of subduing the force of the people. The same malignant aspect in republicanism may be traced in the inequality of fortunes and the opportunities of fraud growing out of a state of war, and in the degeneracy of manners and of morals engendered by both. No nation could reserve its freedom in the midst of continual warfare.

Those truths are well established. They are read in every page which records the progression from a less arbitrary to a more arbitrary government, or the transition from a popular government to an aristocracy or a monarchy.

—**James Madison, "Political Observations," April 20, 1795**

Contents

Prologue

Is It Too Late to Descope This?

IN THE LITTLE TOWN WHERE I LIVE IN HAMPSHIRE COUNTY, Massachusetts, we now have a "Public Safety Complex" around the corner from what used to be our hokey Andy Griffith–esque fire station. In the cascade of post-9/11 Homeland Security money in the first term of the George W. Bush administration, our town's share of the loot bought us a new fire truck—one that turned out to be a few feet longer than the garage where the town kept our old fire truck. So then we got some more Homeland money to build something big enough to house the new truck. In homage to the origin of the funding, the local auto detailer airbrushed on the side of the new truck a patriotic tableau of a billowing flaglike banner, a really big bald eagle, and the burning World Trade Center towers.

The American taxpayers' investment in my town's security didn't stop at the new safety complex. I can see further fruit of those Homeland dollars just beyond my neighbor's back fence. While most of us in town depend on well water, there are a few houses that for the past decade or so have been hooked up to a municipal water supply. And when I say "a few," I mean a few: I think there are seven houses on municipal water. Around the time we got our awesome giant new fire truck, we also got a serious security upgrade to that town water system. Its tiny pump house is about the size of two phone booths and accessible by a dirt driveway behind my neighbor's back lot. Or at least it used to be. The entire half-acre parcel of land around that pump house is now ringed by an eight-foot-tall chain-link fence topped with barbed wire, and fronted with a motion-sensitive electronically controlled motorized gate. On our side of town we call it "Little Guantánamo." Mostly it's funny, but there is some neighborly consternation over how frowsy Little Guantánamo gets every summer. Even though it's town-owned land, access to Little Guantánamo is apparently above the security clearance of the guy paid to mow and brush-hog. Right up to the fence, it's my neighbors' land and they keep everything trim and tidy. But inside that fence, the grass gets eye-high. It's going feral in there.

It's not just the small-potatoes post-9/11 Homeland spending that feels a little off mission. It's the big-ticket stuff too. Nobody ever made an argument to the American people, for instance, that the thing we ought to do in Afghanistan, the way we ought to stick it to Osama bin Laden, the way to dispense American tax dollars to maximize American aims in that faraway country, would be to build a brand-new neighborhood in that country's capital city full of rococo narco-chic McMansions and apartment/office buildings with giant sculptures of eagles on their roofs and stoned guards lounging on the sidewalks, wearing bandoliers and plastic boots. No one ever made the case that this is what America ought to build in response to 9/11. But that is what we built. An average outlay of almost $5 billion a month over ten years (and counting) has created a twisted war economy in Kabul. Afghanistan is still one of the four poorest countries on earth; but now it's one of the four poorest countries on earth with a neighborhood in its capital city that looks like New Jersey in the 1930s and '40s, when Newark mobsters built garish mansions and dotted the grounds with lawn jockeys and hand-painted neo-neoclassic marble statues.

Walking around this Zircon-studded neighborhood of Wazir Akbar Khān (named for the general who commanded the Afghan Army's rout of the British in 1842), one of the weirdest things is that the roads and the sewage and trash situation are palpably worse here than in many other Kabul neighborhoods. Even torqued-up steel-frame SUVs have a hard time making it down some of these desolate streets; evasive driving techniques in Wazir Akbar Khān often have more to do with potholes than potshots. One of the bigger crossroads in the neighborhood is an ad hoc dump. Street kids are there all day, picking through the newest leavings for food and for stuff to salvage or sell.

There's nothing all that remarkable about a rich-looking neighborhood in a poor country. What's remarkable here is that there aren't rich Afghan people in this rich Afghan neighborhood. Whether or not the owners of these giant houses would stand for these undrivable streets, the piles of garbage, the sewage running down the sidewalk right outside their security walls, they're not here to see it. They've moved to Dubai, or to the United States, or somewhere else that's safer for themselves and their money. (Or our money.) Most of these fancy properties in Wazir Akbar Khān were built by the Afghan elite with profits from the international influx of cash that accompanied the mostly American influx of war a decade ago—built to display status or to reap still more war dollars from the Western aid agencies and journalists and politicians and diplocrats and private contractors who need proper places to stay in the capital. The surges big and small have been good to the property barons of Wazir Akbar Khān: residential real estate values were reportedly up 75 percent in 2008 alone. Check the listings under Kabul "villas" today and you'll find properties priced from $7,000 to $25,000 a month with specs like this: four floors, a dozen rooms, nine toilets, three big kitchens, sleeps twenty.

No one sold the American people on this incarnation of Wazir Akbar Khān as one of the desired outcomes of all those hundreds of billions of tax dollars spent in Afghanistan. But it is what we have built at Ground Zero Afghanistan. Whatever we were aiming at, this is the manifest result.

Consider also the new hundred-million-dollar wastewater treatment facility in Fallujah, Anbar Province, Iraq, which provides only spotty wastewater treatment to the people of that city. In 2004, after the US military all but demolished Fallujah in the deadliest urban battle of the Iraq War, it was decided that the way to turn the residents of the recalcitrant Sunni Triangle away from Al-Qaeda and toward their country's fledgling government would be to build a sewage system for all of Fallujah. The initial $33 million contract was let to a South Carolina company in June 2004, while the city was still smoldering. There was no time to waste. The Bush administration's Iraqi Reconstruction Management Office identified the sewage system as a "key national reconciliation issue." The goal was to have it up and running by the beginning of 2006.

Nearly five years after the deadline, having clocked in at three times its initial budget, there was still not a single residence on line. Accordingly, the plan was "descoped"—scaled down—to serve just a third of the city. In the midst then of doing a third of the work for triple the money, there was talk of walking away from the project without connecting even that one-third of Fallujah residences to the aborted plant. We had built a shit-processing plant that didn't process shit.

And it gets worse. According to a 2008 report by the Special Inspector General for Iraq Reconstruction, about 10 percent of the money paid to Iraqi subcontractors for the Fallujah project ended up in the hands of "terrorist organizations." According to that same report, residents near two particular pump stations "[might] become angry" if the system ever did come on line, because "funding constraints" made "odor control facilities" impractical. Even households that were not part of the collection system would still be subject to what the Iraqi minister of municipalities and public works delicately called the "big stink." The eighty-page report also noted, with dry finality, "The project file lacked any documentation to support that the provisional Iraqi government wanted this project in the first place."

When, finally, late in 2011, seven years into the project, at a cost of $108 million, we managed to get a quarter of the homes in Fallujah hooked into that system, this partial accomplishment was not met with resounding huzzahs. "In the end it would be dubious to conclude that this project helped stabilize the city, enhanced the local citizenry's faith in government, built local service capacity, won hearts or minds, or stimulated the economy," the Special Inspector General said in 2011. "It is difficult to conclude that the project was worth the investment." A hundred million American dollars, partially diverted to the groups fighting US troops, to build (poorly) a giant, unwanted wastewater-treatment project that provides nothing but the "big stink" for three-quarters of the city. No one would argue for something like this as a good use of US tax dollars. But it is in fact what we bought.

Here at home, according to an exhaustive and impressive two-year-long investigation by the *Washington Post,* the taxpayer-funded Global War on Terror also built enough ultra-high-security office space (Sensitive Compartmentalized Information Facilities, or SCIF, in bureaucrat-speak) to fill twenty-two US Capitol Buildings: seventeen million square feet of offices in thirty-three handsome and generously funded new complexes powered up twenty-four hours a day, where an army of nearly one million American professionals spies on the world and the homeland. It's as if we turned the entire working population of Detroit and Milwaukee into high-security-clearance spooks and analysts.

The spy boom has been a beautiful windfall for architects, construction companies, IT specialists, and above all defense contractors, enriching thousands of private companies and dozens of local economies hugging the Capital Beltway. All those SCIFs and the rest of the government-contractor gravy train have made suburban Washington, DC, home to six of the ten wealthiest counties in America. Falls Church, Loudoun County, and Fairfax County in Virginia are one, two, and three. Goodbye, Nassau County, New York. Take that, Oyster Bay.

The crown jewel of this sprawling intelligopolis is Liberty Crossing, in the Virginia suburbs of Washington—an 850,000-square-foot (and growing) complex that houses the National Counterterrorism Center. The agency was created and funded in 2004 because, despite spending $30 billion on intelligence before 9/11, the various spy agencies in our country did not talk to one another. So the $30 billion annual intelligence budget was boosted by 250 percent, and with that increase we built ourselves a clean, well-lighted edifice, concealed by GPS jammers and reflective windows, where intelligence collected by 1,271 government agencies and 1,931 private companies under government contract is supposedly coordinated.

It is a big, big idea, and perhaps necessary—the financial commitment to it implies at least that we think it is. But it turns out Liberty Crossing is a bureaucratic haystack into which the now even more vast intelligence community tosses its shiniest needles. When a businessman relayed to CIA agents in Nigeria that his son seemed to be under the spell of terrorists and had gone to Yemen, perhaps for training, that duly reported needle got sucked into the fifty-thousand-reports-per-year haystack, only to be discovered *after* Umar Farouk Abdulmutallab boarded a Northwest Airlines flight from Amsterdam to Detroit and tried to set off a bomb he'd stuffed into his underpants. "The complexity of this system defies description," a retired Army lieutenant general and intelligence specialist told the *Post* reporters. "We can't effectively assess whether it's making us more safe."

If no one knows if it's making us safer, why have we built it? Why are we still building it, at breakneck speed? Liberty Crossing is slated to almost double in size over the next decade. Remember the fierce debate in Congress over whether or not it's worth it to do that? No? Me neither. But we keep building it. We keep chugging along.

National security is a real imperative for our country—for any country. But the connection between that imperative and what we do about it has gone as frowsy as my hometown's little pump station in high August. Our national security policy isn't much related to its stated justifications anymore. To whatever extent we do argue and debate what defense and intelligence policy ought to be, that debate—our political process—doesn't actually determine what we do. We're not directing that policy anymore; it just follows its own course. Which means we've effectively lost control of a big part of who we are as a country. And we've broken faith with some of the best advice the founders ever gave us.

Our constitutional inheritance didn't point us in this direction. If the colonists hadn't rejected British militarism and the massive financial burden of maintaining the British military, America wouldn't exist. The Constitutional Convention debated whether America should even have a standing army. The founders feared that maintaining one would drain our resources in the same way that maintaining the eighteenth-century British military had burdened the colonies. They worried that a powerful military could rival civilian government for power in our new country, and of course they worried that having a standing army around would create too much of a temptation to use it. Those worries about the inevitable incentives to war were part of what led to the division of government at the heart of our Constitution, building into the structure of our new country a deliberate peaceable bias.

But in the past generation or two, we've drifted off that historical course. The steering's gone wobbly, the brakes have failed. It's not a conspiracy, there aren't rogue elements pushing us to subvert our national interests to instead serve theirs. It's been more entertaining and more boneheaded than that.

The good news is we don't need a radical new vision of post–Cold War American power. We just need a "small *c*" conservative return to our constitutional roots, a course correction. This book is about how and why we've drifted. It wasn't inevitable. And it's fixable.

Chapter 1

G.I. Joe, Ho Chi Minh, and the American Art of Fighting About Fighting

THOMAS JEFFERSON WAS A LIFELONG AND HABITUAL FRETTER. He was wary of animal foods, spirituous liquors, state religion, national debt, abolitionists, embittered slaves, unelected federal judges, Yankee politicians, Yankee professors, and Yankees in general. But his predominant and animating worry was the centralization and consolidation of power—in large banks, in closed and secret societies, and, most of all, in governments: the enemy within. "There are instruments so dangerous to the rights of the nation and which place them so totally at the mercy of their governors, that those governors, whether legislative or executive, should be restrained from keeping such instruments on foot, but in well-defined cases," Jefferson wrote as the Constitution of the United States was being debated. "Such an instrument is a standing army."

His feelings didn't much change with time. In 1792 he wrote that one of his "favorite ideas" was "never keeping an unnecessary soldier." In 1799 he wrote to a political friend that he was "not for a standing army in a time of peace, which may overwhelm public sentiment."

Classicist that he was, Jefferson was apt to bolster his arguments with well-polished (if not strictly accurate) examples of early Western history: "The Greeks and Romans had no standing armies, yet they defended themselves. . . . Their system was to make every man a soldier and oblige him to repair to the standard of his country whenever that was reared. This made them invincible; and the same remedy will make us so."

That's at best a loose military history of Greece and Rome—they did rely at times on standing armies. But you see where he's going with this. Jefferson acted on his pet "unnecessary soldier" idea when he became president in 1801. He cut the standing army by a third and left the defense against foreign invasion largely to a "well-regulated militia" under the control of the various states and localities. And he remained unmoved by what he viewed as alarmist and cynical calls for a large nationalized active military. "Were armies to be raised whenever a speck of war is visible in our horizon," he warned Congress in his sixth annual presidential message, "we never should have been without them. Our resources would have been exhausted on dangers which never happened, instead of being reserved for what is really to take place."

Jeffersonian prudence held sway in this country for a century and a half. The professional military was an institution of limited reach and power; in times of peace we kept the regulars busy building defense works and ports and bridges. Whenever we went to war in a big way, we went to war with citizen-soldiers; the small nucleus of an active-duty army swelled with militiamen, reservists, National Guardsmen, enlisted persons, and draftees. When the United States went to war, the entire United States went to war. And no nation's military demobilized with such verve and velocity when the fighting was over. Hell, volunteers on the battlefields were legally separating themselves from the US Army while the Mexican War still raged in 1847. The War of 1812, the Creek War, the Civil War, the Spanish-American War, they were all the same: the clarion call to duty, the citizens' eager answer, the victory parades (having picked our fights judiciously, we were, by the mid-twentieth century, something like 9–0), and the return to home and hearth. Within eighteen months of the conclusion of World War I, Congress had completely dismantled the American Expeditionary Forces and reduced the active-duty military from four million soldiers back to the prewar number of less than three hundred thousand. The effect of tossing more than three million suddenly unemployed men back into an ailing job market did not have an altogether sanguinary effect on the national economy, or on the national mood . . . but hey, nobody ever said war was supposed to be a jobs program.

Mobilization for World War II was even larger, and the postwar drawdown nearly as dramatic. In 1945 there were twelve million people on active duty in the US Armed Forces; five years later, that number had dropped 88 percent, to just one and a half million. But that stunning demobilization had few concomitant dislocations. Call it the War-and-Peace Dividend or the World's Greatest Stimulus Package. A country that left a Great Depression at home to confront the Axis powers overseas converted the massive government spending of the war effort into an unprecedented civilian economic boom when that war was won. Factories that had been making jeeps and warplanes and submarine engines and ammunition were now turning out new Chevrolet Bel Airs, Allis-Chalmers tractors, Cessna 170 airplanes, and Frigidaire iceboxes. It didn't hurt our standing in the world economy that about one in five able-bodied young men in Germany and the Soviet Union had been killed in the war, and at least one in ten of Japan's. And it didn't hurt that the industrial cities of Japan and Germany (and much of Western

Europe, for that matter) were smoking holes; of the 10.5 million cars manufactured worldwide in 1950, the United States made more than 8 million of them, and sold 'em all over the world.

We were a country that could afford to be generous to our returning veterans, and more than sixty years later we're still reaping the benefits of that generosity. The post–World War II GI Bill assured returning vets a year's worth of wages whether they worked or not, and paid college tuition and a living stipend, too. Nearly half of the male students on college campuses in 1948 had been to war. And it also offered low-interest government-guaranteed loans for buying a home. Housing construction and manufacturing boomed. The curve of GNP, household income, and personal spending trended up, up, and up.

The United States of America was a robust nation—a nation of means—and we rebuilt and reconfigured our institutions after World War II in a way that reflected this. Yes, the military demobilization after the war was massive and fast, but even the dramatically shrunk-down US military of 1950 was three times the size it had been before World War II—and with a big footprint. The US soldiers, sailors, airmen, and Marines, right alongside all those consumer goods, were already leading exports. We had 150,000 troops in the Far East, 125,000 in Western Europe, and a smattering in such diverse and far-flung locations as Panama, Cuba, Guatemala, Morocco, Eritrea, Libya, Saudi Arabia, Samoa, and Indochina. Wary as never before of the Communist threat—now a constant "speck of war visible in our horizon"—America had come to see Jefferson's preoccupation with standing armies and threats from inside our own power structure as a bit moldy. We were, after all, the only country still capable of keeping the planet safe for democracy.

Through the fifteen years that followed World War II, we trusted our commanders in chief—Truman, Eisenhower, Kennedy, they'd all served!—to project our military power in measured and meaningful ways. We ratcheted up our extraordinary nuclear program, broke a Soviet blockade of Berlin with a dramatic airlift, beat the Commies back in Formosa and Thailand, fought them to a standstill in Korea, and stared down Khrushchev when our spy planes caught him red-handed putting missiles in Cuba. When President Kennedy decided to engage the Soviets in the space race, the nation's finest military pilots were the chosen first team.

The United States military was an institution of unsurpassed public esteem, top to bottom. You could measure that regard in a hundred different ways. Take, for instance, the plaything metric. In 1964 one of the hottest new toys on the market was a doll, for boys: G.I. Joe.

There was not a whiff of peacetime, soon-to-be civilian in this toy; these were not Ken dolls in dress uniforms at the debutante ball. G.I. Joe was olive drab, M1 rifle, canned Spam, scar-faced, down-and-dirty. The hard-plastic soldiers (petroleum-based all the way) were built to take a pounding. In the spring of 1965, in GI Bill–built suburbs from Levittown, New York, to Castro Valley, California, ten-year-old boys were digging miniature foxholes and jerry-rigging Dad's old handkerchiefs to make paratroopers out of their new dolls. Hasbro had an instant hit; G.I. Joe did close to $20 million in sales that first year. Early indications pointed to steady growth.

But sales reports later in the '60s made for unhappy reading in the Hasbro boardroom, and by the early 1970s the toy company found itself leaning on gimmicks to sell G.I. Joe. These included fuzzy flocked hair (they called it "realistic"), a nonregulation beard, colorful new uniform choices, swiveling "Eagle-Eyes," and a fighting hand formed into a "Kung Fu Grip" (Bruce Lee had taken off by then). Hasbro folded G.I. Joe into "The Adventure

Team . . . ready to go wherever adventure leads." The company was at pains to minimize the militaryness of its military doll.

You can't blame the Hasbro marketers and their sell-side analysts for having been optimistic in those first heady months of 1964. They were sure they were riding the long wave of good feeling for US soldierdom. How could they have known that the ground under G.I. Joe was beginning to shift, even in the happy springtime of his advent?

The first tectonic tremor came from the White House in the early months of 1965 when President Lyndon Baines Johnson began the prosecution of his own hot war in Vietnam. He had campaigned in '64 by promising, "We are not about to send American boys nine or ten thousand miles away from home to do what Asian boys ought to be doing for themselves." He'd painted his Republican opponent, Barry Goldwater, as a dangerous hair-trigger warmonger (with some help from Goldwater himself, who, in a May 1963 ABC interview, proposed dropping low-yield nuclear bombs on Vietnam to destroy supply lines and achieve "defoliation of the forests." And why not? Among their many-splendored uses, nuclear explosions can be excellent pruners).

Yes, in 1961, Johnson's predecessor John F. Kennedy had promised at his inauguration, "We shall pay any price, bear any burden, meet any hardship, support any friend, oppose any foe, to assure the survival and the success of liberty." But Johnson's promise was not Kennedy's; Johnson promised to resist the expensive temptations of foreign wars and to build a Great Society at home instead. He promised not to escalate in Vietnam. He promised he would not allow the United States to get "tied down in a land war in Asia." But then, despite the promises, despite his determination not to, Johnson got dragged to the conclusion that the United States needed to be fighting in Vietnam. He moved to convince the American people and Congress that he should have the authority to use military force there—the wildly exaggerated Gulf of Tonkin incident in 1964 would be the basis for the only congressional authorization Johnson ever sought for war. Then, with only halfhearted gestures toward trying to keep the country on board with a war he never really wanted to fight, Johnson set about trying to fight his war in a way the American people might hopefully not notice too much. "We don't think we'll ask for much money," Johnson confided to the chairman of the Senate Armed Services Committee, Richard Russell, in the summer of 1965, as he made plans to increase the ground forces in Vietnam from 80,000 to 180,000, "because we don't want to blow this thing up."

LBJ "tried to fight a war on the cheap," one of the Johnson administration's key intelligence men, George A. Carver, would say years later, "and tried to fight a war without acknowledging that he was fighting a war."

The agonized president was trying to thread a new and difficult needle: taking the nation's armed forces to war without taking the nation as a whole to war. And central to that effort was one crucial decision. Against the advice of his secretary of defense and the Joint Chiefs of Staff, over the outright objection of the chief of staff of the US Army, Johnson simply refused to call up the modern parallel to those old Jeffersonian state militias, all those men living in our neighborhoods: the US Army Reserve and the National Guard. The Guard or Reserves had been called to fight in every American war in the nation's history—even in the nonwar that was the Cuban Missile Crisis in 1962—but in Vietnam, Johnson hesitated. In part he was worried that a full-scale mobilization would draw the Russians and the Chinese into the war, but mostly he didn't want to get Congress and the rest of the country all het up and asking too many questions.

"I don't think I'll have to call [the Reserves] up now," he told Russell. "I think it's too dramatic. I think it commits me where I can't get out. And it puts me out there further than I wanna get right at the moment. . . . You don't think I oughta have a joint session, do you?"

"Not as long as you don't call up any Reserves and all I wouldn't," Russell answered. The six-term senator from Georgia was sympathetic to the president's predicament. ("I never worked on anything as hard in my life," Johnson complained to the man who had been his mentor and champion in the Senate.)

"It woulda driven me mad," Russell told Johnson. "It's the only thing I've ever hit in my life I didn't have some quick answer to, but I haven't got one to this."

But the seasoned senator also reminded Johnson that failing to mobilize the Reserves would send a signal to the Soviets, the North Vietnamese Communists, and the rest of the world that we lacked will. "It adds to ol' Ho Chi Minh's argument that we ain't gonna stay in there, that we gonna pull out. . . . Call up the Reserves, they understand that language. They understood it in Berlin. They understand that."

"Well, if I extend the enlistments and if I put a hundred thousand out there they'll understand it," Johnson answered with a chuckle, though he did not mean to amuse. "And I'm gonna step up my draft calls. Double 'em."

The draft wasn't new for Vietnam; it had been plugging holes in the active-duty armed forces since 1917. For a president trying to flesh out a Vietnam fighting force without causing too much consternation, increasing the draft seemed a better choice than calling up Reserves. In 1965, the Guard and Reserves were the things you quietly signed up for to avoid service, and Johnson was already hearing from congressmen, who were hearing from prominent constituents, who were in nowise interested in having their sons' Guard and Reserve units called up to fight in some godforsaken war in the jungles of Southeast Asia. And Johnson agreed! This was, after all, not a major war, at least not a war with a major effect on the home front. And there was also Johnson's hope that his war would be a US rout, soldiers in and out in a matter of months: *Ho Chi Minh got anything to match this?* Johnson supposedly bragged to reporters during a bathroom break.

But even as the war's Phase II, "the preparing-to-win phase," as Vietnam historian Neil Sheehan called it, stretched into its second and third years and then started to look like an ugly, viciously prosecuted, no-end-in-sight, preparing-to-lose phase, Johnson stubbornly refused to call up the Reserves, and stubbornly refused to come clean with the country that we—all of us—were in a real war. So from the first 3,500 combat Marines Johnson sent ashore near Da Nang on March 8, 1965, to support the first sustained bombing of North Vietnam to the 535,000 American troops who were in Vietnam at the end of his presidency, something like 1 percent would be Guard and Reserves. The active-duty armed forces shouldered the burdens of Johnson's land war in Asia—fleshed out by draftees, chosen at random from among the ranks of young American men who were unable or unwilling to get themselves out of it.

Whether or not Johnson's decision had any effect on the outcome of the war in Vietnam is debatable, and ultimately unknowable, but there was an enormous cost inside the United States—it tore the military from the heart of the country, and it tore the country from the heart of the military. One young company-commander-turned-novelist saw that wrenching in its inglorious entirety. Jim Webb showed himself to be an extraordinary warrior in Vietnam; he won two Purple Hearts, two Bronze Stars, a Silver Star, and, for bravery under fire, the

Navy Cross. But what really set him apart was his remarkable acuity. From the darkest jungle trenches, the twenty-three-year-old lieutenant managed to apprehend the big picture. And in his Vietnam War novel, *Fields of Fire*, Webb distilled the national tragedy in pitch-perfect dialogue between a battle-tested career-military NCO and a young lieutenant:

> "I'll tell you a little story, maybe it'll make sense. When I came back from Vietnam the first time I went to the Reserve Training Center, like I said. It wasn't really big over here yet. We all knew it would get bigger, though, and we figured Johnson would call up the Reserves. We kept telling all the Weekend Warriors that they'd better get their shit in one bag, because they were going to war. Like Korea. And it got bigger, but Johnson didn't have the balls to call up the Reserves. Reserves can vote. And they drive airplanes for United. And they run businesses. Instead, Johnson just made a bigger draft, filled it with loopholes, and went after certain groups of kids."
>
> "You said yourself the kids were great."
>
> "It ain't what happens here that's important. It's what's happening back there. Shit, Lieutenant, you'd hardly know there was a war on. It's in the papers, and college kids run around screaming about it instead of doing panty raids or whatever they were running around doing before but that's it. Airplane drivers still drive their airplanes. Businessmen still run their businesses. College kids still go to college. It's like nothing really happened, except to other people. It isn't touching anybody except us. It makes me sick, Lieutenant. . . . We been abandoned, Lieutenant. We been kicked off the edge of the goddamn cliff. They don't know how to fight it, and they don't know

how to stop fighting it. And back home it's too complicated, so they forget about it and do their rooting at football games. Well, fuck 'em. They ain't worth dying for."

The American troops' disenchantment with the country's civilian cohort was real, but so was civilian disenchantment with
the Vietnam War, and with the military itself. And it was not
confined to student activists and peaceniks. The worst of the
war had been beamed into middle-class living rooms all across
America—the blood and gore, the death, the waste, the atrocities. The public's idea of the country and what it stood for had
taken a holy beating. One active-duty company commander who
returned from Vietnam to a job at a recruiting station in Kansas
City was stung by the overriding sentiment he found among his
new neighbors. "This is a horrible war and our troops are doing
terrible things over there," they'd say, "but we know you're not
like that, Paul."

Much as the military man tried—"I am them. I am typical. I
am what the Marine Corps is all about"—he never felt able to convince his civilian friends that they had a military to be proud of.

Said one veteran: "There's a wall ten miles high and fifty
miles thick between those of us who went and those who didn't,
and that wall is never going to come down."

We'd gone to war in Vietnam in a way that we'd never gone to war
before, and no one liked how it turned out. So while we did what
we'd done after every war, while we dramatically drew down
ground troops in Vietnam—from 510,054 in 1969 to 212,925 in
1971 to 265 in 1973—this time the brass decided it would be done
differently: in the future, presidents wouldn't have the option
Johnson chose. The next time America went to war, it wouldn't

be the military out there alone, "kicked off the goddamn cliff" as Webb's NCO would say. Officially, the post-Vietnam restructuring of the military was called the Total Force Policy; unofficially, everyone called it the Abrams Doctrine.

Creighton Abrams was the US commander in Vietnam from 1968 to 1972, while troop strength there went from more than half a million to one-fifteenth of that number. Then he returned to Washington, where he served as Army chief of staff from 1972 until he died in 1974. And as chief, while winding down that increasingly unpopular and costly war, Abrams restructured the United States Army in a way that made it harder for a commander in chief to go to war, or at least harder to fight a war without having first sought the support of the American people for that war.

It's hard to make the case that Abrams began his reorganization with the intent to remake the nation's political structures, or with the express purpose of closing off options available to America's elected officials. He certainly never talked about it that way. His overriding concern was the restoration of the institution to which he'd devoted his entire life: the United States Army. Vietnam had bled that institution dry. Its combat readiness around the world had been greatly diminished; the Seventh Army in Germany had become little more than a pricey replacement depot for Southeast Asia. The Guard and Reserves were in shambles, viewed as a haven for shirkers. And Abrams had seen firsthand how even the soldiers who had served honorably and proudly in Vietnam were demoralized. He personally knew the sting of civilian criticism: Johnson's successor, Richard Nixon, had trouble hiding his contempt for Abrams. In 1971, Nixon said to Secretary of State Henry Kissinger that Abrams "had his shot" to win a military victory in Vietnam, "and he's not going to get any more." The following year, he wrote to Kissinger of

Abrams, "Our military leadership has been a sad chapter in the proud military history of this country."

As commander on the ground of a hated war, Abrams grew to love the Army and its soldiers all the more. "In a changing world, changing times and changing attitude and the various political motivations that have thrust themselves upon our country," he told the First Infantry Division in their last hours before returning home, "[you] represent a constancy of those essential virtues of mankind: humility, courage, devotion, and sacrifice. The world is changed a lot, but this division continues to serve as it had in the beginning. I choose to feel that this is part of the cement and the rock and the steel that holds our great country together."

Abrams's passion as Army chief at the end of Vietnam was to manage the nation's demobilization from that conflict in a way that protected the military. Even as wartime appropriations dried up and the size of the Army shrunk dramatically and the now-hated draft was abolished, Abrams wanted a big national investment in military readiness. He had served in three American wars, and he described how calling up an unprepared Army out of an unprepared nation meant shedding too much American blood when it came time to fight: "We have paid, and paid, and paid again in blood and sacrifice for our unpreparedness. . . . I don't want war, but I am appalled at the human cost that we've paid because we wouldn't prepare to fight."

His solution was elegant in its simplicity and its financial efficiency. Under Abrams's Total Force Policy, the Guard and Reserves would no longer be shelters to avoid service but rather integral parts of the nation's fighting capacity. It would be operationally impossible to go to war without calling them up. Abrams wove the Guard and Reserves into the fabric of the active-duty military; he made those in-your-neighborhood citizen-soldiers responsible for functions without which we could not wage a major military campaign. And in weaving the Guard and Reserves into the active-duty military, he also wove the military back into the country.

John Vessey, who worked under Abrams during the restructuring, remembered the general's central focus: "He thought about [the kind of nation America was] an awful lot, and concluded that whatever we're going to do we ought to do right as we are a nation. Let's not build an Army off here in the corner someplace. The Armed Forces are an expression of the nation. If you take them out of the national context, you are likely to screw them up. That was his lesson from Vietnam. He wasn't going to leave them in that position ever again."

And so the political threshold for going to war was raised. The Abrams Doctrine—the Total Force Policy—put American politicians in the position of being "designed out" of waging war in a way that was dislocated from the everyday experience of American families. Remember Russell's advice to Johnson when the president wondered whether he'd have to address a joint session of Congress about a huge escalation in Vietnam: *"Not as long as you don't call up any Reserves I wouldn't."* With the Abrams Doctrine, calling up the Reserves would no longer be optional, and therefore neither would that pilgrimage to Congress. The president's hand was forced: if America was to fight a war, the life of that "airplane driver for United" would have to be profoundly disrupted, civilians would have to be pried out of their civilian jobs. What Johnson had resisted as "too dramatic" in the last war would become the political price of admission to the next one.

The loudest story of the summer and fall of 1973 may have been the Senate slowly tightening the noose of Watergate around

President Nixon's neck, but at the same time Congress was also busy writing "A Joint Resolution Concerning the War Powers of Congress and the President." The War Powers Resolution of 1973 would be an explicit reassertion of the prerogative spelled out under Article 1, Section 8, "to fulfill the intent of the framers of the Constitution of the United States" that Congress—and Congress alone—had the power to declare war.

The framers had been voluble in their rationale for and in their defense of Article 1, Section 8. "The Constitution supposes, what the History of all Governments demonstrates," wrote James Madison, "that the Executive is the branch of power most interested in war, and most prone to it. It has accordingly with studied care vested the question of war in the Legislature." Even that suspected monarchist Alexander Hamilton saw the wisdom of keeping the power to declare war out of the hands of a single executive. Madison, Hamilton, and their fellow framers were building structural barriers against what they saw as the darker aspects of human nature. The lures to war—personal hatreds, political glory, material spoils, and the simple atavistic enthusiasm for violence—might be too enticing for one man to resist, and might be too easy to promote "by fixing the public gaze upon the exceeding brightness of military glory," as a later congressman, Abraham Lincoln, put it, "that attractive rainbow that rises in showers of blood—that serpent's eye that charms to destroy." Madison wrote in his notes during the constitutional debates that Virginia delegate George Mason "was for clogging rather than facilitating war; but for facilitating peace."

The framers clogged up the works by making the decision to go to war a communal one. By vesting it in the Congress—a large, slow-moving deliberative body of varied and often competing viewpoints—the Constitution assured that the case for any war would have to be loud, well argued, and made in plain view. The people's representatives would be forced to take time and care to weigh the costs against the benefits.

This structure did not make the young United States what you'd call pacifist; we didn't spread ourselves from sea to shining sea on high ideals and impeccable manners alone. But the wisdom of erecting high barriers to war making traveled unimpeded through early generations of Americans. In his first term in Congress, Abraham Lincoln reiterated the founding principle with a low-born frontiersman's understanding of who pays the costs of martial élan: "The provision of the Constitution giving the war-making power to Congress was dictated, as I understand it, by the following reasons: kings had always been involving and impoverishing their people in wars, pretending generally, if not always, that the good of the people was the object. This our convention understood to be the most oppressive of all kingly oppressions, and they resolved to so frame the Constitution that no one man should hold the power of bringing this oppression upon us."

In 1973, the successors of that frontier congressman had just had a painful refresher course in the perils of lowering the barriers to war. They had allowed Johnson to exercise tremendous prerogative; he'd shoved more than half a million troops into Southeast Asia without taking his case through Congress and the American people. So in 1973, the United States Congress reasserted itself. It passed legislation to raise and reinforce the structural barriers to a president waging his own wars. The post-Vietnam Congress wanted no future president to be able to act with that sort of impunity. (As the crotchety old Justice Hugo Black would remind folks who complained about the roadblocks to criminal prosecution embedded in the Constitution's Bill of Rights: "They were written to make it more difficult!").

The War Powers Resolution of 1973 was an imperfect law.

But by passing it, the legislative branch was putting the executive on notice—it no longer would settle for being a backbencher on vital questions of war and peace. If the president wanted to execute a military operation (*any* military operation), he had to petition Congress for the authority to do so within thirty days; if Congress didn't grant explicit authorization, that operation would have to end after sixty days by law. The Oval Office would no longer have open-ended war-making powers.

The assertion of congressional power had strong support across party lines. When an incensed President Nixon vetoed the War Powers Resolution, both the House and the Senate overrode that veto with votes to spare.

And the legislature didn't stop there, especially not when the subject was once again Vietnam. In April 1975, members of the Senate Foreign Relations Committee suspected that Nixon's replacement, President Gerald Ford, wasn't telling all about his latest request for financial support for our allies in South Vietnam, President Nguyen Van Thieu's failing army. As far as the committee members could discern from the parade of witnesses sent from the White House, President Ford wasn't willing to accept the facts on the ground: the North Vietnamese Army was about to overrun the friendly government in Saigon and there wasn't a thing he could do about it. American combat troops were long gone.

During an executive session of the committee, the senators worried aloud that the Ford administration had not made a real plan for the coming collapse of Thieu's government. They worried that the president's stubborn support for a failing South Vietnamese military might lead us back into a hot war there, with combat troops once again on the ground. Congress had given Johnson and Nixon too many chances, and these presidents had made too many costly mistakes and miscalculations.

The Senate was not in a mood to give Ford free rein. The game was up. Ford wasn't going to get his $722 million appropriation. He needed to understand that.

So the committee, in the middle of that executive session, dialed up and requested a nearly unprecedented face-to-face consultation with the president, and then marched en masse down to the White House and into the Cabinet Room. "We wanted to tell you our concerns and hear from you your concerns," Ford's fellow Republican, Sen. Howard Baker, told the new president. "We hope when we have, we will have established a new era of negotiation between the Executive and Legislative branches."

Ford was horrified. He wrote in his memoir that the last time the Senate Foreign Relations Committee had showed up at the White House demanding a meeting was back in the Woodrow Wilson administration. Ford—having just come from the House of Representatives himself—was floored by the legislators' presumption. He described the meeting as "extremely tense."

And it was. The minutes show the senators pointedly suggesting that the president get control of his ungovernable and unrealistic ambassador in Saigon, that he make a *real* plan to evacuate the 6,000 Americans and the 175,000 South Vietnamese friendlies, and that he drop his appropriations request by two-thirds and limit it to funds for safe evacuation . . . or forget it. There wasn't going to be any more open-ended aid to stand up additional South Vietnamese infantry divisions.

"If there isn't some indication of aid," Ford harrumphed, "the situation could disintegrate rapidly."

"I will give you large sums for evacuation," Sen. Jacob Javits told the president point-blank, "but not one nickel for military aid for Thieu."

"We are not wanting to put American troops in, but we have to have enough funds to make it look like we plan to hold for some period," Ford offered at the end of the meeting. But the senators damn sure weren't going to get sucked into any more combat missions, even in the effort to evacuate.

"This is a reentry of a magnitude we had not envisioned," Sen. John Glenn, the famed pilot and astronaut, told the president. "I can see North Vietnam deciding not to let us get these people out and attacking our bridgehead. Then we would have to send forces to protect our security forces. That fills me with fear." The Senate had dug in its heels, and there was little the president could do.

Oh, but those days stuck in the craw of the inhabitants of the West Wing circa 1975. Gerald Ford's chief of staff would still be complaining bitterly about that "congressional backlash" and the War Powers Resolution nearly forty years later. "The resolution, despite its questionable and still untested constitutionality," Donald Rumsfeld huffed in his 2011 memoir, "undercut the President's ability to convince troublemakers of America's staying power." Ford complained aloud to his cabinet that Congress had stepped in where it had no business, forcing him to become the president who would, as he put it, "cut and run," who would "bug out" of Vietnam. Secretary of State Kissinger actually whined to Ford that a few Republican senators had been *really* mean to him.

But this wasn't about mean. This wasn't about Kissinger, it wasn't about Ford, it wasn't personal at all. This was about the fundamental question of American martial power and how it's wielded.

In the aftermath of America's decade-long tragedy in Vietnam—in the military demobilization, in the course corrections, and in the political recriminations that followed—something important happened. The new structures that grew out of that searing experience—the Abrams Doctrine, the War Powers

Resolution, a newly muscular Congress—had real, fundamental, change-the-country force. Taken as a whole, they had the sort of salubrious outcome old George Mason would have cheered: they clogged up the country's war-making apparatus.

The questions of how we provide for the common defense, how we apportion our limited resources to the military, how we prepare for war, and whether or not we go to war were back where they belonged, out in the open, subject to loud and jangly political debate.

It must be noted for the record, however, that sales of G.I. Joe remained soft, even with the Kung Fu Grip.

Chapter 2

A Nation at Peace
Everywhere in the World

WHEN RONALD REAGAN SPOKE A THING ALOUD, HE BELIEVED
it forever and for always. By the time he started running for president, in 1976, he had already developed an unwavering and stead-
fast faith in the correctness of whatever came out of his mouth.
"Once he had made an emotional commitment to this or that
policy or story," Reagan's most sympathetic biographer, Edmund
Morris, would write, "no amount of disproof would cause him to
alter his belief in it." Facts and contrary evidence did not get in
the way of a good story—especially one that appeared to set his
audiences' heads bobbing in knowing assent. Welfare queens were
driving around Chicago's South Side in Cadillacs, he'd say out on
the stump; one had defrauded the clueless federal government to
the tune of $150,000 a year *tax-free*! Public housing in East Har-
lem had gone luxury: "You can get an apartment with eleven-foot
ceilings," Reagan told a group in the early primary state of New
Hampshire, "with a twenty-foot balcony, a swimming pool, laun-
dry room, and play room." The federal government was spending
$90 billion a year on welfare and other programs the states should
be administering. So let 'em do it. That'd balance the federal

budget right there. It all sounded about right to Reagan, and to a lot of the people who showed up for his rallies.

And still, the Gipper could not seem to get the necessary traction in that first race for the Republican nomination. The sitting (though unelected, as Reagan would point out) president, Gerald Ford, defeated the onetime governor in the first six primaries that year, including the one in Reagan's birth state of Illinois by nearly twenty points. By early spring, Nancy Reagan was trying to gentle her husband out of the race; the campaign was so broke his managers weren't sure they could afford the jet fuel to get his yellow Hughes Airwest DC-9 charter plane (the Big Banana, the press corps was calling it) to the next contest in North Carolina. But Reagan thought he still had one more card to play, maybe the trump card, against the president who knuckled under to Congress and bailed on the last war.

For Reagan, it wasn't just that Ford had "bugged out" of Vietnam, or that the president was playing footsie with Congress about cutting defense spending. It was the whole issue of national security—the politically potent, unbearably humiliating idea that the United States of America appeared weak in the eyes of the world. Just look at what was happening right under our noses, Reagan told audiences in North Carolina. They might not be aware of it, but President Ford was about to give in to the veiled threats of Panamanian leader Gen. Omar Torrijos. "What are the quiet, almost secret, negotiations we're engaged in to give away the Panama Canal?" Reagan began to ask his audiences. "The Canal Zone is not a colonial possession. It is not a long-term lease. It is sovereign United States territory every bit the same as Alaska and all the states that were carved from the Louisiana Purchase. We should end those negotiations and tell the general: We bought it, we paid for it, we built it, and *we intend to keep it!*"

Oh, that was the line his audiences responded to. Reagan's wide-eyed pollster could see his numbers rising in North Carolina and egged him on. Voters might not know a damn thing about the tangled history of Panama and the canal, or of the agreements the United States already had in place there, or of the actual workings of the canal. But they sure liked a politician who stood up and said, *They're not gonna take it away from us.* It struck the same nerve as that movie that was just out, *Network,* with its catchphrase "I'm mad as hell! . . . And I'm not going to take it anymore!"

"Wrong-headed as it is," noted *Time* magazine, "Reagan's jingoism on the canal has apparently struck a nerve among parts of the electorate, arousing post-Vietnam sentiments that the U.S. should not be pushed around in its own hemisphere by, in Reagan's words, 'a tinhorn dictator.' Insists Reagan, 'The Latin American countries have a respect for macho. I think if the United States reacts with firmness and fairness, we might not earn their love, but we would earn their respect.'"

Reagan won North Carolina going away.

There was blowback. That old nuclear tree-pruning superhawk Barry Goldwater called out Reagan for thoroughgoing dishonesty on the Canal issue. Plenty of journalists took Reagan to task for his absolute and complete fabrication about the Canal Zone being sovereign US territory. But Reagan did not back away. Like a good spokesman armed with a memorable Madison Avenue–like tagline, he just said it louder and more often. "We bought it, we paid for it, we built it, and *we intend to keep it!*" And by all appearances, he really believed it, with all his heart.

The week after his North Carolina victory Reagan bought half an hour of prime-time television—nine thirty on a Wednesday night—and he used it to goose the pretend threat level:

"There is one problem which must be solved or everything else is meaningless. I am speaking of the problem of our national security. Our nation is in danger, and the danger grows greater with each passing day." The Ford administration was asleep at the wheel while Cuba's Communist strongman Fidel Castro continued to "export revolution" to Puerto Rico and Angola and a score of places in between, Reagan said. We had sacrificed democratic Taiwan to Communist China. Then there was the Panama giveaway. And worst of all, the Soviets were cleaning our clocks in war-making capabilities: "The Soviet Army outnumbers ours more than two to one and in Reserves four to one. They outspend us on weapons by fifty percent. Their Navy outnumbers ours in surface ships and submarines two to one. We're outgunned in artillery three to one and their tanks outnumber ours four to one. Their strategic nuclear missiles are larger, more powerful, and more numerous than ours."

None of these stark and terrifying "facts" about Soviet military superiority were true, but really, that was beside the point. "The evidence mounts that we are Number Two in a world where it's dangerous, if not fatal, to be second best." He believed in peace "as much as any man," he said. "But peace does not come from weakness or from retreat. It comes from the restoration of American military superiority."

The turnaround after North Carolina was dramatic: After going 0 for 6 at the start of the primary season, Reagan won four of the next six primaries, swept up every delegate in Texas, Alabama, and Georgia, and extended the race all the way to the convention that summer. He did grudgingly concede to Gerald Ford at that convention, but Ronald Reagan never again took his eyes off the White House. He had made himself a big pin on the political map and he understood exactly how he'd done it. When something worked for Reagan, he stuck with it. So while the new Democratic president who defeated Ford, Jimmy Carter, picked up the Ford policy and negotiated a strategically beneficial treaty with Panama, while mainstream Democrats and Republicans in the Senate joined together to work toward the two-thirds vote necessary for ratification, while right-wing archbishop William F. Buckley and America's beloved tough guy John Wayne (yes, *that* John Wayne) campaigned full-on for the ratification of Carter's treaty, Reagan demagogued with a vengeance. "The loss of the Panama Canal," Reagan said in one of his weekly radio addresses, "would contribute to the encirclement of the US by hostile naval forces, and thereby [threaten] our ability to survive."

Even after John Wayne sent Reagan a private and personal note offering to show him "point by goddamn point in the treaty where you are misinforming people," and offering fair warning that it was time for the Gipper to shut his piehole ("If you continue to make these erroneous remarks, someone will publicize your letter to prove that you are not as thorough in your reviewing of this treaty as you say or are damned obtuse when it comes to reading the English language"), Ronald Reagan doubled down. He cited a former "defense intelligence" expert, Gen. Daniel O. Graham (and put a pin in that name), who said rumors of Castro's Communist minions at work in the fields of Panama were based on "pretty solid evidence." He also cited a former chairman of the Joint Chiefs who "expressed the gravest concern about surrendering the canal to a leftist oriented government allied with Cuba, citing the danger of giving this advantage to a man who might permit Soviet power and influence to prevail by proxy over the canal. He said the 'economic lifeline of the entire Western hemisphere would be jeopardized.'"

In private correspondence with his good friend Bill Buckley, leading up to their nationally televised 1978 *Firing Line* debate

on the Panama issue, Reagan professed a much more accom-
modating view, one that involved maybe internationalizing the
operation of the Canal. But on TV he stuck to his crowd-pleasing
hard line. "We bought it, we paid for it, we built it, and we intend
to keep it!" was not a slogan that invited waffling. "We would
become a laughingstock by surrendering to unreasonable de-
mands, and by doing so, I think we cloak weakness in the suit of
virtue" was how Reagan closed the *Firing Line* debate. "I think
that the world would see it as, once again, Uncle Sam putting his
tail between his legs and creeping away rather than face trouble."

Buckley was on the right side of history in his argument for the
treaty. Panama's subsequent control of the Canal did not create a
threat to "the economic lifeline of the entire western hemisphere,"
or any other kind of threat to the United States. It's been a technocratic nonissue for the most part. But the intellectual father of the
modern conservative movement still marveled at the rewarding
political vein Reagan had tapped. "I think that Governor Reagan
put his finger on it when he said the reason this treaty is unpopular is because we're tired of being pushed around."

By the time the Canal treaty made it to the Senate floor for
ratification, Reagan's histrionics had almost torpedoed the
thing, aided by millions of desperate, pants-on-fire direct-mail
appeals from the Conservative Caucus, and by the American
Conservative Union's "documentary" with the self-parodying
title "There Is No Panama Canal . . . There Is an American
Canal in Panama." "This may be the most important TV program you've ever watched," an ACU spokesman blared on the
eve of the broadcast. What should have been a slam-dunk ratification became an act of political courage in the Senate. Reagan
and his growing right-wing "truth" machine had stirred public
opinion to such a frothy head that Senate Minority Leader Howard Baker was warned that a vote for the treaty would cost him

any chance at the GOP presidential nomination in 1980. On the way to the Senate floor to cast his aye vote, a popular centrist Democrat from New Hampshire asked his wife to "come on and watch me lose my seat."

The treaty squeaked through by a single vote, but it gave Reagan and the right wing of the Republican Party an issue that kept on giving. The next two election cycles were bloodbaths for the Senate Democrats. That New Hampshire senator lost his seat; so did the treaty's floor manager, four-term senator Frank Church, who could not overcome a last-minute conservative ad blitz funded by the National Conservative Political Action Committee: "Now that all the shouting is over, remember the Panama Canal, built with American blood and treasure. Frank Church voted to give it away." Birch Bayh of Indiana lost to a callow, lightweight Republican named Dan Quayle, and the 1972 presidential nominee George McGovern lost his South Dakota seat in an embarrassing 58–39 landslide.

But the Reagan assault didn't stop at the party line. A slew of moderate Republicans who had supported the treaty were swept aside for being weak-kneed, such as Kansan James B. Pearson, who retired amid catcalls that he was not "Republican enough," and old lions like Clifford Case and Jacob Javits, who lost ignominiously in the primary to a county supervisor from Long Island named Alfonse D'Amato. In November 1980, when Republicans gained control of the Senate for the first time since the end of 1954, this was not your father's Republican Party. The Senate newbies were amped up, doctrinaire, undistracted by facts on the ground, and primed for a fight in which America could prove itself mighty once again. And at the head of the parade was the new president-elect, Ronald Wilson Reagan.

· · ·

Just a few months before Ronald Reagan became America's fortieth president, a former director of the White House Military Office wrote a book revealing the contents held within the world's most terrifying valise, America's "nuclear football." They included an eight-to-ten-page list of secure and comfortable accommodations available to the president in the event of nuclear war; a black book full of cartoonish illustrations, with a constantly updated menu of retaliation possibilities ("Rare," "Medium," and "Well-Done") thoughtfully highlighted in red; and a simple three-by-five-inch recipe card with the authentication codes the president needed to unleash our nation's full lethal fury.

Protocol regarding the nuclear football was well established by the time Reagan entered the White House. The military aide carrying the Zero Halliburton briefcase for the day was tasked to stick close to the president. The first reason was operational. Our commander in chief had to have that case at the ready at all hours, with the authentication codes easy to find, just in case. At a moment's notice, the president could dial up anything from "firing a tactical nuclear weapon, one of them," remembered a later nuclear-football-toting aide, "to full-bore Armageddon." The second reason for full-time proximity was more in the realm of public relations. Photojournalists were always snapping pictures of the president, so the Soviets were certain to get constant pictorial reminders that our nuclear button was never beyond reach. Consequently, White House military aides saw a lot of the president, which perhaps bred a certain amount of familiarity, which could be why one aide, John Kline, wondered aloud if maybe Ronald Reagan was doing something out of line. Kline noticed that his boss was *saluting* members of the armed forces. Soldiers were supposed to salute their president; the president was not supposed to salute the soldiers. No modern president, not even old General Eisenhower, had saluted military personnel. It might even be, well, sort of, improper. Reagan seemed disappointed at this news. Kline suggested he talk to the commandant of the United States Marine Corps and get his advice, and the commandant's advice ran something like this: *You're the goddamn president. You can salute whoever you goddamn well please.* So Ronald Reagan continued saluting his soldiers, and he encouraged his own vice president and successor, George H. W. Bush, to do the same. And every president since has followed.

Ronald Reagan loved the military; even long after he left the presidency he was still extolling the virtues of martial efficiency as compared to the federal government's bloated, bureaucrat-driven civil service system. When he saluted the military, Reagan really meant it. He'd been a soldier himself, he'd sometimes remind people, a captain in fact, with a pretty high security clearance. Way back in 1937, Reagan had done the patriotic thing and signed up as a reserve officer in the US Army Cavalry. Because of the actor's debilitating nearsightedness, the Reserves had deemed Reagan capable of only "limited duty." But then, after Pearl Harbor, and just as his movie career seemed finally to be taking off, the cavalry unceremoniously plucked him out of his $5,000-a-week job as a contract player at Warner Bros. and sent him to a San Francisco supply depot loading ships bound for Australia. Lt. Reagan never complained. His country was at war and this was what he'd signed on for.

The Army physical didn't do much for Reagan's self-esteem, as he described it in one of his autobiographies: "One of the doctors who was administering the test told me after checking my eyes that if they sent me overseas, I'd shoot a general. The other doctor said, 'Yes, and you'd miss him.' My report read: 'Confined to the continental limits, eligible for corps area service command or War Department overhead only.'" He'd be good for pushing paper, in other words, and that was about it.

As luck would have it, Reagan's old studio boss, Jack Warner, had just been sworn into the Army as a lieutenant colonel, though unlike Lt. Reagan, Warner got to keep drawing his civilian salary. Warner's orders were to stand up a movie-making team within the Army Air Corps. The First Motion Picture Unit, Fum-Poo in Army acronym speak, would be responsible for the Air Corps' total celluloid output, from combat photography of bombing runs to full-blown rah-rah morale-building motion pictures to training films for pilots and their crews such as *Aircraft Wood Repair: Parts 1 thru 4; Uncrating and Assembly of the Thunderbolt Airplane; Oil Fires, Their Prevention and Extinguishment;* and *Land and Live in the Jungle* and its sequels *Land and Live in the Desert* and *How to Survive in the Arctic.*

Warner needed men familiar with movie production. So two months into his tour at the port in San Francisco, Reagan received orders to report to the old Hal Roach Studios in Culver City for his new job as Fum-Poo's personnel officer, where he could also moonlight as needed as an actor and narrator for the unit films. His commander in San Francisco, a career officer from Virginia Military Institute, was flabbergasted by Reagan's new assignment. The Army had a long history of mismatching men and jobs, but Reagan's assignment to the Army's in-house movie studio was a move of exquisite logic and thoroughgoing good sense. "In thirty-four years, this is the first time I've ever seen the Army make sense," said the colonel. "This is putting a square peg in a square hole." Reagan might not have had great potential as a soldier, but few men were better equipped to perform the role of a soul-stirring make-believe soldier.

Reagan could be amused by the goings-on at Fort Roach—"a completely unofficial title, and one, I think, that was not intended to be complimentary," he wrote in his autobiography. He always got a chuckle out of seeing some visiting regular

Army colonel saluting an actor-private who was costumed as a general. But the mission of Fum-Poo was no joke to Reagan. Even the simplest training films required mastery of both the craft of filmmaking and the technical know-how of flying and maintaining America's expensive new weapons—an array of advanced high-altitude bombers and aerobatic fighter planes with the latest electronic control systems.

But the real Hollywood magic was reserved, in the dark days after Pearl Harbor, for the Big Sell. At the beginning of the war, Army Air Corps chief Hap Arnold figured he needed fifty thousand pilots and maybe triple that number of crewmen. The general needed a recruiting tool, and wanted movies with heart-thumping scenes of the "full inspirational splendor of roaring engines," he said, "of tight bomber formations gliding through the clouds," to be distributed in target-rich environments like high schools and colleges. Pilots signed up by the droves. Reagan's future vice president enlisted right out of high school, against his own father's advice. But when the Air Corps fell short of the enlistment quota for its most notoriously dangerous assignment, rear gunner, Arnold turned to Jack Warner and Fum-Poo to help him invest that job with "some romantic appeal."

The result was a twenty-six-minute short film, *Rear Gunner*, starring Burgess Meredith as milquetoast Kansas farm boy Pee Wee Williams and Ronald Reagan as an eagle-eye lieutenant who thought Private Pee Wee might have bigger things in store for him than aircraft maintenance. "Pee Wee," Reagan asks, "how'd you like to go to gunnery school?" In short order, Pee Wee would be molded into an ice-veined, steel-eyed warrior—"one of aviation's mightiest little men . . . a Galahad of gunnery"—and then shipped off to the Pacific to serve on the flight crew headed by that same eagle-eyed lieutenant. By the time the film ended,

Pee Wee had won the Distinguished Service Medal, and potential recruits had been reminded that "the fire from your guns is the fire of freedom."

Rear Gunner worked on a variety of levels. American audiences knew nothing of Reagan's trepidation about actual flying, but they'd seen his previous turns as a hero pilot in movies such as *Secret Service of the Air*, *International Squadron*, and *Desperate Journey*. And publicity for *Rear Gunner* noted that both Meredith and Reagan were active-duty lieutenants: "Perhaps they were more than acting their parts in the film—perhaps they were living them."

Reagan really never did more than act the part of a combat soldier. He spent his entire war at that Culver City back lot, with Hollywood's once and future stars, directors, and producers, helping the 1,200-man-strong motion-picture unit churn out more than four hundred training, recruiting, or booster films. He never busted out to fly combat missions like Clark Gable or Jimmy Stewart; he never got a chance to fight the Japs like his actor friend Eddie Albert did. But Reagan took pride in the fact that he'd done what was asked of him, and he'd taken to heart one of Fum-Poo's central missions: to keep reminding the folks at home (the ones who could buy the war bonds, for instance) that the United States and its military power was all that stood between our freedoms and the maniacal world-enslaving designs of Adolf Hitler and his Japanese allies. Nearly forty years later, he'd hauled himself into the White House by reminding the folks at home that US military might was all that stood between our freedoms and the maniacal world-enslaving designs of the Soviets and their energetic and ruthless agent in the Western Hemisphere, Fidel Castro.

By the time Reagan became president he'd long since come to understand that good enemies (even welfare queens and tinhorn

dictators) make good politics. The two previous Oval Office inhabitants had made plenty of hay with war metaphors, but they
never really set up suitably threatening or concrete antagonists.
Gerald Ford had declared war on the high cost of living ("Whip
Inflation Now!") . . . and lost the presidency. His successor,
Jimmy Carter, had declared war on our national dependence on
foreign oil. Carter's renowned 1979 "malaise speech"—the one
in which he never uttered the word "malaise"—is little remembered as what it actually was: a call to arms for fixing our nation's dire energy future. "Beginning this moment, this nation
will never use more foreign oil than we did in 1977—never,"
President Carter said in his nationally televised address to the
nation. "The generation-long growth in our dependence on foreign oil will be stopped dead in its tracks right now and then
reversed as we move through the 1980s, for I am tonight setting the further goal of cutting our dependence on foreign oil
by one-half by the end of the next decade." Carter was going
to use all the weapons at his disposal: import quotas, public
investment in coal, solar power and alternative fuel, and—
drum-roll, please—"a bold conservation program" where "every
act of energy conservation . . . is more than just common sense;
I tell you it is an act of patriotism." He tried to make it all
sound as martial as possible: "Just as a similar synthetic rubber
corporation helped us win World War II, so will we mobilize
American determination and ability to win the energy war. . . .
We must deal with the energy problem on a war footing . . . the
moral equivalent of war . . . a fundamental threat to American
democracy . . . the threat . . . the crisis . . . threatening to destroy
the social and the political fabric of America . . . a clear and
present danger to our nation." Name-checking the world wars
repeatedly, Carter declared that "energy . . . can also be the
standard around which we rally!"

But somehow Carter's "battlefield of energy" never really filled up with eager American combatants. It just never felt like anybody was going to be draped in glory for taking public transportation, or carpooling, or turning down the thermostat and wearing a cardigan.

Lost in President Carter's ten-car pileup of war metaphors was a line that probably should have been his headline that night: that America was "a nation that is at peace tonight everywhere in the world." But Jimmy Carter did not try to sell that; instead, he declared a "war" on the energy crisis . . . and lost the presidency.

The founders were onto something with their cautions about that whole military vainglory thing. There really is nothing that approaches war's political potency. Carter proved this point in failure—shouting into the void that something other than a war, if maybe you *called* it a war, "can rekindle our sense of unity, our confidence in the future, and give our nation and all of us individually a new sense of purpose." No, it can't. Or at least, no, it hasn't.

In 1895, at a time when America had enjoyed peace for more than a generation, a fifty-five-year-old Massachusetts judge named Oliver Wendell Holmes Jr. delivered a Memorial Day speech called "A Soldier's Faith" that, as well as anything before or since, described Americans' attraction to war. It's not just the mistake of kings—even in a government that is by, for, and of the people, the people's own understandable, emotional inclination to war can make it hard for a country to remain peaceable.

"War, when you are at it, is horrible and dull. It is only when time has passed that you see that its message was divine. . . . In this snug, over-safe corner of the world we need it that we may realize that our comfortable routine is no eternal necessity of things, but merely a little space of calm in the midst of the tempestuous, untamed streaming of the world, and in order that we may be ready for danger." Thousands of citizens had assembled to hear Holmes's Memorial Day oration, but the judge was speaking mainly for the benefit of the stooped and grizzled old soldiers in the crowd that day.

More than thirty years earlier, Holmes had fought in the Civil War, in what remain, to this day, America's most terrifying and costly battles. He was shot through the neck and left to die at Antietam, where nearly twenty thousand of his countrymen were killed or wounded in a single afternoon. Nearly two years later, he was still up and in the fight. In the Wilderness campaign, he saw a man instantaneously decapitated by flying shrapnel and noted in his diary the carnage at the Bloody Angle: "the dead of both sides lay piled in the trenches 5 or 6 deep—wounded often writhing under the superincumbent dead." And only then, aged twenty-three years and two months, did Holmes finally choke on the blood. He walked away from that war before the outcome was decided, with little concern for which side won or lost. "I have felt for sometime," he wrote to his parents in May 1864, "that I didn't any longer believe in this being a duty."

But as he delivered "A Soldier's Faith" thirty years later, Oliver Wendell Holmes had been enveloped by the practiced amnesia of a willful romantic. "It is not well for soldiers to think much about wounds," he said that day. "Sooner or later we fall, but meantime it is for us to fix our eyes upon the point to be stormed, and to get there if we can." After walking away from his own war when he lost his sense of its purpose, decades later, Holmes made that purpose war itself; war, regardless of its cause, as its own reward, its own sublime virtue, an inevitable consequence simply of life as man, and man's need for a reason to need one another. He continued:

> As long as man dwells upon the globe, his destiny is battle. I do not know what is true. I do not know the meaning of the universe. But in the midst of doubt, in the collapse of creeds, there is one thing I do not doubt, that no man who lives in the same world with most of us can doubt, and that is that the faith is true and adorable which leads a soldier to throw away his life in obedience to a blindly accepted duty, in a cause which he little understands, in a plan of campaign of which he has no notion, under tactics of which he does not see the use. . . .
>
> Perhaps it is not vain for us to tell the new generation what we learned in our day, and what we still believe. That the joy of life is living, is to put out all one's powers as far as they will go; that the measure of power is obstacles overcome; to ride boldly at what is in front of you, be it fence or enemy; to pray, not for comfort, but for combat; to keep the soldier's faith against the doubts of civil life, more besetting and harder to overcome than all the misgivings of the battlefield, and to remember that duty is not to be proved in the evil day, but then to be obeyed unquestioning; to love glory more than the temptations of wallowing ease. . . .
>
> We have shared the incommunicable experience of war; we have felt, we still feel, the passion of life to its top.

If the eighty years that followed Holmes's ode to soldiering is any guide, Americans share his suspicion of peace and his conviction that battle can be a source of existential meaning and personal uplift. This country developed a serious war jones.

Even a bookish and bespectacled Princeton professor named Woodrow Wilson cheered "the young men who prefer dying in the ditches of the Philippines to spending their lives behind the counters of a dry-goods store in our eastern cities. I think I should prefer that myself." We'd got in the habit of being at war, and not against some economic crisis, but real war—big, small, hot, cold, air, sea, or ground—and against real enemies. Sometimes they'd attacked us, and sometimes we'd gone out of our way to find them. It had got to the point that being "at peace everywhere in the world, with unmatched economic power and military might" was a condition to be downplayed, a losing political message, as if being at peace, in our "snug, over-safe corner of the world," made us edgy, as if we no longer knew, absent an armed conflict, how to be our best selves.

Chapter 3

Let 'Er Fly

JOHN TRAVOLTA'S APPEARANCE IN AN ARMY PUBLIC SERVICE announcement—with production values on a par with early public-access cable television—is an oddly reassuring artifact from the '70s, and a useful marker to show just how deeply Ronald Reagan changed the way Americans think about their military. Here was the not-yet-famous teenage Travolta, a fresh-faced if slightly confused-looking new recruit not long removed from the hallways of his New Jersey high school, pillow-lipped, goofily coiffed, weaponless, with his future star wattage tucked neatly into Army-issue olive drabs, receiving a ceremonial lei and a kiss on the cheek from a lovely and inviting Asian American woman. He was all smiles at the bargain the Army was offering him: free housing, thirty days of paid vacation (could be Hawaii!), a starting salary of $288 a month ("*every* month"), and, with so much paid for, enough cash left over to finance a new car.

The military marketers had started retooling their sales pitch when the unspooling Vietnam disaster had convinced politicians the time had come to end the draft. The Army brass had to get people to *volunteer* for military service, and they found themselves thrown into the business of devising new ways to improve its sagging public image and to showcase its most alluring features to

potential recruits—give it "some romantic appeal," as old Hap
Arnold used to say. The good news was that recruiters no longer had to trundle their reels of film around to high schools
and colleges; they could get to the boys right in their own living rooms while they watched popular TV shows like *Laugh-In,
Bonanza, Mannix,* and—"Here come da Judge! Here come da
Judge!"—*The Flip Wilson Show.*

"To achieve the goal of voluntary accessions, it will be necessary to greatly increase the reach and frequency of our advertising delivery, particularly against the prime target audience of
young men," the Army's director of advertising and information
confessed. "We must follow the lead of the razor blades, shaving
creams, and automobiles, and buy the time necessary to deliver
the audiences we need to reach." Recruiting specialists found
$10 million in the Army's annual budget to begin selling itself
in this mod new way, and handed the account to the venerable
old agency N. W. Ayer & Son, who convinced the generals that
they knew just how to talk to civilians. The officers in charge,
however, were less than pleased when the admen pitched them
the slogan "Today's Army Wants to Join You."

"Do you have to say it that way?" said the Army chief of staff.
The retired general in charge of the Defense Manpower Commission was more blunt: "God, I just wanted to vomit." But they
grudgingly signed off, surprising even some of the ad executives
at Ayer.

The "Today's Army Wants to Join You" campaign flipped on
its head the old ethos. The message was no longer about what
you could do for Uncle Sam. *Honor, Duty, Country? The fire
from your guns is the fire of freedom?* Whatever. Gunnery wasn't
a big part of the pitch. The Army was now selling all the wonderful ways Uncle Sam and the military could improve your life.
And he wouldn't even make you cut your hair *that* short. "We

care more about how you think than how you cut your hair," the Army reassured potential recruits. The initial test run of paid television advertising turned out to be a success—recruitment in the period jumped by four thousand over the previous year—but the ads also induced nausea in the chairman of the House Armed Services Committee. He cut off funding for the advertising campaign, and the Army fell back to its mainstays: public service announcements and print ads.

Still, those print ads were stylish four-color magazine deals, featuring shirtless young men playing touch football on the beach, promising the opportunity to enlist with your buddies and go through basic training together . . . guaranteed in writing. "The Army wants to accommodate you. And the guys." There were ads featuring the exotic emoluments of an extended European vacation: here you are in a green velvet jacket, high collar, long sideburns, sitting *intime* in a fashionable Parisian café with a beautiful blonde (could she be Swedish?), sporting a comely crocheted beret. This could be available to you from your posting with "one of seven crack outfits stationed in Germany . . . within easy reach of any free weekend, Italy and the Riviera are just a few hours away. . . . If you want to live and work where tourists only visit, drop us the coupon."

For teenagers less enticed by continental savoir faire, like the guys who might have gone in for the old G.I. Joe Adventure Team, there were the ads in *Field & Stream* ("You get 12 matches, a knife, some twine, and 3 days to enjoy yourself") that made military service appear to be a minimally weaponized Boy Scout troop where you could design your own special training mission. "And if your unit commander likes the idea," promised the Army, "we'll even supply the equipment."

The Army's new pitch was simple. Good pay, good benefits, a manageable amount of adventure . . . but don't worry, we're not looking to pick fights these days. For a country that had paid so dear a price for its recent military buccaneering, the message was comforting. We still had the largest and most technologically advanced standing army in the world, the most nuclear weapons, the best and most powerful conventional weapons systems, the biggest navy. At the same time, to the average recruit the promise wasn't some imminent and dangerous combat deployment; it was 288 bucks a month (*every* month), training, travel, and experience. Selling the post-Vietnam military as a career choice meant selling the idea of peacetime service. It meant selling the idea of peacetime. Barf.

Ronald Reagan's election in 1980 changed all that in a hurry. Although it's laughable enough in retrospect to have been deliberately forgotten by a Reagan-worshipping country only one thin generation later, "Reagan did not forget the impact, especially among conservatives, of his stand on the Panama Canal," William F. Buckley would write in *The Reagan I Knew*. Reagan knew provocations to American strength and pride ("Uncle Sam putting his tail between his legs and creeping away rather than face trouble") could easily mow down commonsense arguments where national security was concerned. Revving the American fighting machine into high idle, he'd discovered by the time he entered the Oval Office, made very good politics. And he was trained to be good at it.

During World War II, the Army Air Corps film unit had not only shown the Gipper the importance of public relations, it had made him a practiced hand at stirring America's martial moxie. That had been his part to play, and he was proud of it. He'd starred in the Fum-Poo training short *Jap Zero* ("How soon do I get a chance to knock one of 'em down?"). He'd narrated

Target Tokyo, the film story of the bomber crews who flew, as he intoned, "almost halfway around the world, to return a visit that had been paid to Pearl Harbor three years before. Pearl Harbor was on their minds now: the two thousand American men dead. Hickam Field in flames . . . there were other things on their minds. There was a triumphant feeling of being first, the advance guard of a long procession of superforts that would smash Tokyo." Here was a spokesman who could utter, without betraying a hint of self-consciousness, lines such as "It's shooting like this that will knock them on their axis" or "The Japanese—a people we used to think of as small, dainty, polite, concerning themselves only with floral arrangements and rock gardens, and the cultivation of silk worms."

In his inaugural address in 1981, President Reagan got up and thrummed for all it was worth that old tried-and-not-quite-true Holmesian melody about duty and soldiering. He even made a point to buck tradition and make his speech from the back side of the Capitol Building, facing west, so that, near the end of that talk, he could steer the nation's gaze toward

> the sloping hills of Arlington National Cemetery with its
> row on row of simple white markers. . . . They add up to
> only a tiny fraction of the price that has been paid for our
> freedoms. Each one of those markers is a monument to
> the kinds of hero I spoke of earlier. Their lives ended in
> places called Belleau Wood, the Argonne, Omaha Beach,
> Salerno . . . on Guadalcanal, Tarawa, Pork Chop Hill,
> the Chosin Reservoir, and in a hundred rice paddies and
> jungles of a place called Vietnam. Under one such marker
> lies a young man—Martin Treptow—who left his job in a
> small-town barber shop in 1917 to go to France with the
> famed Rainbow Division. There, on the Western Front, he

was killed trying to carry a message between battalions
under heavy artillery fire. We are told that on his body
was found a diary. On the flyleaf under the heading "My
Pledge," he had written these words: "America must win
this war. Therefore, I will work, I will save, I will sacrifice,
I will endure, I will fight cheerfully and do my utmost, as
if the issue of the whole struggle depended on me alone."

Private Treptow, it turns out, is actually buried back home in
Bloomer, Wisconsin, and nobody on Reagan's team was able to
verify the contents of this battlefield diary. These problematic
actualities had been pointed out to Reagan before he gave the
speech. But he waved off the fact-checkers. He wasn't going to
let them get in the way of a useful bit of salesmanship.

Our military leaders heard this new tune and instantly recognized it as something they could dance to. They'd grown weary
of falling short of recruitment quotas, and they chafed at the
news that the public approval ratings of the military, as measured by Gallup pollsters, were at an all-time low. The general
in charge of Army recruiting had already read the riot act to the
boys at the N. W. Ayer agency. The era of selling velvet jackets
and vacation pay was coming to an end. "I got it straight with
them that I was in charge of the advertising," he later said. "They
weren't in charge of it, I was."

Beginning in 1981, the Army started spending money on
high-production-value, high-testosterone action ads featuring airborne jumps, attack helicopters, tanks with laser-guided
firing systems and the latest computers, stirring music with
one-off lyrics ("There's a hungry kind of feeling, and every day it
grows"), can-do copy ("In the Army, we do more before nine a.m.
than most people do all day"), and, of course, the toe-tapping
jingle you couldn't get out of your head: "Be . . . all that you can

be . . . 'cause we need you . . . in the Aaaaaaaar-my." And just at the moment the Army sales force took this bold and combative new tack, the Reagan administration buried them in money; the Army's ad budget arced to more than $100 million during Reagan's years in office.

The new president was ready to put our money where his mouth was; he was anxious to expend enormous pots of the national resources to improve our war-making capabilities. And it was an easy sell at first. He'd run on cutting taxes, gutting welfare programs, and spending big on the military. By the time his first budget came up for a vote, Ronald Reagan was also riding a wave of public popularity, largely on the strength of having survived a near-fatal assassination attempt with remarkable grace, at least according to the information released by the White House public relations officers. His personal approval rating in the country was more than 70 percent. So Congress—its members could read a poll—overwhelmingly passed Reagan's initial defense appropriation request, which clocked in at a nearly 20 percent increase. In something as huge as the Pentagon budget, a 5 percent increase would have been enough to rattle desks all over Washington; 10 percent was almost unimaginable; getting up toward 20 percent was fantasy talk. That kind of enormous one-year jump was unprecedented—at least it was without our troops actively fighting on a battlefield somewhere. And that play-money request from Reagan came with a promise of more: the administration's announced strategy was to *double* the defense budget in five years.

By the time that first massive defense appropriation passed, coupled with the largest tax cuts in American history, Reagan's budget director, David Stockman, was already trying to flag to the president a new threat. The projected annual budget deficit had ballooned to $62 billion, Stockman advised, and—at current taxing and spending levels—was sure to hit $112 billion within five years. The yearly deficit, which had generally hovered around 2 percent of GDP in the postwar years, would jump to unprecedented peacetime levels, as much as 4 or 5 percent. When Stockman suggested that the country's financial situation would benefit from a small reduction to the planned increase of the annual defense budget in the coming years, Reagan would have none of it. "When I was asked during the campaign about what I would do if it came down to a choice between defense and deficits," he explained to Stockman, "I always said national security had to come first, and the people applauded every time."

Reagan had plenty of politically astute advisers on his team who knew that they could not count on the president's personal popularity for the long haul. And they knew they could not count on Americans to forever turn a blind eye to exploding budget deficits. Key to managing public expectations and acceptance of this massive defense spending spree was to manage the public's perception of the need for it.

The more or less paranoid contention that America was a nation under existential threat was the propulsive force of the Reagan presidency. The threat that Reagan exalted above all others—the Enemy—remained an important and lasting mental bedfellow for the president, even as other things faded for him. Just a year after he left office, while reluctantly testifying at the federal criminal trial of one of his former staff members, Reagan could no longer place the name of the man who served him for more than three years as chairman of the Joint Chiefs of Staff ("Oh dear. I have to ask for your help here. His name is very familiar") or recognize the leader of the Nicaraguan military group he'd pledged to support "body and soul." He could not recall the specifics of a single meeting with the defendant, Adm. John Poindexter, with whom he'd met one-on-one every day for nearly a year. He had virtually no recollection of signing the momentous presidential finding that could have led to his impeachment in the Iran-Contra scandal.

Looking back now, it is sadly apparent that this was not simply a legal tactic but a physical manifestation of the Alzheimer's disease that had already begun to eat away his mind. When attorneys presented him with transcripts of his speeches and press statements, Reagan beheld them with the delight of first discovery. But in the middle of this arduous and, as he admitted, confusing day and a half of back-and-forth with lawyers, in an instant of unexpected and shocking clarity, Reagan offered an unsolicited reminder to these young attorneys of just what he'd been up against as president: "We only had to heed the words of Lenin, which was what was guiding them, when Lenin said that the Soviet Union would take Eastern Europe, it would organize the hordes of Asia and then it would move on Latin America. And, once having taken that, it wouldn't have to take the last bastion of capitalism, the United States. The United States would fall into their outstretched hand like overripe fruit. Well, history reveals that the Soviet Union followed that policy." It was a stirring moment in an otherwise sad and dreary courtroom exercise, when the ex-president let loose with his eloquent little peroration and showed a flash of the ol' Gipper. He could still remember his best lines. And deliver them too.

Never mind that Lenin didn't ever say or write this. Reagan likely got the quote from *The Blue Book of the John Birch Society,* circa 1958, which had cribbed it from the fanciful US Senate testimony of a youngish Russian exile by the name of Nicholas Goncharoff, who was just three years old when Lenin died. The fake Lenin quote in the original Goncharoff-Bircher rendering did not in fact mention Latin America, but Reagan was never shy about ad-libbing an update here, an improvement there. His point was, when he walked into the Oval Office, the Soviet Union, "the evil empire" bent on world domination, was out to enslave the citizens of the United States. And the Soviets had fellow travelers lurking right here on our own continent: the Cuban strongman Fidel Castro and a growing contingent of Marxist revolutionaries who were working hard to make Communist satellites of El Salvador, Honduras, Costa Rica, Nicaragua. There was a Bolshevik in every *baño*.

When Team Reagan started down the road to military buildup, its ideological and quasi-intellectual backup came from the post–World War II phenomenon of the permanent national security hawk nest, the out-of-power roost for ex-military, ex-intelligence, ex–Capitol Hill, defense industry, academic, and self-proclaimed experts on threats to the United States and how (inevitably) those threats were being ignored by the naïve government apparatchiks these restless hawks were eager to replace. The Think Tanks and Very Important Committees of the permanent national security peanut gallery are now so mature and entrenched that almost no one thinks they're creepy anymore, and national security liberals have simply decided it's best to add their own voices to them rather than criticize them. But like we lefties learned in trying (and failing) to add a liberal network to the all-right-wing, decades-old medium of political talk radio, the permanent defense gadfly world can't really grow a liberal wing. It's an inherently hawkish enterprise. Where's the inherent urgency in arguing that the threats aren't as bad as the hype, that military power is being overused, that the defense budget could safely and wisely be scaled back, that maybe this next war doesn't need us? The only audience for defense wonk-ery is defense enthusiasts, and they're not paying the price of admission to hear that defense is overrated.

Even before President Carter was losing the nation's attention with his talk of "a nation that is at peace tonight everywhere in the world," the oh-no-you-don't defense-igentsia's alternate po-sition was being proclaimed by a cabal of academics, military officials, and businessmen (a director of the defense contrac-tor Boeing, for instance), who liked to meet for lunch over the starched white tablecloths of Washington's exclusive Metropoli-tan Club; they called themselves the Committee on the Present Danger. Among the committee members were the rabid anti-communists Paul "Missile Gap" Nitze, who was well known for his frightening and incorrect assertions in the 1950s that the So-viets had achieved superiority in offensive nuclear missiles; Gen. Daniel O. Graham, Reagan's go-to guy on Panama and godfather of the Star Wars defense shield; James R. Schlesinger, who was at that moment eloquently and vociferously sick and tired of the nation's neurotic hand-wringing; and historian Richard Pipes, who liked to bash his lefty academic colleagues while using his Harvard faculty credentials as proof of his own intellectual bona fides. The mélange of suit-and-tie warriors fancied themselves latter-day Paul Reveres, and in the spring of 1976, in the cos-seted world of the Metropolitan Club, they began scripting the dire warning that the Russians were coming, the Russians were coming—that the Soviet Union had *surpassed* the West in both nuclear and conventional force capabilities. The Russians were building their strategic (aka offensive) capabilities, they said, toward not just starting and not just fighting, but starting and fighting and *winning* a nuclear war. And there was nobody in the United States intelligence apparatus clever enough to under-stand it, not like the Present Danger luncheoneers.

The Committee on the Present Danger might have finished its career as a forgotten lot of kooks if it weren't for Ronald Reagan. The first thing he did for them was to prove that you could get real political traction with their kind of scare tactics. "The evidence mounts that we are Number Two in a world where it's dangerous, if not fatal, to be second best," Reagan had said on the campaign trail, on his way to nearly upsetting sitting president Gerald Ford in the primaries. When Reagan began roughing up Ford in that election season, Ford's new CIA head decided he could provide the president some political cover from the tough-talking right by acquiescing to the Present Danger luncheoneers' demand to participate in the government's official top secret estimate of Soviet military and political strength. "Let 'er fly!" Director George H. W. Bush wrote, inviting this group of "outside experts" (they would be called Team B) to look over the shoulder of his agency analysts and come up with a parallel assessment of the Soviet threat.

From the start, Team B was much more interested in the political and public relations benefits of participating in the National Intelligence Estimate than in the final product itself. When Team B looked at the intelligence data, it was sure to misread it, and not by a matter of slight degree. Team B wildly overhyped the flight range of the Soviets' Backfire bomber, rendering it a threat to America's East Coast when in fact it had a proven combat radius that left it about three thousand miles short. Their estimate of future production numbers of the bomber was off by more than 100 percent. They asserted, falsely, that the Soviets were working furiously on laser-beam weapons that were nearing deployment. Because the United States had developed acoustic devices for tracking nuclear subs, Team B assumed the Soviets had them too. When it was unable to find a whit of evidence that the Russians had developed these acoustic devices, Team B simply invented for the Soviets "non-acoustic" devices. As Anne Hessing Cahn, a former Defense Department official who wrote a book about the Team B fiasco, noted: "They're saying, 'We can't find any evidence that they're doing it the way everyone thinks they're doing it, so they must be doing it a different way. We don't know what that different way is, but they must be doing it.'"

The obfuscations and make-believe continued for fifty-five breathless pages. The Team B report incorrectly asserted that Soviet military spending, especially on new nuclear weapons, was on a steady upward trajectory. Team B was so wrong about the Soviets, so invested in hyperinflating the Soviet threat, that they even claimed that the USSR was exempt from the basic guns-versus-butter tradeoff that everyone learns on day one of macroeconomics class. In Team B's imaginings, the Soviets were so all-powerful that they didn't have to trade off anything. "Soviet strategic forces have yet to reflect any constraining effect of civil economy competition, and are unlikely to do so in the foreseeable future," wrote Team B, conjuring a world in which the Soviets could build all the tanks and tractors they wanted, without limit. In this, Team B simply brushed aside the settled historical fact that the Politburo could hardly keep its own people fed. "The spectacle," noted an official CIA analysis in 1964, "of the USSR, after boastful claims and plans a few years ago, coming to the West hat in hand to buy wheat and ask for long-term credits . . . These phenomena are not passing difficulties, nor are they merely consequences of misfortune. The source is deeper, and the problem will not soon go away." In fact, at the time Team B imagined for the Soviets an impossible sustained upward arc, Soviet military expenditures were flat or even falling.

Team B further asserted, with no hard evidence, that the Soviet Union had "hardened" its command-and-control structure to permit the Communists to win a nuclear war against the

United States, and was training its citizenry in a civil defense system that would ensure the survival of a large enough cohort of its population to maintain a viable nation after that war. Team B was apparently unaware of the joke among Muscovites about Soviet civil defense:

"What do you do in the event of a nuclear attack?"

"Wrap yourself in a white sheet and crawl slowly to the cemetery."

"Why slowly?"

"To avoid causing a panic."

In Team B's defense, not that many ordinary Russians made it to the Metropolitan Club for lunch in those days.

The umbrella assertion made by Team B—and the most inflammatory—was that the previous National Intelligence Estimates "substantially misperceived the motivations behind Soviet strategic programs, and thereby tended consistently to underestimate their intensity, scope, and implicit threat." Soviet military leaders weren't simply trying to defend their territory and their people; they were readying a First Strike option, and the US intelligence community had missed it. What led to this "grave and dangerous flaw" in threat assessment, according to Team B, was an overreliance on hard technical facts, and a lamentable tendency to downplay "the large body of soft data." This "soft" data, the ideological leader of Team B, Richard Pipes, would later say, included "his deep knowledge of the Russian soul."

Historian Pipes had not lived for any extended time in Eastern Europe since his family fled Poland at the beginning of World War II when he was still a teenager, and his area of expertise in Russian history stopped somewhere around 1923. America's self-proclaimed Kremlinologist never claimed any real sources of information inside the Kremlin. But that didn't mean he was shy about explaining "the grand strategy" of the Soviet leaders circa

1976; neither was he shy about parsing their psyches without a license. The Soviet Union, according to Pipes, was more than ever hell-bent on world domination. The old aristocracy sympathetic to the West had been killed off long ago; the people in charge were descended from a mindless and bitter peasantry, and they were wielding a lot more than pitchforks these days.

The Team B report may have been an exhilarating exercise for its members, allowing them the endorphin-producing experience of beating on the crania of the CIA's analysts, but the nation that Team B meant to wholly reorient to the ... uh ... "present danger" remained unaware of Team B's warnings. Their entire output was for the eyes of the president and his intelligence hands only. Pipes's efforts to get Team B's addendum to the NIE report declassified and into the widest possible circulation were rebuffed.

But that could be fixed: somebody from Team B started leaking its findings to the press, and then the Committee on the Present Danger published their own white-linen manifesto: "The principal threat to our nation, to world peace and to the cause of human freedom is the Soviet drive for dominance based upon an unparalleled military build-up."

They also published articles under unforgettable headlines such as "Why the Soviet Union Thinks It Could Fight & Win a Nuclear War" by Richard Pipes, who now had the imprimatur of his recent participation in the National Intelligence Estimate, and who therefore had, as far as his readers believed, the inside dope. The Committee on the Present Danger had gotten their message out there: The Soviet Union was actively trying to off us. *Now*. While the naïve among us thought we were at peace!

Ronald Reagan was a big fan of the Present Danger crowd; they would later claim he was a member. And it is certainly true that

he hired on many Present Danger men to serve in his administration, and not as bureaucratic pikers but as national security
adviser (Richard Allen), as director of Eastern European and Soviet Affairs (Richard Pipes), as chief negotiator on the Interme-
diate Range Nuclear Forces Treaty and later special adviser on
arms control (Paul Nitze), and as director of Central Intelligence
(William Casey). Casey, in particular, represented an incredible
shift to the . . . well, incredible. Willard C. Matthias, one of the
CIA's best-known and best-respected analysts going back to the
1950s, a man who tried to warn the Johnson administration in
1964 that a war in Vietnam was not winnable, summed it up
like this: "With Casey's arrival at the CIA, the campaign to shift
control of national estimates to the hard-line anti-Communist
faction of the intelligence community was over. The rational approach, with its commitment to keeping Soviet behavior under
continuing review, was replaced by one that simply identified the
USSR as an implacable and changeless enemy determined to enslave the world. The only question was when and how the Soviets
would attempt to do so. The issue was 'slavery' versus 'freedom.'"

Even before he was elected, Reagan had been making Casey's
slavery-versus-freedom argument himself, and he really believed it. He could occasionally be shocked when presented
with the logical operational extension of his hard-line rhetoric,
as when his first secretary of state, Alexander Haig, suggested
a US military attack on Cuba. "Give me the word," the nation's
chief of diplomacy said to the new president in March 1981, "and
I'll turn that island into a fucking parking lot." One of Reagan's
most loyal and longtime aides, Mike Deaver, later said that
Haig's pronouncement had "scared the shit out of me" and had
also shaken the boss. Deaver asked Chief of Staff James Baker
to make certain Haig was never again in a room alone with the
president.

But Reagan did not soften his own tough talk. In a nationally televised interview in March of 1981, when *CBS Evening
News* anchor Walter Cronkite suggested that Reagan might be
laying it on a little thick about the Soviet leaders being "liars
and thieves," the president stuck by his assessment, paraphrasing another hysterical Bircher trope: "We're naïve if we don't
remember their ideology is without God, without our idea of
morality in the religious sense—their statement about morality is that nothing is immoral if it furthers their cause, which
means that they can resort to lying or stealing or cheating or
even murder if it furthers their cause. . . . If we're going to deal
with them, then we have to keep that in mind."

That same month, the Reagan administration went into production on a new publication called *Soviet Military Power*. The
illustrated, ninety-nine-page booklet, released just as Reagan
was asking for added funding for MX missiles and B-1 bombers, was no internal government-eyes-only threat assessment.
This was straight-up politics, complete with dozens of specially
commissioned artists' renderings of the Soviet military's 25,000-
ton ballistic missile submarines, MiG-23 Flogger counter-air jet
fighters and MIRVed intercontinental missiles, each of which
looked like a cel from a deranged Team B–authored episode of
Jonny Quest. On one page was the outline of the Soviets' Nizhny
Tagil Tank Plant ominously superimposed on a map of Washington, DC. The tank factory covered the Mall from the Capitol
Building to the Lincoln Memorial. "There are 135 major military industrial plants now operating in the Soviet Union with
over 40 million square meters in floor space, a 34 percent increase since 1970," the booklet informed readers. High-tech Soviet shop classes, the booklet noted, were graduating thousands
of welding engineers every year. And they had "perfected two

new methods for refining steel and other alloys—electroslag re-melting and plasma-arc melting." Nine hundred thousand mad Soviet scientists were at work designing and testing new weapons systems, giving the Soviets, according to best guesstimates, a running head start on twenty-first-century weapons technology: "The Soviet high energy laser program is three-to-five times the U.S. level of effort . . . they have worked on the gas dynamic laser, the electric discharge laser and the chemical laser . . . in the latter half of [the 1980s] it is possible that the Soviets could demonstrate laser weapons in a wide variety of ground, ship and aerospace applications. . . . Research in behavioral modification, biological warfare and genetic engineering all have the potential to result in the development of new and extremely effective weapons."

"Its purpose," noted *Time* magazine of the *Soviet Military Power* booklet, "[is to] send a red alert to Americans and their allies that the U.S.S.R. is gaining a military edge over the West. Naturally, there was suspicion that the timing was designed to help the Pentagon justify the vast sums needed for the new strategic systems." Reagan's secretary of defense Caspar Weinberger denied this allegation. "There is a very real and growing threat," he said when unveiling the booklet produced by the Pentagon's public affairs team. "It is not scare talk or any kind of propaganda."

Of course, it *was* scare talk and propaganda, but it was *quality* scare talk and propaganda. In 1981, and 1983, and every year thereafter, right around budget time, the Pentagon released its newest installment of *Soviet Military Power* to the public, and then Reagan sent his chairman of the Joint Chiefs up to Capitol Hill to make headlines. A typical pronouncement from 1983: "The Soviets have armed themselves to the teeth and they continue to do so at a rate far in excess of any legitimate defense needs by any measure—theirs or ours. The plain fact of the matter is that, in the last ten years, Soviet military investment in hardware alone has exceeded ours by some 500 billion dollars." And every year the Pentagon bite of the federal dollar got bigger and bigger. In Reagan's eight years in office, military expenditure doubled from around $150 billion to $300 billion a year, until it represented nearly 30 percent of our overall annual budget and more than 6 percent of GDP. And all to chase the giant shadow projected on the wall by the *Fantasia* boys at the Committee on the Present Danger.

You didn't have to be a defense contractor to cash in on this '80s political phenomenon. Hollywood studios, those great coastal reflecting pools of received wisdom, had pretty much dispensed with introspective films like *Deer Hunter* and *Coming Home* that picked at the old scabs of the Vietnam War. Now they were happy to produce box-office gold while feeding the Soviets-as-maniacs paranoia. In *Red Dawn*, schoolboys C. Thomas Howell, Patrick Swayze, and Charlie Sheen went guerrilla to fight a spectacularly armed force of Soviets, Cubans, and Nicaraguans who had invaded their peaceful Colorado town after (yes, Richard Pipes!) a Kremlin-ordered nuclear first strike destroyed most major American cities. The biggest moneymaking movie of 1986 was a Knights-of-the-Sky adventure pic that would have made Burgess Meredith and Hap Arnold blush: *Top Gun*. "Gentlemen," says our flight instructor, "this school is about combat. There are no points for second place." Young Tom Cruise was the lasciviously oiled, sun-burnished, leather-jacket-wearing, motorcycle-driving, soul-singing fighter pilot who overcomes self-doubt (a psychic leftover from his father's service record in Vietnam) and the training-exercise death of his best buddy/navigator ("Talk to me, Goose") to air-joust the Soviet MiG jets into bloodless submission and win the girl. *Top Gun* sold nearly fifty million tickets in US theaters.

And who was pushing back at this hypermilitarism? Well, it didn't much matter. When a million people gathered at a Central Park rally to protest nuclear arms proliferation—the biggest single demonstration in American history—Team Reagan initially wrote them off as well-intentioned but hopelessly naïve. But the administration soon moved on to suggesting the demonstrators were stooges in a Soviet plot. "In the organization of some of the big demonstrations, the one in New York and so forth," Reagan asserted in a press conference a few months after the rally, "there is no question about foreign agents that were sent to instigate and help create and keep such a big movement going." Reagan refused to elaborate on this theory "because I don't discuss intelligence matters." And it was true that the publications providing the most cogent and consistent counterweight to the new American militarization were generally the magazines whose ad revenue depended on discount-priced Oriental herbs, futons, prefab geodesic homes, all-cotton drawstring pants, send-a-crystal-to-a-friend, and the magic of Feldenkrais's Awareness Through Movement seminars.

Not many mainstream American publications gave much play to the statement of Soviet General Secretary Leonid Brezhnev a month after Reagan's first *Soviet Military Power* was issued: "It is dangerous madness to try to defeat each other in the arms race and to count on victory in nuclear war. I shall add that only he who has decided to commit suicide can start a nuclear war in the hope of emerging a victor from it. No matter what the attacker might possess, no matter what method of unleashing nuclear war he chooses, he will not attain his aims. Retributions will ensue ineluctably." Nor that of Brezhnev's deputy Konstantin Chernenko, who said nuclear war "must not be permitted. . . .

It is criminal to look upon nuclear war as a rational, almost legitimate continuation of policy." Nor that of Brezhnev's other
deputy, Yuri Andropov, who said that "any attempt to resolve
the historic conflict between these systems by means of military
clash would be fatal for mankind."

But, hey, those guys were liars. The president said so. And in
1981 Reagan went on the record with a dark warning, saying,
"Unlike us, the Soviet Union believes that a nuclear war is possible and they believe it is winnable."

America's actor president and his hard-right turn looked like
madness to the Soviets. What Team B was making up about
the Soviet mind-set actually seemed true about the American
one. The Soviets saw the US defense budget go up by 10 percent a year; they saw us rolling out ever more lethal strategic weapons and investing in new military technology. They
watched with growing alarm as Reagan convinced NATO to
plant nuclear-armed missiles all over Western Europe. And
they watched as Reagan convinced a skeptical but apparently
spineless Congress to fund General Graham's defense system
designed to knock down any missiles the Soviets fired, a system
popularly known as Star Wars, as in the blockbuster film. Star
Wars was as much a fantasy as Ewoks and lightsabers. Thirty
years later we're still futzing with it and it doesn't really work,
or even really make sense. But from the point of view of the Soviets, who had no way of knowing how close to science fiction
Star Wars was, this signaled an alarming move by Reagan to
free the United States from the fearsome but stabilizing deterrent of Mutually Assured Destruction. With Star Wars defenses
in place, the Soviets feared, our nukes would hit Russia first, but
then any retaliatory missiles from them would be shot out of the

sky before they even entered American airspace. It would take the safety off America's nuclear trigger.

The Soviets put their own intelligence services on high alert, watching for any and every sign of American military movement. And their ambassador to the United States, Anatoly Dobrynin, who spent much of his adult life in Washington, was gently passing the word to his bosses in the Kremlin that Reagan really did believe what he was saying. Dobrynin later wrote in his memoir that "considering the continuous political and military rivalry and tension between the two superpowers, and an adventurous president such as Reagan, there was no lack of concern in Moscow that American bellicosity and simple human miscalculation could combine with fatal results."

In 1983, when fear at the Kremlin was at an all-time high, the Reagan administration was more or less oblivious to it. "While we in American intelligence saw the tension," Deputy CIA Director Robert Gates (yes, *that* Robert Gates) wrote in his memoir, "we did not really grasp just how much the Soviet leadership felt increasingly threatened by the U.S. and by the course of events."

There was, remarkably, according to Dobrynin's later memoir, one article of faith inside the Kremlin that gave the Soviets some measure of solace: the American system of government. They understood that a president had a lot of hoops to jump through before he could take the United States to war. Dobrynin had been in Washington to watch the Congress erect the would-be barrier to presidential war making that was the War Powers Act. Reagan's Soviet counterparts—Brezhnev, Chernenko, Gorbachev—believed, as Dobrynin wrote, that the "political and social structure of the United States was the best guarantee against an unprovoked strike." Yuri Andropov, who was Soviet general secretary in 1983, that year of living most dangerously, was not so sanguine. "Reagan is unpredictable," a nervous Andropov confided to Dobrynin. "You should expect anything from him."

Plenty of Americans will always believe that it was the economic and psychological pressure of the arms race that hastened or even caused the collapse of the Soviet Union in 1991, two years after Reagan left office. And there might be some truth to that. It is certainly the narrative the Reagan hagiographers have sold us. But it's also true that the Soviet Union was already teetering badly by the time Reagan took office. And it's impossible to say how Russia might look today if we had spent more of our national energy helping Gorbachev find his way toward democracy and less time convincing Western European leaders to point the world's most potent weapons of mass destruction at Red Square.

Counterfactuals aside, what is demonstrably clear and empirically measurable is the damage that our country suffered from the enormity of the defense spending of the Reagan presidency. David Stockman's initial dire deficit projections, it turns out, were rosy; Reagan's annual budget deficit ballooned from 2 percent to a record 6.3 percent of GDP in his first two years in office, a fiscal sinkhole it would take us nearly twenty years to climb out of. But as the yearly budget shortfalls grew from $50 billion to $100 billion to $150 billion to $220 billion, the Reagan administration waved them off like so many anti-nuke protesters. The self-proclaimed fiscal conservatives just kept asking for and getting more dollars for more weapons. Reagan's continual appeals to American strength and pride, his vivid emotional doomsaying, all his overhyped talk about the Commies enslaving the world . . . it worked. He conjured for us an enemy worthy of our cause, something big to push back against. And he convinced us to reach deep, deep, deep into our pockets to fund that push.

"For more than a third of a century, assertions of Soviet superiority created calls for the United States to 're-arm.' In the 1980s, the call was heeded so thoroughly that the United States embarked on a trillion dollar defense buildup," Anne Hessing Cahn wrote in 1993. "As a result, the country neglected its schools, cities, roads and bridges and health care system. From the world's greatest creditor nation, the United States became the world's greatest debtor—in order to pay for the arms to counter the threat of a nation that was collapsing."

A lot of important things got back-burnered to make way for "re-arming." After Carter's insistence that "our dependence on foreign oil will be stopped dead in its tracks right now and then reversed as we move through the 1980s," American oil consumption grew in the Reagan years, and in George H. W. Bush's, and in Bill Clinton's, and in George W. Bush's. Our oil imports, which took a big jump in Reagan's second term, just kept rising. In 1973, the United States of America imported a third of the oil we consumed; by 2005 we imported about 60 percent.

But again, who got excited about joining Jimmy Carter in the fight against energy dependence, or against his unspoken national malaise? Who wanted to be told our most threatening enemy was our own lack of faith and fortitude, our commitment to competing with the world on terms beyond shooting at them? Reagan convinced us that there was a world full of evildoers to fight out there, and not just behind the Iron Curtain. There were also bad guys who were a lot more convenient to get to.

Chapter 4

Isle of Spice

WHEN THE REAR RAMP OF THE LEAD C-130 AIR FORCE TRANS-port plane fell open, somewhere over the Atlantic, the jumpmaster for Navy SEAL Team Six got his first surprise. He and his team-mates had been well briefed on their top secret mission. They were to be the phantom vanguard, the crucial eyes and ears, of the United States' first major combat mission since Vietnam, in and out before anyone ever knew they were there. The sixteen SEALs, along with two eighteen-foot Boston Whaler patrol boats, were to make a 1,200-foot parachute drop into deep water well away from commercial shipping lanes, forty miles northeast of the still-under-construction Point Salines airfield on the edge of a Ca-ribbean island few of the men could have found on a map a few days earlier. Once in the water, the frogmen would swim to the boats, meet up with an Air Force Combat Control team from the nearby USS *Sprague*, and, after darkness fell, motor forty miles to shore. The SEALs would suss out the situation at the airfield and radio back what they found: Were the runways complete enough for landing a couple of battalions of Army Rangers? Were the run-ways clear? Was the airfield defended by local soldiers? How big was the Cuban construction and engineering crew, and how many of the Cubans were armed? Did they know we were coming?

Intelligence about the airfield was spotty at best, which was why the SEALs were infiltrating the island a day and a half before the invasion was to begin, even before President Reagan had made the final decision on whether or not to launch the overall operation.

SEAL Team Six had been given to understand that there was nothing complicated about its reconnaissance mission. In fact, the SEALs' commander had taken himself off the offshore drop so he would be available to lead a different SEALs mission: the rescue of the island's governor general thirty-six hours later.

The SEALs approached their drop site right on schedule. Weather reports promised clear skies, low winds, and calm seas. And then the ramp dropped, and, well, it seemed the planners had forgotten to take into account the daylight saving time change, and a one-hour miscalculation is no small thing twelve degrees north of the equator, where the sun drops in a hurry. As the jumpmaster remembered it years later, "It was pitch-black outside. We couldn't see a thing. I grabbed a flashlight off the air crewman and tried to stick it on the boat. . . . We had no lights rigged anywhere. We were told it was going to be a daylight drop."

Secrecy. That was the controlling force in the planning and execution of Operation Urgent Fury, the October 1983 invasion of the Caribbean island of Grenada. When the SEALs commander had suggested, in the early planning stages, that it might be simplest to fly his men and their Boston Whalers directly to the *Sprague*, he had been waved off for reasons of "operational security." The planning team, wrote the leader of the Air Force Combat Control team, "was afraid that word might leak of the pending operation." Flying to the *Sprague* would let too many people in on the secret. In fact, the Air Force crews flying the SEALs south in the two cargo planes still thought this open-water drop was just another training exercise.

President Reagan's national security team and his chief military advisers meant to keep this operation under wraps until the last possible moment. Reagan had stuck to his announced public schedule, making many of the crucial decisions about Urgent Fury from the Eisenhower Cottage at Augusta National during a presidential golf weekend. Less than twenty-four hours before the operation began, key planning officers gave up valuable hours to attend an annual military ball. Not going to the dance, commanders reckoned, would be a big red flag that something was up. At least one member of the Air Force planning team suspected that nobody had requested pre-invasion intelligence on Grenada from the National Security Agency, which monitored international phone calls and radio traffic ("probably the richest source of intelligence" on the island). Planners feared that operatives at the NSA, the most secretive agency in government, would leak. And apparently nobody in the chain of command had asked the Defense Mapping Agency for detailed tactical maps of Grenada, which is why planning teams were occasionally working with maps dating from 1895, and commanders on the ground ended up depending on fold-out tourist maps like "Grenada: The Isle of Spice."

President Reagan did not even risk alerting British prime minister Margaret Thatcher of the operation until after Urgent Fury was under way, despite the compelling fact that Grenada was a member of the British Commonwealth. And the American press corps? They were getting nowhere near Operation Urgent Fury. No provisions were made to attach pool reporters to the mission, a remarkable break from traditional US policy. And Reagan officials did more than simply evade the press. On the eve of the invasion, when asked point-blank to confirm an NBC reporter's question about an impending military action in Grenada, Deputy National Security Adviser John Poindexter flat-out lied. "Preposterous," he said.

Team Reagan also made the executive decision that it would be imprudent to bring Congress into the loop too early. Somebody on the intelligence committee was sure to leak if informed, the president and his closest advisers believed, and that would jeopardize the entire mission. As far as the White House was concerned, there was simply too much at stake. Secrecy!

As soon as the Boston Whalers went out the rear door of the lead C-130, eight SEALs followed into the unexpected darkness ... and into a squall. Clear skies forecast notwithstanding, windswept rain pelted the jumpers, and they hit the water a lot faster than they had expected. A few later estimated that instead of their planned 1,200-foot drop, they'd gone out of the planes at a dangerously low height of about six hundred feet. The first eight SEALs hit the water so hard that fins and equipment pouches sheared off. The swells were as high as ten feet, and the wind on the water so stiff that the parachutes would not deflate.

"It ... started dragging me through the water, almost from wave to wave, dragging me facedown, swallowing water rapidly," one SEAL said later. "I reached up and grabbed the lines of the parachute and started dragging them in, trying to collapse the parachute. ... I had a lot of lines all around me. ... But I had time to get to my knife and start cutting lines and got enough of them cut so it didn't start dragging me again."

The second team of eight had been flung out of its C-130 well away from the assigned drop point, and the scattered men had trouble finding the Boston Whalers on the dark and stormy seas.

After a long scramble through the dangerous waters, a few managed to get into one of the boats, but the other SEALs finally gave up and swam toward the lights of the *Sprague*. Twelve of the sixteen men were fished out of the Atlantic that night; they could hear one of their teammates shouting and firing off shots in hopes of bringing help. After hours of frantic searching for their lost teammates, the SEALs ceded the rescue operations to the crew of the *Sprague* and, along with the Air Force team, cobbled together enough men to attempt the shore landing near the airfield. But by the time they finally neared the coastline, Grenadian patrol boats were panning searchlights across the open water, forcing the SEALs to give up the mission and return to the *Sprague*.

When they got back early the next morning, the four missing comrades were still lost at sea. The men never would be found, and were likely pulled underwater by their parachutes. The death of four friends did not deter Team Six. They called back to base to request the drop of another Boston Whaler. They'd try again when the sun fell later that evening.

When word reached the Pentagon planners that the SEALs failed to reach land as scheduled—and that they were determined to try again later that evening—the Joint Chiefs suggested a prudent twenty-four-hour delay in the operation, but a State Department liaison surprised the military brass by shooting down that idea. The coalition of Caribbean states that had agreed to back the US overthrow of the Grenadian government, he admitted, was already coming apart at the seams. It might not hold together for another twenty-four hours. If the US military was going to effect this coup, they had to go at the appointed hour. "Besides," the State Department aide told the military chieftains, "how could the world's strongest military power need any more time against what is probably the world's weakest?"

The avowed reason for the urgency of Urgent Fury—planned from scratch in about seventy-two hours—was that American citizens were in grave danger on the island of Grenada. And they had to be rescued in a flash. An intramural scrap inside the island's Marxist-Leninist government had left the prime minister and a number of his supporters dead and sent his number two and rival into hiding. Power had devolved to a military council and a somewhat rattled general who announced a four-day curfew enforced by armed soldiers. "No one is to leave their house," the general said. "Anyone violating this curfew will be shot on sight."

The Reagan administration's diplomat in the region, the ambassador to Barbados, was a former Nebraska highway commissioner with no experience in foreign affairs. He'd been so offended by the Communists in Grenada that he forbade anybody from his diplomatic team from visiting the island or having contact with its leaders. The advantage of this strategy: it sure looked tough. The disadvantage: it ensured that America had no active Grenadian contacts, no one in-country, no way to make real-time observations on this island we were so concerned with. As best the Reagan national security team could determine (lacking actual on-the-ground information), law and order had completely broken down, leaving more than five hundred US students attending the American-owned and -operated St. George's University School of Medicine cowering in their rooms, potential hostages. The administration's draft decision memorandum, written in the main by a Marine lieutenant colonel named Oliver North, called first and foremost for "ensuring the safety of American citizens on Grenada," but also for standing up a new democratic (aka pro-American) government in

Grenada and ridding the island of the biggest Bolsheviks in the *baño*, the Cubans and their Soviet friends. When Vice President George Herbert Walker Bush questioned the (probably illegal) objective of a regime change by force, Reagan barely blinked: "Well, if we've got to go there, we might as well do everything that needs to be done." Those med students had just become an important hook for a grand American scheme.

By October 1983, the time of the invasion, Reagan had been beating the presidential tom-toms about the Central America peril for more than two years, and he was growing ever more frustrated that he had been unable to get Congress to fall in step. When the House Intelligence Committee chairman learned from press reports in November 1982 that Reagan's ambassador in Honduras was secretly training rebels to overthrow the popular but Marxist-leaning government in Nicaragua, he pointedly introduced legislation (which passed) that specifically prohibited the Department of Defense or the CIA from allocating any of their approved budgets to assist and foment a coup in Nicaragua. The usually unflappable Reagan was visibly angered by what he thought was congressional interference. "The Sandinistas have openly proclaimed Communism in their country and their support of Marxist revolutions throughout Central America," he blurted in evident exasperation in a meeting with Democratic Speaker of the House Thomas P. "Tip" O'Neill. "They're killing and torturing people! Now, what the hell does Congress expect me to do about that?"

Reagan went on one of his signature public relations offensives. In a speech to the nation from the Oval Office in March 1983, wherein the president warned that his record-breaking defense budget had been "trimmed to the limits of safety" by the soft-on-Communism Congress, Reagan revealed some hazy satellite photos of an airfield under construction. "On the small island of Grenada, at the southern end of the Caribbean chain," he'd said, "the Cubans, with Soviet financing and backing, are in the process of building an airfield with a ten-thousand-foot runway. Grenada doesn't even have an air force. Who is it intended for?"

Reagan meant this as an ominous rhetorical question, but it did have rather less ominous empirical answers. To wit: there were airfields of similar size and capacity already dotting the Caribbean; the Grenadian government wanted to build a new modern airport to increase tourism, which was their only source of income outside nutmeg, bananas, and servicing those medical students at St. George's University. The Grenadian government had asked the United States for money to help build it so they could bring in big jetfuls of tourists directly from Miami and New York and Dallas; the tourists wouldn't have to wait around Bridgetown, Barbados, to catch a puddle-jumper connection. The United States had said no to the aid request, but Great Britain and Canada had been happy to help. The main contractor for construction of the Point Salines airfield was a British company underwritten by a grant from the British government. None of this was secret. But according to Reagan there was a much more nefarious plot afoot. The president said he wanted to reveal more to the American people on TV that night, but, alas, he claimed, the stakes were too high. "These pictures only tell a small part of the story. I wish I could show you more without compromising our most sensitive intelligence sources and methods."

Here's what he could say: "The Soviet-Cuban militarization of Grenada, in short, can only be seen as power projection into the region. And it is in this important economic and strategic area that we're trying to help the governments of El Salvador, Costa Rica, Honduras, and others in their struggles for democracy against guerrillas supported through Cuba and Nicaragua.

"This is why I'm speaking to you tonight—to urge you to tell your senators and congressmen that you know we must continue to restore our military strength. If we stop in midstream, we will send a signal of decline, of lessened will, to friends and adversaries alike."

Reagan's national plea did not shake loose the cash he'd desired from the legislature, so a month later he called a rare and dramatic joint session of Congress to ask members to stop resisting his budget requests for fighting the Commies in Central America. "The national security of all the Americas is at stake in Central America. If we cannot defend ourselves there, we cannot expect to prevail elsewhere. Our credibility would collapse, our alliances would crumble, and the safety of the homeland would be put in jeopardy."

But Congress kept whittling away at funding for El Salvador, and for the Contra rebels in Nicaragua. The Senate blocked a specific request to have the CIA actively undermine the Communist-friendly runway-happy Grenadian government—effectively a slow-motion coup. But when Congress said no on Grenada, Reagan simply prepared an end run. On October 4, 1983, the president signed National Security Decision Directive 105, which ordered his own national security team to draw up plans for destabilizing the economy and the institutions of Grenada (among other Central American countries), to overthrow its Socialist government, and to rid the island once and for all of Cuban and Soviet influence. Senate be damned.

When the news hit that something was afoot in Grenada (just nine days after the secret presidential directive was issued), Reagan's national security adviser for Latin American Affairs immediately brought up the possible perils to the Americans living on the island. "In crises there is opportunity," he said later, "and I believed that this emergency just might present an excellent chance to restore democracy to Grenada while assuring the safety of our citizens." What better way to do all that—and to prove that America was back—than military action. Military action in Grenada was a first resort for the Reagan team, not a last resort. It's not like they tried much else. They didn't even bother to get good information about what was actually happening on the island, or to verify what little they did get. They were under the spell of their old Team B Soviet-military hype. The Russians were running a takeover in Grenada.

And frankly, this was an administration eager to use the military in a way that would let the president say things like "America is back." He had been using the idea of military strength to political effect for years; now he could use *actual* military strength. The purported justification sold to the American people about Grenada—the rescue of these American medical students—was so far from the operational point of Urgent Fury that the White House would send the president out to make his victory speech even before all the students were secure.

As the Grenadian government tore itself apart over the next week, Reagan's administration made plans for the "rescue" of the British queen's representative in Grenada, Governor-General Paul Scoon, a ceremonial figurehead who governed nothing and didn't know we were coming. The military rescue team for Scoon would also include a US State Department representative who made sure that the governor-general went up on the island's radio network and said all the right things about how the Americans had been officially invited in to restore order and good government. There was considerably less diplomatic push to ensure the actual safety of the American students living on the island. Little or no effort was made to contact anybody in student housing or to talk to the faculty and staff of St. George's University, whose bursar had been receiving personal assurances from Grenadian government officials that the students were safe and would be assured a safe departure if they wished to leave. (The retired chief actuary of the US Social Security system flew out of the small airport on the northeast part of the island the day that SEAL Team Six made its second attempt to infiltrate the island.)

No, the real energy inside the Reagan administration was expended on preparing a full-out combat operation, and preparing to justify it after the fact. Every branch of the military was anxious to get a piece of the action: the SEAL teams, an Army Ranger battalion, a second Army Ranger battalion, the Air Force for transport, the Navy for air and gun support. Everybody had a piece of the little spice island. The Marines didn't get much, but they did get a little real estate to take up north.

But then, less than thirty hours before the invasion was to commence, events on the other side of the world changed the plans in a big way. On the morning of October 23, 1983, a suicide bomber drove a truck containing six tons of explosives and a variety of highly flammable gases into the US barracks at the airport in Beirut, Lebanon, killing 241 Marines there on a don't-shoot peacekeeping mission. Fourteen months into the deployment, and after an earlier suicide bombing at the US embassy in Beirut, Reagan was still unable to make clear to the American people exactly why US Marines were there. Were we keeping the peace in the civil war there, or were we taking sides with the Christians against the Muslims? The Reagan administration was still mixed on that message in the wake of the bombing, but the president was damned sure not going to let anybody question American resolve. Reagan dispatched Vice President

Bush to Beirut to make sure the world knew we were going to be staying the course in Lebanon, that we weren't going to be frightened off by terrorists.

That afternoon the chairman of the Joint Chiefs of Staff suggested that perhaps the Grenada operation was a dangerous exercise, at least where the president's political standing was involved. Reagan was headed into reelection season, the chairman reminded him, and he didn't need a double whammy of military complications. It might be less fraught to let the diplomats work out a deal to extricate the American students from Grenada. But Reagan was not about to back down. Not now. This was not the time to show weakness.

Word of a change in plans for Operation Urgent Fury started to filter through the chain of command within eight hours of the Lebanon bombing. "Now that the Marines had been bloodied in Beirut, they wanted an active role," SEALs commander Robert Gormly wrote later. "Politics took over and the island was divided down the middle, with the Joint Headquarters retaining the southwest part and the Marines given the go-ahead to make an amphibious landing at the smaller airfield in the northeast." The next day, as Gormly mourned his four dead SEAL colleagues and continued planning for the rescue of the governor-general, he found himself in a meeting with the State Department official who was going to go along on the operation. "[He] offered me some interesting information: that the Cuban 'engineers' on the island wouldn't be a problem, because their government had informally agreed to keep its people in their barracks during our incursion. In other words, the Cubans knew we were coming."

Funny thing, that secrecy business. Our putative enemy, Fidel Castro, knew about the invasion well before the Speaker of the

United States House of Representatives. In fact, when President
Reagan finally had a group of congressional leaders to the White
House residence on the night of October 24, 1983, secretly, to
explain the plans for Grenada, the Army Rangers were already
collecting their ammo and loading into their transport planes.
The secretary of state briefed the three Democratic leaders and
two Republicans on the situation on the ground in Grenada, and
the chairman of the Joint Chiefs laid out plans for a military operation involving two thousand American soldiers, sailors, and
Marines. Only House Republican leader Bob Michel offered un-
questioning support. The majority leader in the Senate, Tennes-
see Republican Howard Baker, wondered if Reagan was making
a serious political mistake, and perhaps a military one. House
Democratic majority leader Jim Wright thought the situation
called for a stronger diplomatic effort, not military force. Senate
Minority Leader Robert Byrd said point-blank he was against
the invasion, and he'd say so in public.

Tip O'Neill, the venerable old big-city liberal and the Democratic Speaker of the House, was torn. He was sympathetic to
Reagan's worry that American hostages would be taken in Grenada; the 444-day hostage crisis in Iran just a few years earlier had been a grim national nightmare, and Jimmy Carter's
inability to free them had torpedoed his presidency. But O'Neill,
like the other Democrats at the meeting, thought diplomacy was
the wiser course to take in Grenada. There were no reports of
Americans being menaced on the island, let alone being taken
hostage. He saw no compelling reason for the United States
military to execute a full-scale regime change; and he knew of
no compelling constitutional argument that permitted Reagan
to launch the operation simply on presidential say-so. Even if
Operation Urgent Fury wrapped up within the sixty-day window that compelled Reagan, under the War Powers Resolution,

to consult Congress and secure specific statutory authority for
the war, it was hard to make the case that Grenada represented
a "national emergency created by an attack upon the United
States, its territories or possessions, or its armed forces." At the
very least, the president should have *begun* the process of seeking approval from Congress before hitting the Go button. "You
are informing us," O'Neill pointedly told the president at the end
of the administration's presentation, "not asking us."

Reagan reminded the congressional leaders that the rush of
events had simply overtaken constitutional prerogatives. The
safety of the American students was paramount; there was no
time to lose. And then, prompted by something his national
security adviser said, Reagan told the congressional leaders a
story about how the Filipino people had cheered American soldiers after their liberation in World War II. "I can see the day,
not too many weeks from now," Reagan told the group, "when
the Lebanese people will be standing at the shore, waving and
cheering our Marines when they depart."

O'Neill grew increasingly uncomfortable as Reagan kept
going on about Lebanon in the middle of a meeting about Grenada. The Speaker began to suspect that part of the rationale for
the invasion of Grenada was to use a quick-and-easy triumph as
a distraction from the hideousness of the Beirut bombing.

Tip O'Neill was old-school. He worked hard to find common
ground with the president, no matter how divergent their political philosophies. He'd always given the president the benefit
of the doubt when White House factotums grabbed for a little
extra on every deal the two men made—give a little, get a little was how O'Neill's politics worked. Just three weeks earlier
the Speaker had gone to bat for the president on the mission
in Beirut, convincing skeptical House Democrats to vote for an
eighteen-month extension of the 1,200-Marine US presence in

the multinational peacekeeping force there. Reagan's team had assured the Speaker that things were improving; that they could get Israeli and Syrian military units out of Lebanon, stand up a viable coalition government in Beirut, and train and equip a Lebanese Army capable of defending the country without an American presence. They just needed a little time.

Grenada was a tougher mission to back, but Tip O'Neill was also convinced that partisanship ended at the water's edge in wartime. Even in a war against a tiny, poorly armed island military, he was not going to criticize the president while American troops were in a fight, and he would implore the House Democratic Caucus to do the same. On the way out of the meeting, O'Neill wished Reagan good luck, sincerely. He wasn't interested in seeing American boys die. But he privately worried that Reagan's insistence on making war in Grenada would start our own country down a dangerous new road.

The United States military might have been facing one of the weakest foes on the planet, but Operation Urgent Fury was no cakewalk. The Grenadian soldiers put up more of a fight than intelligence had suggested they would, but still, resistance melted away pretty quickly. Most of the damage the United States suffered in the invasion was self-inflicted. The lack of intelligence and basic tactical maps along with the inability of the various services to communicate with one another led to results ranging from comic to mortal. The SEALs sent to rescue Governor-General Scoon had to be rescued themselves. They had to use the house phone to call Fort Bragg to request fire from the US naval ships off the coast. The radio station selected to be used for Scoon's address to the people of Grenada turned out to be nothing more than a remote transmission tower. Navy

Corsair pilots accidentally blew up a mental hospital, killing eighteen patients. A US Marine liaison team mistakenly called in a naval air raid on a nearby US Army command post, wounding seventeen American soldiers and killing one. Helicopters were lost to small-arms fire, to the rotors from another chopper, and to a confrontation with a palm tree.

When word of the invasion began to reach home that first day, the early results were a cold slap in the face for Team Reagan. Members of the United Nations Security Council immediately began debating a resolution "deeply deploring" the US invasion of Grenada as a "flagrant violation of international law." (The vote would go 11–1, with the United States exercising its veto power.) Prime Minister Margaret Thatcher called to register her anger with Reagan. Democrats and Republicans alike in Congress were not happy about being kept in the dark about this multimillion-dollar military adventure. "I was the designated person on the day of the beginning of the action when it became public to go to the Congress," Secretary of State George Shultz told an audience a few years ago. "I spent all day long and there was hardly a good word said." Sen. Lawton Chiles told reporters: "One day we've got the numbers of Marines' deaths, which shocked us all, the next day we find we're invading Grenada. Are we looking for a war we can win?"

The press corps, meanwhile, was apoplectic that they had not been brought along on the combat mission, and that a White House official had flat-out lied ("Preposterous!") when asked in advance about the operation. The executive vice president of the National Newspaper Publishers Association called for a full-on congressional investigation into Reagan's "policy of secret wars hidden from the American people." Four years later, the conservative columnist and Republican defender William Safire was still pitching into Reagan's national security team. "The United

States Government may on rare occasion fall silent for a time, but it must not deliberately lie; only the presence of reporters pledged to temporary secrecy can help justify a news blackout. By breaching the democratic precedent, and by issuing a lie, the Reagan Administration engaged in self-corruption far more important than one victory in the Caribbean."

Meanwhile, on Grenada, the way operations were unfolding did not exactly bolster the administration's case that the point of Urgent Fury was saving the St. George's University medical students. The plan to pluck the students from what was called the True Blue campus just a short hop north from the Point Salines airfield was executed to perfection. The Army Rangers swept in and secured all the students living on the campus without a serious hitch on the first day. But the Rangers found fewer than a third of the six hundred American students they'd been expecting on the campus. That's because, the students explained, *most* of the students lived at the Grand Anse campus a few miles north.

Oops. In the full week after the crisis came to a head, nobody in the Pentagon or the White House made an effort to contact the school to see where everybody lived. Nobody picked up the telephone and called the dorms. Nobody checked the student-loan records to get actual addresses for the Americans studying at St. George's. There was no plan to rescue students at the Grand Anse campus *because nobody in the United States government knew there was a Grand Anse campus.* Now the Army Rangers picked up the phone and called Grand Anse, and the students told them they thought a small group of Grenadian and Cuban soldiers had dug in around the campus. Whether they were to protect the American students or to hold them was anybody's guess. But it must be noted that those Grenadians and Cubans had more than thirty-six hours after the first American troops landed to do as they pleased with the students. And they did them no harm.

While the Rangers made plans for a new commando assault/resue on the Grand Anse campus, the military kept reporters at bay, in Barbados. The last thing they needed now was reporters crawling around, which meant the media missed the most seamless operation of Urgent Fury. Firepower from the USS *Independence* took out a couple of hotels near the campus (part *deux*), and then three waves of helicopters came roaring in over the Atlantic, blasting their .50-caliber guns into the smoke and haze and off-loading dozens of Army Rangers. In a matter of half an hour, another 224 American students had been freed from their beachside apartments and shipped off to safety in military helicopters.

The triumph would have been complete, except for one sour note. The Grand Anse students inquired about the condition of their classmates who lived across the island at Prickly Bay; must be another two hundred or so people over there. Prickly Bay? What's Prickly Bay?

The rationale of Operation Urgent Fury—this $135 million, 8,000-strong expedition—may have been to save these Americans from being kidnapped by ruthless Caribbean Commie thugs, but that wasn't much of an operational focus for what happened on the ground in Grenada.

Once some of the students had been "rescued," the administration wasn't sure what to expect from them. The chancellor of the medical school had already been telling reporters that their students hadn't needed rescuing. And frankly, the students' scariest moments may have been when US Army Rangers came in with guns blazing. Oliver North later said the State Department had failed to get its operative on board the plane home to work on convincing the students of the danger they had been in. So when the plane full of students touched down in Charleston, South Carolina, Reagan and George Shultz were watching the live television feed with some trepidation until one of the first kids off the plane knelt down and kissed the tarmac. "Mr. President," Shultz claims to have said, "the fat lady just sang." By the time Reagan went on the air to address Congress, that tarmac-kissing scene had been seared into the American brainpan. Nearly two-thirds of the country professed approval for Operation Urgent Fury. And that was before the speech!

Reagan led his Urgent Fury speech to the nation not with Grenada but with an explanation of the bombing at the Marine barracks in Beirut. Although just fifteen weeks later, in February, Reagan would order a full US withdrawal from Lebanon, that night in prime-time in October 1983, he promised to stand strong:

> Let me ask those who say we should get out of Lebanon: If we were to leave Lebanon now, what message would that send to those who foment instability and terrorism? . . . Brave young men have been taken from us. Many others have been grievously wounded. Are we to tell them their sacrifice was wasted? They gave their lives in defense of our national security every bit as much as any man who ever died fighting in a war. We must not strip every ounce of meaning and purpose from their courageous sacrifice.

Only at the end did the president turn to the daring liberation of all those young Americans in the Caribbean:

> The events in Lebanon and Grenada, though oceans apart, are closely related. Not only has Moscow assisted

and encouraged the violence in both countries, but it provides direct support through a network of surrogates and
terrorists. It is no coincidence that when the thugs tried to
wrest control over Grenada, there were thirty Soviet advisers and hundreds of Cuban military and paramilitary
forces on the island. . . .

In these last few days, I've been more sure than I've
ever been that we Americans of today will keep freedom
and maintain peace. I've been made to feel that by the
magnificent spirit of our young men and women in uniform and by something here in our nation's capital. In this
city, where political strife is so much a part of our lives,
I've seen Democratic leaders in the Congress join their
Republican colleagues, send a message to the world that
we're all Americans before we're anything else, and when
our country is threatened, we stand shoulder to shoulder
in support of our men and women in the Armed Forces.

President Reagan may have "believed in peace . . . as much as
any man," but in Washington a war like this one sure felt good.

After that speech, approval for the American peacekeeping
mission in Beirut jumped more than ten points; approval for Operation Urgent Fury spiked even higher. Of course, at the time
the president spoke, there were still two hundred or so Americans as yet unrescued at Prickly Bay in Grenada—probably won-
dering if they needed to stick around home in case the Army
was coming to rescue them, too, or if they could maybe get in an
afternoon at the beach.

The toll in the end was this: 19 American servicemen killed
(17 from friendly fire or accidents), 120 Americans wounded,
300 Grenadians killed or wounded, including those 18 mental
patients killed in their beds. And also, precedent: operational

secrecy justifying flat-out lying to the press corps and therein to the public. Secrecy, again, and the blunt assertion of executive prerogative justifying a cursory dismissal of the constitutional role of Congress in declaring war, and even of the need to consult them.

Whatever the costs, the Reagan White House reaped the benefits: in the American mind, the toll and humiliation and political inexplicability of Lebanon was now "closely related" to this much more satisfying rescue mission. And for a president who had traded on the emotional potential of American military strength and glory for his political aims, it was a chance to put taxpayer money where his mouth had long been, to let the US Armed Forces flex their arguably atrophied muscles.

"For all of its shortcomings, for all of the derisive commentary about the pathetic stature of the enemy against which American power was hurled, the invasion of Grenada was a victory," journalist Rick Atkinson wrote in *The Long Gray Line*. "Armies fight with morale and esprit as much as they fight with tanks and bullets; after Grenada, soldiers walked a little taller, not because of their battlefield exploits but because of the huzzahs from the rescued students and an appreciative citizenry at home. The United States Army, its self-esteem battered in Southeast Asia, needed to win a war, any war. That slender campaign streamer from Grenada buried beneath it the seventeen preceding ribbons from Vietnam."

And it wasn't just the military that was walking taller. Reagan was enveloped by the glorious success of the first war of his presidency—even this small one. In terms of public approval ratings, it turned out to be better than getting shot. The founders had been right about the politics of war: the benefits of military victory really do accrue to the Executive.

Not that there weren't a few thorns in the laurels. Republican senator Lowell Weicker accused his president of "flouting the law." Congress took a little time away from raising the debt ceiling to vote through a resolution invoking the War Powers Act, forcing the Reagan administration to pull the troops out of Grenada within sixty days or face begging explicit permission from Congress to prolong the mission. And Tip O'Neill—now that the fighting was done in Grenada—laid down a spray of verbal fire on the president: "You can't justify any government, whether it's Russia or the United States, trampling on another nation," O'Neill confided to the equally venerable *New York Times* reporter Scotty Reston. "I'm worried about the effects of this. Where do you go from here? . . . This is Machiavelli: If they can't love ya, make 'em feel ya. He is wrong in his policy. He's caused us continuous harm." And that was just on policy; then O'Neill got personal: "He only works three and a half hours a day. He doesn't do his homework. He doesn't read his briefing papers. It's sinful that this man is President of the United States. He lacks the knowledge that he should have, on every sphere, whether it's the domestic or whether it's the international sphere." It was time for Reagan to pack it in and take Nancy back home where she could be the "Queen of Beverly Hills," he told Reston. *Damn.*

O'Neill's opposite number in the House rushed to the president's defense: "I am willing to concede that any leader of the majority party knows more about sin than we Republicans do." Gerald Ford's onetime White House chief of staff, now a congressman from Wyoming, jumped in too: "A lot of folks around the world," said Dick Cheney, "feel we are more steady and reliable than heretofore."

The White House floated mostly above the fray. When asked what he thought of a hundred nations at the UN voting for the resolution deploring the US invasion of Grenada, Reagan waved it off, saying, "It didn't upset my breakfast at all." Team Reagan

had the footage of the rescued medical student kissing the Carolina tarmac to rely on. They had unnamed "senior administration" sources out leaking to reporters that US troops had found
smoking-gun evidence that the Grenadians and their Cuban advisers had been planning to grab Americans. The senior officials
wished they could release the details and specifics of this plan,
but of course all enemy correspondence had to be translated and
analyzed first. They were happy, however, to characterize what
they'd found. "It is clear from these documents and other information we now have that serious consideration was being given
to seizing Americans as hostages and holding them for reasons
that are not entirely clear, but seem to involve an effort to embar-
rass the United States and, more immediately, to forestall American military action in Grenada," one senior official said.

Reagan himself remained adamant about the size of the
danger averted: "Grenada, we were told, was a friendly island
paradise for tourism. Well, it wasn't. It was a Soviet-Cuban
colony, being readied as a major military bastion to export terror and undermine democracy. We got there just in time." This
statement became a Spice Island touchstone for other White
House officials: "It appears we got there just in time to prevent
a tragedy."

After about ten days of postgame back-and-forth, O'Neill
and the other skeptics on both sides of the congressional aisle
were beating what one of them admitted was "a strategic retreat." Reagan had bested them. He knew he still had that old
Fum-Poo flair, and that if he could get the American public behind him, he could roll Tip O'Neill and Congress on just about
any issue he wished. The night of his Grenada speech, Reagan
had noted in his diary, with obvious pleasure, that he'd "hit a
few nerves. . . . ABC News polled 250 people before the speech,
the majority were against us. They polled the same right after

the speech & there had been a complete turnaround. 1000s of phone calls & wires from all over the country flooded us, more than on any speech or issue since we've been here—10 to 1 in our favor." Not for nothing was Ronald Reagan known as the Great Communicator. The country's overall approval ratings for the Grenada invasion soared to nearly 90 percent. And however much Congress disagreed, they knew that there wasn't much margin in arguing the merits of the case against the invasion when more than eight in ten Americans were for it. "Public opinion is what's behind things," Democratic congressman Robert Torricelli told reporters. "I hardly get a call in my office about Grenada where people don't mention the Iranian hostage situation. So people feel their frustration relieved and members of Congress sense that."

What was the connection between the Iranian hostage situation and Grenada? None, exactly. But if the people were erasing a bad memory and replacing it with a better one, who was to argue? The point was, as Ronald Reagan would say at his next State of the Union address: "America is back—standing tall."

Chapter 5

Stupid Regulations

THE THING TO DO IN NICARAGUA SEEMED SO GLARINGLY OBVI-
ous to President Reagan that it almost didn't need explaining ("It
seems to me that the issue was so plain," he was still saying years
later. "We were talking about preventing the presence of a Soviet
satellite in the Americas!"). "The Sandinista rule is a Communist
reign of terror," he implored in a May 1984 address to the nation.
"If the Soviet Union can aid and abet subversion in our hemisphere, then the United States has a legal right and a moral duty
to help resist it."

But the more he explained it, the more clear it became that he
would not be able to move the public to his way of thinking; on
this one question, the nation would not dance to his tune. It didn't
matter how hard the president beat the drum about the frightening prospect of a Central American country being sucked into the
sphere of Soviet influence. (Remember, we got there just in time in
Grenada! Might not be so lucky in Managua.) Didn't matter how
hard the president beat the drum about the need to forestall what
he described in his diary as "another Cuba on the American main-
land." Didn't matter how adoringly he extolled the virtues of the
brave Nicaraguan resistance. ("They are our brothers, these freedom fighters, and we owe them our help," he'd offered. "They are

the moral equal of our Founding Fathers and the brave men and women of the French Resistance. We cannot turn away from them.") Didn't matter what he said, it seemed to him, he could not get traction on the issue.

"Dick Wirthlin's poll figures were interesting & holding up well—except for the Nicaragua issue," Reagan wrote in his diary in the spring of 1985. "We have to do a job of education with the people—they just don't understand." It was a failure he stewed over again and again in that diary: "Our communications on Nicaragua have been a failure, 90% of the people know it is a communist country but almost as many don't want us to give the [anti-Communists] $14 million for weapons. I have to believe it is the old Vietnam syndrome." After meetings with members of Congress on Nicaragua, Reagan wrote, "The meetings went well & I think I answered some of their worries. It's apparent though that the lack of support on the part of the people due to the drum beat of propaganda 'a la Vietnam' is influencing some of them."

When Reagan wrote about the "Vietnam syndrome," what he meant was that the American body politic suffered from a real pathology. He was sure that his failure to rally the country on Nicaragua, that all the impediments he found to making war on the Commies in Central America (or even to doing just a little energetic saber rattling)—the public's disinclination to call up our troops to fight on foreign soil, the press asking questions about it, Congress asserting its power to stop war or limit it—were symptoms of this dread disease.

"In the last ten years," Reagan complained at one press conference near the end of his first term, "the Congress has imposed about 150 restrictions on the President's power in international diplomacy. And I think that the Constitution made it pretty plain way back in the beginning as to how diplomacy was to be conducted. And I just don't think that a committee of 535 individuals, no matter how well intentioned, can offer what is needed in actions of this kind or where there's a necessity. Do you know that prior to the Vietnamese War, while this country had four declared wars, Presidents of this country had found it necessary to use military forces 125 times in our history?"

But the "Vietnamese War" didn't break anything. America's structural disinclination toward war is not a sign that something's gone wrong. It's not a bug in the system. It *is* the system. It's the way the founders set us up—to ensure our continuing national health. Every Congress is meddlesome, disinclined toward war, and obstructive of a president's desire for it—on purpose. On Nicaragua, Congress was doing its constitutional duty, and what the founders expected.

In the run-up to the 1984 election, Congress had stayed late and built a big wall the president could not easily scale where his Nicaragua policy was concerned. After being *told* and not *asked* about the Grenada invasion, Tip O'Neill was not going to be gone around on this one. The lesson of Grenada (and Lebanon) for Speaker O'Neill was that passivity didn't pay. Against a president who seemed bent on war, Congress needed to vigorously (and sometimes preemptively) assert its own authority.

This new barrier erected by Congress—the Boland Amendment—was no garden-variety, cut-off-some-funding restriction but rather an explicit legislative move to block the president from doing exactly what he wanted to do, to stop him from doing what he was *already* doing: conducting a secret, CIA-funded, CIA-run war fought by a CIA-created, CIA-led army of local insurgents to overthrow the Nicaraguan government. The Reagan administration had been training those insurgents—called Contras—in Honduras, as well as running attacks on Nicaraguan military patrols, on fuel tanks at Nicaraguan ports, and even on the airport in Managua. When a secret CIA-led operation to mine Nicaraguan harbors became public in the spring of 1984, the chairman of the Senate Intelligence Committee, Barry Goldwater, blew up. Goldwater was as much of an anti-Communist badass as anyone in the Senate, but the fact that what Reagan was doing was anti-Communist didn't trump that what Reagan was doing seemed to Goldwater anti-American. The Reagan team had been legally obligated to inform Goldwater, the Senate Intelligence chairman, that these covert missions were happening, and they'd been violating that law, among others. "The President has asked us to back his foreign policy. Bill, how can we back his foreign policy when we don't know what the hell he is doing?" Senator Goldwater wrote to the director of Central Intelligence, William Casey. "Lebanon, yes, we all know that he sent troops over there. But mine the harbors in Nicaragua? This is an act violating international law. It is an act of war. For the life of me, I don't see how we are going to explain it."

Senior senators muscled Director Casey into making a pilgrimage to Capitol Hill to apologize to a closed session of the *entire* Senate Intelligence Committee. The full Senate voted 84–12 to condemn the mining; even staunch anti-Communist Republicans stood up to be counted. The message was clear: no president was vested with this kind of power. That summer, both houses of Congress debated the merits of Reagan's secret war in Nicaragua, and that fall, the Democratic-controlled House and the Republican-controlled Senate voted to put the brakes on it.

"During fiscal year 1985," read the Boland Amendment of October 12, 1984, "no funds available to the Central Intelligence Agency, the Department of Defense, or any other agency or entity of the United States involved in intelligence activities may be obligated or expended for the purpose or which would have the effect of supporting, directly or indirectly, military or para-military operations in Nicaragua by any action, group, organization, movement or individual." The amendment was written in purposefully broad language ("any other agency or entity of the United States involved in intelligence activities," "purpose or . . . effect of supporting," "directly or indirectly," "military or paramilitary") to make sure the Reagan team could not evade congressional will. "There are no exceptions to the prohibition" was how the amendment's author explained it.

And yet in a separate provision of the amendment, Congress gave Reagan a way to try to win back the funding for his secret war; they invited the president to make his case for his Nicaraguan operation. To them. Maintaining their constitutional prerogative as the arbiter of war, they *asked* the administration, in effect, to *ask them;* to submit to Congress the evidence that Nicaragua was exporting Communist revolution to other Central American countries, to make a formal and specific dollar request of Congress for US support of Contra military or paramilitary operations, to justify the need and the amount, and to explain in full the goal of this effort.

When asked years later about congressional requests for this sort of information, Reagan explained them as a clever political maneuver by Tip O'Neill and his soft-on-Communism liberal chums in Congress: "Well, frankly," Reagan said, "I just believe it was part of the constant effort of the Congress to discredit those who wanted to support the Contras."

Actually, it was a wide-open invitation for Reagan to make his case to Congress about why they, too, should support the Contras. But Reagan refused to see it that way. The president's nearly unprecedented electoral romp in 1984—Reagan had won forty-nine of fifty states and 525 electoral votes to Walter Mondale's paltry thirteen—hardened his conviction that Congress shouldn't be sticking its nose into his business (like into Nicaragua, for instance).

His commitment to act in Nicaragua despite Congress was both procedural and substantive. He could not have been more certain that he was on the right side of history. "The Contras," Reagan liked to say, "wanted to have what we had in our own country, and that was [that] the result of the revolution would be democracy." In March 1986 he told a group of elected officials at the White House, "So I guess in a way [the Nicaraguan rebels] are counterrevolutionary, and God bless them for being that way. And I guess that makes them Contras, and so it makes me a Contra too." To a president who saw not only George Washington as a Contra, but saw *himself* as a Contra too, the Congress and the American people being opposed to helping those freedom fighters was simply a nuisance to be got around, not a real impediment to action.

By the time he embarked on his second term, Ronald Reagan had moved well beyond the built-in resentment and disdain presidents have for members of the Senate or the House or the press. (Which one of *them* had received *fifty million votes*?) Somewhere along the way, Reagan had taken the remarkable posture that even just public debate on issues of war and peace was detrimental to our national security. Reagan had said it plain in the days after he'd grudgingly pulled US military troops from the misbegotten mission he had ordered in Lebanon: "When you're engaged in this kind of a diplomatic attempt and you have forces there, and there is an effort made to oust them, a debate as public as was conducted here, raging, with the Congress demanding, 'Oh, bring our men home, take them away.' All this can do is stimulate the terrorists and urge them on to further attacks because they see a possibility of success in getting the force out, which is keeping them from having their way. It should be understood by everyone in government that once this is committed, you have rendered [our military] ineffective when you conduct that kind of a debate in public."

In other words, according to Reagan, having a spirited argument about where, when, and why to put United States soldiers in harm's way (as well as how long to keep them there) and forcing a president to engage in a real argument about the wisdom of his foreign policy initiatives, to make his case in public, was akin to giving aid and comfort to the enemy—to Communists and terrorists.

By the middle of his second term, this radical ethic had become fully operational in the White House. Forget open debate. Forget making your case to Congress or the public. Even a congressional request for information on a matter like Nicaragua was an offense to the presidency. Reagan didn't need a permission slip from anyone. He wouldn't even take one if offered. Forget the Boland Amendment. He was the president! He had personally approved all the covert activities in Nicaragua. His administration had not always met the legal requirements of keeping Congress up to speed on this secret war, but that was his call. He didn't trust the legislature. And frankly, Congress needed a brushback.

Reagan was convinced that a president needed unconstrained authority on national security. He was also convinced that he knew best (after all, he was the only person getting that daily secret intelligence briefing). These twin certainties led him into two unpopular and illegal foreign policy adventures that became a single hyphenated mega-scandal that nearly scuttled his second term and his legacy, and created a crisis from which we still have not recovered. In his scramble to save himself from that scandal, Reagan's after-the-fact justification for his illegal and secret operations left a nasty residue of official radicalism on the subjects of executive power and how America cooks up its wars.

The day after President Reagan complained in his diary about that old Vietnam syndrome, in March 1985, the militant Islamic group Hezbollah abducted an American journalist in Lebanon, bringing the total number of US hostages there to four. "Was shown the photo recently taken by the bastards who are holding our kidnap victims in Lebanon," Reagan wrote five days later. "Heartbreaking, there is no question but that they are being badly treated." Hezbollah grabbed two more Americans living in Beirut over the next few months, so that by the summer of 1985, the group was holding a journalist, a Catholic priest, a Presbyterian minister, and two administrators from the American University in Beirut. Reagan's national security team was especially concerned about the other known hostage: the CIA station chief in Beirut.

This was Reagan's worst nightmare—American hostages, and in the Middle East again. Nothing was more politically resonant to him than how the long, drawn-out, 444-day water torture of a hostage situation in Iran had worn away what remained of the Carter presidency, demoralized the American people, and made the country look weak. Those fifty-two hostages had been freed in the hours after Reagan's inauguration, and the new president welcomed them to his White House a week later. "It's the most emotional experience of our lives," said Reagan's vice president, George H. W. Bush, of the ceremony in the Blue Room. "You could feel it build until the point it hurt inside." And President Reagan's wife, Nancy, a woman with a reputation for keeping a cool distance from the hoi polloi, could not maintain her composure: "Oh I can't stand this," she exclaimed, and began hugging and kissing the returning victims of Ayatollah Khomeini and his Iranian henchmen.

"Those thenceforth in the representation of this nation will be accorded every means of protection that America can offer," Mr. Reagan said from the Blue Room that day, for the world to hear. "Let terrorists be aware that when the rules of international behavior are violated, our policy will be one of swift and effective retribution. . . . Let it also be understood, there are limits to our patience."

Three years later, the president, in the triumph of bringing home those might-have-been hostages from Grenada, was still speaking it aloud: "The nightmare of our hostages in Iran must never be repeated." But here was Reagan in 1985, in the hostage soup, and with no real channel of communication to Hezbollah. So when the president's national security adviser, Bud McFarlane, came to him in July 1985 with a hush-hush plan that might just free the captive Americans, the president grabbed it and held on for dear life.

"Bud, I've been thinking about this," he said in one call, according to McFarlane. "Couldn't you use some imagination and try to find a way to make it work?"

"Mr. President," McFarlane had answered, "your secretary of state and secretary of defense were against this."

"I know, but I look at it differently. I want to find a way to do this."

The main agent in the hostage-release scheme was a Paris-based exiled Iranian arms dealer, Manucher Ghorbanifar, who claimed to have ties to a buzzing nest of moderates inside Iran's military. These army officers, according to the tale Ghorbanifar told, wanted to overthrow the madman Khomeini and make a fresh start with the United States. As a show of good faith among new future friends, the United States would open up the spigot for weapons sales to Iran, and the Iranian moderates would convince Hezbollah to release all of the American hostages in Beirut.

By the time Ghorbanifar presented his tantalizing arms-for-hostages plot, he was already well known in US intelligence circles. A lengthy CIA report described him as "personable, convincing . . . speaks excellent American-style English." (Not even intelligence guys are immune to the charms of excellent American-style English.) However, the report concluded, Ghorbanifar "had a history of predicting events after they happened and was seen as a rumor-monger. . . . The information collected by him consistently lacked sourcing and detail notwithstanding his exclusive interest in acquiring money. . . . Subject should be regarded as an intelligence fabricator and a nuisance. Any further approaches by subject or his brother Ali should be reported but not taken seriously." In fact, on the occasions the CIA had subjected Ghorbanifar to a polygraph test, he generally proved himself to be a liar on any question more complicated than his name and his place of residence. But still, under cover of secrecy, Reagan decided it would be good policy to get in bed with Ghorbanifar and his French silk jammies.

As the deal unfolded—badly—assessments of Ghorbanifar within Reagan's White House national security team included "corrupt," "devious," "duplicitous," "not to be trusted," and "one of the world's leading sleazebags." National Security Adviser Bud McFarlane even called him a "borderline moron." There was pretty good evidence that Ghorbanifar's main goal was money. And still, Reagan decided it would be good policy to continue to pursue the Ghorbanifar plan.

The way the first arms-for-hostages deal was designed, Israel would sell US-made weapons to Iran, and the US government would replace Israel's weapons from its own stocks. As a favor to us, Israel was allowing itself to be used as a pass-through for America sending missiles to Iran. It was a shame that the first arms shipment of ninety-six TOW antitank missiles to Iran ended up (and this was truly unfortunate, everybody agreed) in the hands of Khomeini's loyal Revolutionary Guard. Worse, no hostage was released. It turned out to be arms-for-no-hostages.

Reagan was undeterred, and, as ever, optimistic. "It seems a man high up in the Iranian govt believes he can deliver all or part of the 7 Am kidnap victims in Lebanon sometime in early Sept," Reagan recorded in his diary a few days after the first failure. "They will be delivered to a point on the beach north of Tripoli & we'll take them off to our 6th fleet. I had some decisions to make about a few points—but they were easy to make. Now we wait."

In spite of Reagan's high hopes, the second weapons delivery of more TOW missiles, also via Israel, shook loose only one hostage, and not the one McFarlane requested. In planning the third shipment, eighteen Hawk antiaircraft missiles, Reagan's operatives managed to piss off Portugal, endanger Turkey, get the CIA illegally involved, raise protests from the Defense Department, and move Secretary of State George Shultz to think about resigning . . . and all for nothing. This time, according to Ghorbanifar, there would be no hostages released at all, because the Iranians were upset at having received substandard weapons. In fact, they'd like to return the Hawks.

Nearly six months and millions of dollars of weapons into the arms-for-hostages deal, Reagan had yet to inform Congress about the status or existence of the operation. The president had his reasons. The way Reagan told it to himself, the success of it hinged on secrecy. The president had kept his secretaries of state and defense largely out of the loop; hell, he withheld information from his own personal record of the events of his presidency. "I won't even write in the diary what we're up to." No one could know, most especially Tip O'Neill and the Democrats in the House; Reagan didn't want them to run crying to the press.

This insistence on secrecy was fueled in part by Reagan's fear that the hostages or the men inside Iran doing the talking would be killed if details of the negotiations became public. Nobody in the Reagan administration had good enough contacts to know if this fear had any basis in reality. Hard data had never been—and would never be—a controlling factor in the Reagan administration's decision-making process. But there was also just the embarrassment factor. Given a choice between secrecy and the public finding out about the operation's Laurel-and-Hardy-worthy failures (up to and including the Iranians sending our weapons back, dissatisfied!), who wouldn't choose secrecy? Finally, there was the fact that much of what Team Reagan was doing was not simply flying in the face of their own stated policy against dealing with terrorists ("We make no concessions," Reagan had said. "We make no deals") or state sponsors of international terrorism (Iran was a gold-plated designee on that list); it was not just shredding the president's own executive orders and national security directives; it was not simply executing a spectacular and hypocritical affront to good sense and good diplomacy; but, in fact, much of this arms-for-hostages operation was quite flagrantly against the law. Flat-out illegal.

Reagan's deal violated the Arms Export Control Act by permitting Israel to secretly transfer US-supplied arms to a third country and failing to report the transfer to the proper officials in the US legislature. And the CIA, in providing access to the jet that flew the Hawk antiaircraft missiles to Iran in November, had violated a post-Vietnam amendment to the Foreign Assistance Act that forbade the agency from undertaking covert

operations in a foreign country unless a president issued a finding that the operation is "important to the national security of
the United States."

At a White House meeting three weeks after the disastrous
and illegal-on-two-counts shipment of the TOW missiles,
most of the president's top advisers tried to pull him out of the
arms-for-hostages racket. A CIA deputy director explained that
the notion of an independent moderate faction in the Iranian
Army was a fiction, which meant that, even if Casey's deputy
didn't say it aloud, selling weapons to Iran meant selling weapons directly to Khomeini. George Shultz and Caspar Weinberger,
who rarely agreed on anything, were agreed on the benighted
nature of the Ghorbanifar operation. Secretary of State Shultz
had never bought Reagan's argument that because we put Israel between ourselves and Iran, and then put some unknown
and unidentified "Iranian moderates" between ourselves and
Hezbollah, this was not an arms-for-hostages deal. Those were
a couple of strands of hair too fine to split. And Secretary of Defense Weinberger pointedly reminded Reagan of the violations
of both the embargo on selling arms to Iran and the Arms Export Control Act. The president was visibly annoyed with both
Shultz and Weinberger, Shultz later said, and "very concerned
about the hostages, as well as very much interested in the Iran
initiative. . . . Fully engaged." Despite the vocal in-house opposition to the operation, the Iranian arms deal remained on the
table for the next month, largely because Reagan himself would
not let it be extinguished.

In the meantime, by the reckoning of the White House's NSC
staff, one good thing had come from this mess of an arms
deal: a smallish but quite useful windfall had dropped into

the Swiss bank account of a private American company set up almost exclusively to further President Reagan's foreign policy agenda. That first arms-for-hostages profit didn't happen by design. The logistics of the third weapons shipment—the Hawks shipment—became so knotty that Israel had to pay a retired US Air Force general to deliver to Iran their four separate planeloads of twenty antiaircraft missiles. They advanced Gen. Richard V. Secord and his partners at Lake Resources, a key subsidiary of what came to be called "the Enterprise," a million dollars for the job. Only one of the four shipments was actually made. The Enterprise spent $150,000 of the $1 million making that one flight to Tehran, but what would become of the remaining $850,000?

As it turned out, the Enterprise, this web of shady little offshore companies, had another client in real need. That extra money became what Secord—and perhaps his contact inside the Reagan White House, Col. Oliver North—called a "Contrabution." And this is where Iran-Contra, the scandal that almost destroyed the Reagan presidency, earned its hyphen.

By the time General Secord got his unexpected windfall, the White House had been for a year secretly running a public-private partnership to keep the Contras in what the many Marines on Reagan's team liked to call "beans, boots, Band-Aids, and bullets." The privatization of the Contra aid operation was an idea first promoted in the highest circle of the Reagan administration in the summer of 1984, when it started to become clear that Congress was going to stop the US government from aiding the Contra military effort directly. According to now-declassified minutes, much of the June 25, 1984, National Security Planning Group meeting in the White House Situation Room was about funding the Contras. And everybody in the room understood they were edging up against legally questionable measures.

"If we can't get the money for the [Contras]," said UN ambassador Jeane Kirkpatrick at the meeting that afternoon, "then we should make the maximum effort to find the money elsewhere."

"I would like to get the money for the Contras also," Secretary of State George Shultz countered, "but another lawyer, Jim Baker, said that if we go out and try to get money from third countries, it is an impeachable offense."

"I am entitled to complete the record," CIA Director Casey chimed in, to remind everybody of the presidential finding on Nicaragua that Reagan had signed. "Jim Baker said that if we tried to get money from third countries without notifying the oversight committees, it could be a problem and he was informed that the [presidential] finding does provide for the participation and cooperation of third countries. Once he learned that the finding does encourage cooperation from third countries, Jim Baker immediately dropped his view that this could be an impeachable offense."

"I think," Shultz suggested, "we need to get an opinion from the attorney general on whether we can help the Contras obtain money from third sources. It would be the prudent thing to do."

After a brief argument about the feeble prospects of a diplomatic push in Central America, Casey circled the conversation back to finding money for the Contras. "It is essential that we tell the Congress what will happen if they fail to provide the funding for the [Contras]. At the same time, we can go ahead in trying to help obtain funding for the [Contras] from other sources; the finding does say explicitly 'the United States should cooperate with other governments and seek support of other governments.'"

"As another nonpracticing lawyer," offered Ed Meese, a longtime presidential counselor, who was then more or less auditioning for the role of attorney general, "I want to emphasize that it's important to tell the Department of Justice that we want them to find the proper and legal basis which will permit the United States to assist in obtaining third party resources for the anti-Sandinistas. You have to give lawyers guidance when asking them a question."

A few minutes later, Casey seconded Meese: "We need the legal opinion which makes clear that the US has the authority to facilitate third country funding for the [Contras]."

As the meeting finally wound down, Vice President George Bush made a rare interjection, a tepid endorsement for the plan, with a tepid caveat: "How can anyone object to the US encouraging third parties to provide help to [Contras] under the finding? The only problem that might come up is if the United States were to promise to give these third parties something in return so that some people could interpret this as some kind of an exchange."

National Security Adviser Bud McFarlane, clearly concerned about a discussion that had led off with the specter of impeachment, suggested extreme caution. "I propose that there be no authority for anyone to seek third-party support for the [Contras] until we have the information we need," he told the group, "and I certainly hope none of this discussion will be made public in any way."

Reagan agreed wholeheartedly with his national security adviser's assertion of the need for absolute discretion. It was clear that he expected his team to keep their traps shut about this plan: "If such a story gets out," the president said to close the meeting, "we'll all be hanging by our thumbs in front of the White House until we found out who did it."

Four months after that meeting, when Congress did cut off money for the US government to carry on with the Contras, the White House did not pause to consider the legal niceties of making its (covert) push for funding from third countries. Good news was that King Fahd bin Abdul Aziz of Saudi Arabia was already on board to the tune of a million dollars a month in direct aid to the Contras; the king was probably most appreciative for the 450 Stinger missiles Reagan had expressed to Saudi Arabia under the guise of presidential emergency powers, and for the US president's promise to ask Congress for more. During Fahd's visit to Washington in February 1985, the king capped a delightful private breakfast with the president with a promise to double his monthly donation. In all, Saudi Arabia would give about $32 million in aid to the Contras, or more precisely to the Enterprise. The only real disappointment for the president in his relations with Fahd was when the king tried to give Reagan a gift of four Arabian horses. He complained in his diary, "I couldn't accept them as a gift—due to our stupid regulations."

Word also got around in our hemisphere that the US president was up for bargaining with any country that would indulge him on his Contra obsession. Reagan used emergency powers to get Honduras $20 million worth of military supplies from the Pentagon. El Salvador wanted trade concessions. The Guatemalan president asked the United States to double its economic assistance package to his country, and triple the military package. Panamanian president Manuel Noriega offered to assassinate the leadership of the Nicaraguan government, but in return he wanted a commitment from the White House to lift the ban on US weapons sales to Panama, and also, maybe, a little help in revitalizing his image would be nice. The whole "dictatorial strongman" thing was apparently beginning to eat at Noriega. Reagan took a pass on the Noriega deal.

President Reagan left no continent undisturbed in his quest for "Contra-butions." When, after Reagan had left office, an independent counsel attorney presented him with a document that suggested he had asked the leader of an Asian country to ship weapons to the Contras, Reagan stammered out a remarkable truth, under oath: "I know this man of course, very well, met with him a number of times in his own country. . . . I don't recall seeing this and . . . my policy was not to involve others in this. I mean, I wanted them involved but I didn't want to be on the record of doing it."

That was the way Reagan liked to work, off the record. But Admiral John Poindexter, and those Marines on the National Security staff—Bud McFarlane and Oliver North—heard the president loud and clear when he tasked them to keep the Contras alive "body and soul." According to an independent counsel's report on the Iran-Contra affair published after more than five years of investigation, "North described how he and Secord, in order to replace the CIA in assisting the Contras, in their covert-action Enterprise created a 'mirror image outside the government of what the CIA had done.' [North] claimed he never made a single trip or contact 'without the permission, express permission, of either Mr. McFarlane or Admiral Poindexter, and usually, when I could, with the concurrence of Director Casey.'"

North turned out to be one hell of an operator; he understood that the president's appreciation for "third party" assistance to the Contras went well beyond foreign royalty and foreign governments. North managed a team of private fund-raisers and arms dealers who kept the Contras alive in the year of living without congressional funding. He'd shake the change out of the pockets of wealthy donors at fund-raisers hosted by the (newly created, not-for-profit, all-contributions-tax-deductible) National Endowment for the Preservation of Liberty, and he'd make sure the best check writers got a private audience—and a picture, of course—with the president. The president was happy to help.

With a combination of Saudi dollars and contributions from private American citizens funneled into the Enterprise's Swiss bank accounts, North and his friend Secord kept those Contras in millions of dollars (though not as many as they raised, but more on that later) of beans, boots, Band-Aids, and bullets. By June 1985, Secord's Enterprise was acting as the sole purchasing agent and weapons supplier of the Nicaraguan Contras. Contra leaders had no access to the money given them; North and Secord controlled it.

By spring 1986 North, Secord and partners also controlled and directed the logistics of the Contra resupply efforts (this would be known as Project Democracy) and its $4 million in assets comprising two C-123 cargo jets, two C-7 planes, and a $75,000 Maule aircraft paid for single-handedly by a wealthy Republican, Ellen Garwood, after a private meeting with the president. Ms. Ellen's two and a half million dollars also helped pay for a maintenance base in Miami, living quarters in El Salvador for eighteen or so resupply employees, and an airstrip in Costa Rica known as "The Plantation." This was essentially the closest North could come to the "mirror image" of the CIA's secret support to the Contras.

But unlike the CIA, which had to depend on money from Congress, this privately funded entity had added value: the privatization of Reagan's foreign policy initiative turned out to be just the ticket for evading all those barriers the legislature had erected. (Stupid regulations!) How could the president be obligated to report the activities of a private enterprise to Congress or anyone else? The Boland Amendment didn't stop the administration from helping concerned citizens who just wanted to help the Contras. This quasi-privatization—with fronts like the National Endowment for the Preservation of Liberty, and for-profit companies like Secord's Stanford Technology

Trading Group International and Project Democracy's Corporate Air Services—allowed the White House to run its Nicaragua operation unmoored from the Constitution and its fetters, free from congressional or statutory constraints, and clear of accountability. If anything went wrong, there was a firewall. Even though the Reagan administration directed the covert activity, there was a break in the formal chain of command; the orders up and down the line weren't really traceable. So confident in the firewall of deniability was the White House that when the House Intelligence Committee got wind of the Contra resupply operation, Reagan's NSC staff simply lied to Congress. "None of us has solicited funds, facilitated contacts for prospective potential donors, or otherwise organized or coordinated the military or paramilitary efforts of the resistance," the national security adviser told House Intelligence Committee members. "There has not been, nor will there be, any such activities by the National Security staff."

If accountability for military action to Congress and to the public was the foundational disincentive to war we got from the Founding Fathers, Reagan was taking a pickax to that foundation. He claimed the private right to go to war, in secret, against the express will of Congress.

The only hard part was keeping the thing funded. Overhead expenses were a bitch, of course. And then, too, private American companies like to show a profit, especially in a high-risk environment. Of the nearly $40 million that was raised toward Contra aid, only about $17 million found its way to the brave freedom fighters.

That's why the windfall from the Iran arms-for-hostages sale was so enticing. North wanted more Iranian profits to divert to the Contras, and he made his case in crew-cut-hair-on-fire memos that made their way to Reagan. North may never have been alone in the same room with the president, but he knew his man. The way he sold the need to continue the Iranian arms deal was simple: if the United States backs off the deal now, the hostages in Lebanon are dead meat.

On January 7, 1986, at that day's NSC meeting, the president surprised his key advisers by talking up a new idea to sweeten the pot: securing the release of twenty Hezbollah associates from Israeli prisons and shipping them along with the newest arms cache from Tel Aviv. The president could see the whole thing unfold. We arrange for Iran to get weapons and the Hezbollah guys from Israel. We sell Israel replacement weapons. Hezbollah frees our hostages. Iran pledges there will be no more kidnappings. "We sit quietly by and never reveal how we got them back," Reagan noted.

In the middle of this presidential reverie, Secretary Weinberger once again started in on Reagan about violating the Arms Export Control Act. But Ed Meese—he had ascended to United States Attorney General by this point—offered the sort of argument that always pricked up the ears of Ronald Reagan. There *was* a way around the Arms Export Control Act: "The president's inherent powers as commander in chief," Meese said. "The president's ability to conduct foreign policy." Reading later descriptions of this moment brings to mind an image of the pink and jowly attorney general, his full girth tucked into circus tights, performing a series of spectacular and acrobatic trapeze feats without a net:

> This opinion was based upon an October 5, 1981, opinion of Attorney General William French Smith that if the President determined that neither the Foreign Assistance

Act nor the Arms Export Control Act could be used, he
could approve a transfer outside the context of these stat-
utes if he determined that the authorities of the Economy
Act and the National Security Act should be utilized
in order to achieve 'a significant intelligence objective.'
Whereas Attorney General Smith advised that reporting requirements . . . required that the House and Senate
Intelligence Committees be informed of the President's
determination, Attorney General Meese took a more
extreme view that the National Security Act implicitly
authorized the President to withhold any prior or contemporaneous notice to Congress, even the limited notice to
the leadership of the two houses of Congress.

Meese was spoiling for this sort of fight; he'd already hired
into the Justice Department a coven of brilliant ultraconser-
vative young lawyers—Federalist Society guys—and set them
to the task of arguing the case for unleashing presidential authority. They were just then at work on a Meese-commissioned
report—"Separation of Powers: Legislative-Executive Relations"—
which invented something called the unitary executive theory,
based on a make-believe version of the Constitution, wherein
the president is given unilateral free rein in the realm of foreign
policy and national security. The report made a science fiction–
like case that the president was within his constitutional rights to
reinterpret congressional legislation to conform more closely to
his own desires, or to simply refuse to carry out laws with which
he did not agree, or that, the report harrumphed, "unconstitu-
tionally encroach on the executive branch." In sum, anything the
president doesn't want to do he doesn't have to do; anything he
wants to do, consider it done.

This "Separation of Powers" report was still a few months

away, but Meese was already living the dream at that January 1986 meeting. The nation's chief legal officer was basically giving the back of his hand not only to all the post-Vietnam, post-Watergate fetters the legislative branch had seen fit to impose in the aftermath of a couple of runaway presidencies, but to the ones written in the Constitution, too. Meese was saying "Fuck Congress," only in Latin. As Jane Mayer and Doyle McManus write in *Landslide*, their book about Reagan's second term in office, this interpretation of the powers of the president "hadn't been made quite so brazenly since Watergate. Following the constitutional crisis, Richard Nixon had been asked, 'When the president does it, that means that it is not illegal, by definition?' And he had answered, 'Exactly, exactly. If the president approves something for national security . . . then the president's decision is the one that enables those who carry it out, to carry it out without violating the law.' Meese's approach to the issue was essentially the same."

Shultz was taken aback by the entire scene at the NSC meeting that day. The lack of opposition, he later said, "almost seemed unreal."

Ten days later Reagan signed a presidential finding authorizing a new type of secret arms-for-hostages operation. On Attorney General Meese's legal advice, it was decided the US government should sell arms directly to the Iranians and cut out the Israelis as the middleman. And as he made clear in earlier discussions of this matter, Attorney General Meese stood ready to give his Justice Department lawyers, you know, a little nudge in the right direction. ("You have to give lawyers guidance when asking them a question.") A month later, the US government secretly shipped a thousand TOW missiles to Iran through a private party by the name of Richard Secord. One of Secord's planes returned with the unwanted Hawks. Not a single hostage was released. And Reagan decided that the wise policy would be not to inform Congress.

Well, they got caught of course. The whole thing was so dunderheaded, how could they not? By November 1986, Reagan's "Secret Dealings with Iran" had supplanted the 1986 midterm election results on the front page of *Time* magazine. Reagan played dumb for a few weeks, until the news broke that the money from the illegal arms sales had been diverted to the illegal Contra aid operation. The Reagan White House tried to get out ahead of the breaking scandal, calling for a special commission to investigate the entire affair and promising cooperation with a full-on congressional investigation. They even appointed an independent counsel to ferret out the scope and specifics of the illegalities. The president took some hard knocks. Before Christmastime that year, *Time* front-paged Iran-Contra twice more: "Probing the Mess," with a grotty close-up of the downcast eyes of "White House Point Man Oliver North," and "How Far Does It Go?" with a distant, lit-from-below White House looming like a murder-scene mansion in a horror movie.

By spring, after the Reagan-friendly Tower Commission had concluded that the administration had in fact traded arms for hostages and diverted some of the proceeds from those weapons sales to the Contras, *Time* had dispensed with the photographic emotional cues. They were no longer necessary to convey the seriousness of the damage to the presidency, or the ugliness of the scandal. With Reagan at the presidential lectern, and the Tower Commission report in the foreground, the cover asked simply, "Can He Recover?" The answer, in short, maybe not so much.

The answer in the magazine was longer, one derisive conclusion piled upon another. Reagan was "the befuddled and intellectually lazy figure so damningly portrayed in the Tower report . . . the picture of an inattentive, out-of-touch President."

And it got worse from there:

> The defects of what the commissioners euphemistically
> called Reagan's "management style," and what some for-
> mer associates more bluntly term mental laziness . . .
> stands exposed as a President willfully ignorant of what
> his aides were doing, myopically unaware of the glaring
> contradictions between his public and secret policies . . .
> unable to recall when, how or even whether he had
> reached the key decision that started the whole arms-
> to-Iran affair . . . the President has consistently and
> vehemently denied that the U.S. was swapping arms
> for hostages, though the voluminous record assembled
> by the Tower commission leaves no question that that is
> what happened. . . . [I]t is far from clear whether Reagan
> has yet admitted that even in his own mind.

Oh, wait, there's more.

"The President who did not understand that arms-for-hostages swaps, in the commission's words, 'ran directly counter to the Administration's own policies on terrorism' is the same Reagan who has never admitted, probably even to himself, that his tax and spending programs were bound to result in gargantuan budget deficits."

Meese did his nimble-for-a-large-man best; he was in full protect-the-president mode. The attorney general threw the military professionals—McFarlane, North, and John Poindexter —to the wolves. He got up some good evidence for a "cabal of zealots" theory arguing that they had operated without presiden-tial knowledge. And in his July 1987 testimony before Congress, Meese did his damnedest to explain why all those activities the cabal had worked so hard to hide from Congress had not, in fact, been illegal at all; he did this by giving legislators a little legal guidance on the meaning of their own Boland Amendment. The Boland Amendment, Ed Meese explained to committee chairman Daniel Inouye in another remarkable high-wire act, didn't apply to national security staff members in the employ of the White House.

> INOUYE: As the chief law enforcement officer of the
> United States, are you suggesting, or is it your opinion,
> that once the Boland Amendment was passed setting
> forth certain activities that are forbidden to the CIA, the
> NSA and others, that the NSC could have assumed these
> forbidden functions without violating the law?

> MEESE: Well, Mr. Chairman, the question was directed to
> me as to whether the Boland Amendment applied to the
> NSC staff. I indicated that this was an issue on which we
> had not rendered an opinion in the Justice Department. I
> also indicated that if you look at the language it is possible
> to make a strong case for the fact that the Boland Amend-
> ment does not apply to the NSC staff. . . . If the Boland
> Amendment does not apply to the NSC staff then they
> would not be included within the prohibitions.

> INOUYE: Are you telling us that the staff of the National
> Security Council can carry out functions that are forbid-
> den to the CIA without evading the laws of the lands of
> the United States?

> MEESE: If the law doesn't apply to them then they can
> without violating the law, obviously. That's a tautology.
> And when I say the law doesn't apply to them, the law by
> its language does not include them.

INOUYE: But if an agent of the CIA carried it out, that would have been a violation of the law?

MEESE: Because the law applies to the CIA by its very terms, but the law by its terms only applies to the CIA, I believe the Defense Department, and entities of the government involved in intelligence activities. Normally, under the list that I read to you, that is not normally deemed to include the National Security Council staff.

INOUYE: Even if they carried out intelligence activities, covert activities?

MEESE: Well, it would depend again on the circumstances. It's a hypothetical question. But by the language there I think a good case can be made that Congress in its enactment of that law did not include the National Security Council staff within the purview of the agencies that are listed in that section as involved in the prohibition.

INOUYE: Then in other words from what you're telling me, employees of the Department of Agriculture could have done the same thing without evading the law? To carry out covert activities?

MEESE: I think that it's entirely possible that as the—that as the law is written here where it says, 'funds available to the Central Intelligence Agency, the Department of Defense or any other agency or entity of the United States involved in intelligence activities may be obligated and expended only as authorized in specific sections.' Now, as I read that, as I said earlier, a strong case can be made I think that that does not apply to the Agriculture Department, that it doesn't apply to Health and Human Services, and a number of other entities which are not involved in intelligence activities.

INOUYE: But if some agent of the Department of Agriculture involved himself with the approval of the president in some covert activity, would that law apply then?

MEESE: By its language, it does not appear to.

INOUYE: Then the Boland Amendment can be evaded very easily.

MEESE: I don't think it would be an evasion if the law itself doesn't apply to a particular entity. It certainly would not be an evasion.

Ta-da!

At the same time Attorney General Meese was turning in that grand performance in the Russell Senate Office Building, conjuring imagined armies of USDA inspectors and epidemiologists marching on Managua (it's all legal), declaring the National Security Council as not being involved in intelligence activities, Meese's Office of Legal Counsel was making the exact opposite argument. Assistant Attorney General Charles Cooper had determined that the first two arms shipments to Iran were perfectly legal because the NSC *was* involved, and it was "clear" that the NSC is an "intelligence agency." Meese's testimony and Cooper's legal opinion were, as one might say, diabolically opposed, and this was—well, should have been anyway—embarrassing in the way they were making it up as they went. But this was all new.

Most informed and sentient onlookers would have thought back in the spring and summer of 1987 that this new Meeseian executive-branch modus operandi was about to meet the fate it deserved—a swift and sure death. Even before all the indictments and the convictions of senior administration officials, Reagan's new way—the president can do anything so long as the president thinks it's okay—looked like toast. In fact, Reagan looked like toast. Whatever his presidency had meant up until that point, Iran-Contra was such an embarrassment, such a toxic combination of illegality and sheer stupidity, that even the conservatives of his own party were disgusted. "He will never again be the Reagan that he was before he blew it," said a little-known Republican congressman from Georgia by the name of Newt Gingrich. "He is not going to regain our trust and our faith easily."

The president had been caught red-handed. Congress had exercised its legal and constitutional prerogative to restrain the executive branch from waging a war in Nicaragua. Reagan responded by breaking the law, waging the war anyway, and funding it by illegal and secret weapons deals that the president insisted weren't happening. The secretary of defense was indicted on multiple counts, as were two national security advisers, an assistant secretary of state, the chief of Covert Ops at the CIA, and two other senior CIA officials. The president himself escaped largely by pleading exhaustive ignorance and confusion: "I'm afraid that I let myself be influenced by others' recollections, not my own . . . the simple truth is, I don't remember—period." The Reagan presidency—the whole mythology of Reagan's leadership—was laid bare. This was competence?

But a funny thing happened on the way to the burial of those tough-guy president-can-do-anything ideas. The lesson of the whole affair didn't really take hold. The Tower Commission and the congressional investigating committee and the independent counsel expended their resources and energies on personalities like North and Secord and McFarlane and Poindexter, and Reagan got a pass. Which meant that in the not very much longer term, Reagan could be reimagined and reinvented by conservatives as an executive who had done no wrong: the gold standard of Republican presidents. By 2011, Newt Gingrich was trying to pave his own path to the presidency with Gingrich Productions "documentaries" like *Ronald Reagan: Rendezvous with Destiny.* "I knew Ronald Reagan; I began working with Ronald Reagan in 1974 when I first ran for Congress," Gingrich was thundering from the podium at conservative conferences. "And I hate to tell this to our friends at MSNBC and elsewhere: Barack Obama is no Ronald Reagan!" (Newt's Reagan movie kind of glossed over the whole Iran-Contra thing, when the extent of Newt Gingrich's "working with" Ronald Reagan was throwing him under the bus, as the untrustworthy president who "blew it.")

The Iran-Contra scandal hasn't exactly turned into a badge of honor for those who had starring roles, but neither does it tarnish the high sheen retrospectively applied to the Reagan presidency or those who did his illegal or extraconstitutional bidding. Reagan's successor, George H. W. Bush, pardoned most of the Iran-Contra convicts; Bush's son George W. hired on a number of the scandal's key players for his own administration. The Obama administration kept W's defense secretary, Robert M. Gates, whose name is the title of chapter 16 of the Iran-Contra independent counsel report. ("The evidence established," said the report, "that Gates was exposed to information about North's connections to the private resupply operation that would have raised concern in the minds of most reasonable persons about the propriety of a Government officer having such an operational role.")

But even more dangerous was the sad fact that the shameful

Meese-made legal arguments about nearly unlimited executive power were not seen as the crazy talk they were, and killed off for good. One leader in Congress was instrumental in making sure this executive-power argument remained politically viable, by loudly declaiming at the time of Iran-Contra, in the midst of the scandal, that Reagan was right to do what he did. As the main author of the minority's 145-page written dissent from the congressional investigation of Iran-Contra, Wyoming Representative Dick Cheney insisted, radically, that Iran-Contra was no crime, that Reagan was right to defy Congress, because there was nothing in Congress, nothing anywhere in America's political structure, that could constrain a president from waging any war he wanted, however he wanted. It was an extreme view of executive power, a minority view when written, but it quickly became a blueprint for the next generation of Republican thinking about war and its limits. "The President was expected to have the primary role of conducting the foreign policy of the United States," Cheney argued in his minority report on Iran-Contra. "Congressional actions to limit the President in this area therefore should be reviewed with a considerable degree of skepticism. If they interfere with core presidential foreign policy functions, they should be struck down. Moreover, the lesson of our constitutional history is that doubtful cases should be decided in favor of the President."

And who won this argument? The answer is kind of surprising, but sadly obvious today, when we find ourselves in a succession of indefinite hot wars the country does not really want.

Remember the words of James Madison: "The Constitution supposes, what the History of all Governments demonstrates, that the Executive is the branch of power most interested in war, and most prone to it. It has accordingly with studied care vested the question of war in the Legislature." The "studied care" Madi-

son describes behind that "vesting" has not been matched by any
equal and opposite studied care in recent decades, as we've di-
vested that same power. It's not a conspiracy. Rational political
actors, acting rationally to achieve rational (if sometimes dumb)
political goals, have attacked and undermined our constitutional inheritance from men like Madison. For the most part,
though, they've not done it to fundamentally alter the country's course but just to get around understandably frustrating
impediments to their political goals. The ropes we had used to
lash down presidential war-making capacity, bindings that by
design made it hard for an American president to use military
force without the nation's full and considered buy-in, have been
hacked at with very little appreciation about why they were put
there in the first place.

When Ronald Reagan extricated himself from the Iran-
Contra scandal by cutting one of those crucial mooring lines—
without considered forethought or specific course headings in
mind—it set the country adrift and heading into a dangerous
tide.

Congress has never since effectively asserted itself to stop
a president with a bead on war. It was true of George Herbert
Walker Bush. It was true of Bill Clinton. And by September 11,
2001, even if there had been real resistance to Vice President
Cheney and President George W. Bush starting the next war (or
two), there were no institutional barriers strong enough to have
realistically stopped them. By 9/11, the war-making authority in
the United States had become, for all intents and purposes, un-
contested and unilateral: one man's decision to make.

It wasn't supposed to be like this.

Chapter 6

Mylanta, 'Tis of Thee

TWO HUNDRED THOUSAND ADDITIONAL TROOPS MINIMUM, nearly double what the president of the United States had already ordered into the hot desert of Saudi Arabia, was what it would take. According to the presentation his top military adviser made at the White House Situation Room meeting of October 30, 1990, that was the minimum manpower price George Herbert Walker Bush would have to pay to forcibly remove Saddam Hussein and his Iraqi Army from Kuwait. This was decision day. If Bush couldn't bear the size of that call-up and he stoppered the military spigot pouring our soldiers into the Persian Gulf, he could do no more than sit his army in the desert and wait for the UN sanctions to pressure Saddam out of Kuwait. If he kept the flow open, he'd leave himself the option of launching a punishing offensive attack on Saddam's army. He'd have the wherewithal to make the biggest war Americans had seen in a generation.

It had been three months since the Iraqi dictator had invaded Kuwait, jettisoned its ruling royal family, and claimed its oil fields, which gave Saddam, the Bush administration claimed, something near to 20 percent of the world's oil reserves. And worse than that, Saddam was now within arm's reach of Saudi oil, which might give him close to half of the planet's most consumed necessity.

In the first days after the invasion, President Bush had made it clear: "This will not stand, this aggression against Kuwait." He said later, "That's not a threat, not a boast. That's just the way it's going to be." Within a week of the Iraqi Army's invasion of Kuwait, the president had deployed a large contingent of American soldiers, sailors, and Marines to the Persian Gulf to make sure Saddam knew the United States was serious about defending Saudi Arabia—and to stand by for further orders. And he had convinced the reluctant Saudi king to play host to this huge American army. (The Saudi king, incidentally, had chosen Bush's offer of military assistance over the offer made by a certain Saudi national who boasted he could defend the kingdom's oil fields with his army of mujahedeen fighters, who had distinguished themselves in battle against the Soviets in Afghanistan. King Fahd's decision to go with the American military instead turned Osama bin Laden against the Saudi royal family forever, and it didn't exactly enhance his feelings toward America, either.)

Bush had been masterful at building international support and a broad coalition of allies. The UN Security Council and almost every nation in the civilized world had agreed to impose strangling economic sanctions meant to bring the Iraqi dictator and his army to heel. And the United States was leading the way. "Recent events have surely proven that there is no substitute for American leadership," Bush reassured Congress and the country. "In the face of tyranny, let no one doubt American credibility and reliability. Let no one doubt our staying power. We will stand by our friends. One way or another, the leader of Iraq must learn this fundamental truth." At Bush's insistent urging, every one of Saddam's Arab neighbors had signed up on our side. Even the Soviet Union was with us.

But still, three months in, George Herbert Walker Bush was not a happy man.

The day before that fish-or-cut-bait National Security Council meeting, Saddam had appeared on television—*US television*—having sport with the president. "If an embargo would force the American people to withdraw from the last state that was linked to the United States—say, Hawaii," Saddam offered, "then the same standards, if they were applied, would probably lead the Iraqis to consider withdrawal from Kuwait." And then, sticking a thumb in Bush's eye: "Whoever commits aggression against Iraq will be the party that shall turn out to be the loser. . . ."

When President Bush met with his national security team the next day, his patience was wearing thin, and he was not, as the chairman of the Joint Chiefs of Staff, Gen. Colin Powell, knew, a patient man to begin with. The president had been agitating the chairman for weeks about launching air strikes on Baghdad; he'd also been confiding in British prime minister Margaret Thatcher as well as his own advisers that he'd really appreciate it if Saddam did something sufficiently provocative—like, say, abusing some of his Western hostages (whom the Iraqi dictator insisted on calling his "guests")—to justify a US-led attack. The longer this stalemate went on, the more nervous Bush seemed to grow. "Dealing with the president," Powell said years later, "was like playing Scheherazade, trying to keep the king calm for a thousand and one nights."

Besides being a man of preternatural impatience—sitting still without a fishing rod in his hand drove him batty—the president had whipped up for himself a furious and frothy head of contempt for Saddam and his invasion of Kuwait. What had started as a strategic national imperative to keep energy prices in check, maintain a balance of power among the oil-producing nations of the Middle East, and show that as the world's lone remaining superpower after the slow-motion dissolution of the Soviet Union, America would remain an active force in the world, had blossomed for Bush into a bigger idea, a vision thing. "As I look at the countries that are chipping in here now, I think we do have a chance at a new world order," he'd said at one formal news conference. "And I'd like to think that out of this dreary performance by Saddam Hussein there could be now an opportunity for peace all through the Middle East." And he got downright poetic in an address to the nation: "A hundred generations have searched for this elusive path to peace while a thousand wars raged across the span of human endeavor. And today, that new world is struggling to be born. A world quite different from the one we've known. A world where the rule of law supplants the rule of the jungle. A world in which nations recognize the shared responsibility for freedom and justice. A world where the strong respect the rights of the weak."

So there was the whole new world order thing. The otherwise grounded and pragmatic George Herbert Walker Bush was nominating himself for a place among the pantheon of politicians and kings who claimed that one, just *one* more war would bring world peace. There was also the matter of standing up to a bully, a matter of honor in Bush's personal code of ethics. Human Rights Watch had reported that Saddam's soldiers were murdering, raping, and generally brutalizing Kuwaiti citizens. "I mean, people on a dialysis machine cut off, the machine sent to Baghdad," Bush had exclaimed. "Babies in incubators heaved out of the incubators and the incubators themselves sent to Baghdad." He was even hearing stories about Kuwaiti children being mowed down and killed on their way to hospitals, or Iraqi soldiers releasing the animals from the Kuwait zoo for target practice. "Their efforts, however, were not completely successful," a Bush administration official told reporters. "A lion escaped and mauled a young Kuwaiti girl."

It wasn't long before Bush, the old World War II fighter pilot, started turning his description of Saddam up to eleven. "Worse than Hitler!" he said. "I began to move from viewing Saddam's aggression exclusively as a dangerous strategic threat and an injustice to its reversal as a moral crusade," Bush later wrote. "I became very emotional about the atrocities. They really gave urgency to my desire to do something active in response. At some point it came through to me that this was not a matter of shades of gray, or of trying to see the other side's point of view. It was good versus evil, right versus wrong. I am sure the change strengthened my determination not to let the invasion stand and encouraged me to contemplate the use of force to reverse it."

Saddam had rolled into Kuwait on August 2, 1990. Bush had sent troops to wait in Saudi Arabia on August 6. By October 30, 1990, the day he summoned what was effectively his war council to the Situation Room, the president was worried that the air was leaking out of his new world order moral crusade. He was getting edgy; he wasn't sure how long the international coalition he had personally gathered would hold together. And he wasn't sure how long the American people would support him in the crisis. He'd had huge backing for his response to Saddam up till then, something near 70 percent of Americans. But he could feel it slipping away.

He'd had a tough month—he'd taken "the damndest pounding I've ever seen" from the Democratic-controlled Congress in the budget battle occasioned by the prodigious deficits Reagan had left in his wake, and then another one from his own party when he'd had to back down from his Eastwoodesque "Read My Lips—No New Taxes" pledge. The tax hike was the right thing to do, Bush knew, but that didn't make it popular with the hard-liners in his party. He was starting to fear the return of that ugly (and he thought unfair) *Newsweek* headline he'd endured during his presidential campaign, "Fighting the Wimp Factor." His recent twenty-one-point drop in the polls was "one of the worst slides in public approval of any modern President," the *New York Times* noted. "That fall is at least as great, although perhaps not quite as sudden, as the decline in President Gerald R. Ford's approval rating after he pardoned former President Richard Nixon for his conduct in the Watergate scandal and the tumble that President Ronald Reagan took after disclosure of the Iran-contra affair."

And now, after pummeling Bush into submission over the budget, Congress was starting to "get in his knickers," as he sometimes said, about his handling of the Iraqi invasion of Kuwait. Just a few hours before the big October 30 war council meeting, he'd had to endure an hour-and-a-half-long sit-down with congressional leaders—they'd demanded it—so they could lecture him about war powers and public sentiment. The Democratic Speaker of the House had opened the proceedings by formally presenting Bush with a letter signed by eighty-one of his colleagues:

> Recent reports and briefings indicate that the United States has shifted from a defensive to an offensive posture and that war may be imminent. We believe that the consequences would be catastrophic—resulting in the massive loss of lives, including 10,000 to 50,000 Americans. This could only be described as war. Under the US Constitution, only the Congress can declare war.

We are emphatically opposed to any offensive military
action. We believe that the UN-sponsored embargo must
be given every opportunity to work and that all multinational, non-military means of resolving the situation must
be pursued. If, after all peaceful means of resolving the
conflict are exhausted, and the President believes that
military action is warranted, then . . . he must seek a declaration of war from the Congress. . . . We firmly believe
that consulting with this group in no way replaces the
President's constitutional obligation to seek a declaration
of war before undertaking any offensive military action.
We demand that the Administration not undertake any
offensive military action without the full deliberation and
declaration required by the Constitution.

Bush sat and listened. Senate majority leader George Mitchell
insisted that the case had not been made that the sanctions had
failed. "I want to plead with you personally before you take the
country into war," Speaker Tom Foley implored. "Unless there is
gross provocation, you won't have public support." Bush listened
some more, and then showed them the door. Oh, he'd "consult."
He'd tell them what he was doing—*what he'd already done,* was
more like it. He wouldn't trust Congress with a decision about
China patterns at a state dinner, let alone war and peace. "As
long as the people are with us, I've got a good chance," he'd written in his diary. "But once there starts to be erosion, [Congress]
is going to do what Lyndon Johnson said: they painted their
asses white and ran with the antelopes."

Bush never bothered to answer that congressional letter. As
far as he was concerned, he required no authorization from
Congress to make war. In fairness to the president, one has to
remember that he had been swimming for eight years in that

muddled soup of reasoning that was the Reagan White House, and particularly in Ed Meese's gooey construct called the "inherent powers of the president." About his unilateral decision to deploy those troops to Saudi Arabia for more than sixty days, well, he said, they were in "no imminent danger of hostilities," so the War Powers Act didn't apply even if he did recognize its reach, which he did not, because it was an unconstitutional check on presidential power. Meese's lawyers had said so. This was a matter of national security, Bush believed. He was commander in chief. He had all the authority he needed.

And as commander in chief the president made it plain in the Situation Room, a few hours after that congressional invasion of the White House, that he wanted *his* military—if not the nation—prepared to launch an air-and-ground attack to remove Saddam from Kuwait, and he meant to provide his generals with whatever they needed to do the job.

But what the generals said they needed to do the job functioned as a bit of a check on the move toward war. The chairman of the Joint Chiefs of Staff, Colin Powell, had not been shy in the ask that afternoon. Powell wanted an overwhelming, decisive use of force to meet American military objectives clearly and quickly. The whole Powell Doctrine of disproportionate force, clear goals, a clear exit strategy, and public support was designed to create a kind of quagmire-free war zone. He was unequivocal—he and his commander on the ground, Norman Schwarzkopf, had agreed: two hundred thousand more troops was what it would take. And they'd already made sure the president understood the numbers would go up if he decided he wanted not only to eject Saddam from Kuwait but to destroy his army, or to depose him. The mission objectives would have to be clearly defined before H-Hour. In any case, Powell and Schwarzkopf wanted five, maybe six, aircraft carrier task forces deployed to the Persian Gulf, which would leave naval power dangerously thin in the rest of the world. By the time the offensive capability was in place, about two months down the road, there would be something in the neighborhood of 500,000 American troops in the Middle East—nearly as many as at the high-water mark in Vietnam. Two-thirds of the combat units in the Marine Corps would be deployed in the Gulf. There would be no more talk of rotating troops home after six months. Soldiers had to understand they were in the Gulf until the job was done, however long that took.

And another thing Powell had long ago made clear: there would have to be a huge reserve contingent. The Department of Defense had already called up a few thousand reservists—mostly pilots and uniformed baggage handlers to get the troops airlifted to the desert. But this new commitment would mean activating tens of thousands of reservists from all over the country. As soon as they announced the call-up, or as soon as word got out, Saddam Hussein would know the United States of America was preparing to commence a war. And so would the American people.

The president insisted the military guys could have what they needed. Not everybody in the room was so cheerfully acquiescent. A lot of the president's advisers, including Powell's own boss, Secretary of Defense Dick Cheney, believed the Joint Chiefs chairman was a carrier of that dread disease, the "Vietnam syndrome." And while Cheney backed Powell's request that day, he was among the men in the war council who thought the chairman of the Joint Chiefs had spent too much time in the previous three months focused on political considerations and too little on military planning. He sometimes questioned whether the general was "on the team."

"Listening to him," Cheney wrote of Powell, "made me think about how Vietnam had shaped the views of America's top generals. They had seen loss of public support for the Vietnam War undermine the war effort as well as damage the reputation of the military. There was a view in the Pentagon, for which I had a lot of sympathy, that the civilian leadership had blown it in Vietnam by failing to make the tough decisions that were required to have a chance at prevailing. I understood where Powell was coming from, but I couldn't accept it. Our responsibility at the Department of Defense was to make sure the president had a full range of options to consider."

If Cheney believed Powell was dragging his heels all through the early stages of Desert Shield, he was partly right. Throughout the process Powell had agitated for a clear statement from the president of mission objectives, a real effort by the president's political team to win the support of the American people, and a commitment of all necessary resources. He would admit to overstepping his bounds in pressing the president on these essentially political questions, but he would not apologize for it. He had observed very little internal debate in the White House about whether or not we *ought* to make this war, and he believed the men and women sent to fight in the Persian Gulf deserved a real and genuine consideration of that question by their civilian leaders. He'd lived through two tours in Vietnam, seen his brother officers demoralized, seen the Army disavowed by the general public and close to broken as an institution. Reluctant warrior? "Guilty," Powell would write in his autobiography. "War is a deadly game; and I do not believe in spending the lives of Americans lightly." There would be no repeat of Vietnam while he was in charge, no lives needlessly thrown away. "Perhaps I was the ghost of Vietnam," he told a television interviewer in 1995. "If it caused me to be the skunk at the picnic," his compatriots in the George Herbert Walker Bush administration could all "take a deep smell."

According to Powell's excellent biographer, Karen DeYoung, the general's presentation at the October 30 meeting gave the president's closest confidant on matters of war and peace, National Security Adviser Brent Scowcroft, a snootful of something he didn't much like. "Scowcroft was taken aback by the size of the attack force Powell was proposing," DeYoung wrote of that moment. "The military, he believed, had moved from reluctance to undertake an offensive operation at all to a deliberately inflated plan designed to make the president think twice about the effort."

Scowcroft . . . he was onto something there.

The thing was, there was no other institutional brake on the war-making machine, at least not one the president acknowledged. One of the last remaining brake lines had been severed by the disintegration of the Soviet Union. In the previous year, since the fall of the Berlin Wall signaled the beginning of the end for the United States' Cold War foe of more than forty years, the Department of Defense had been fighting a fierce bureaucratic battle to hold on to the lion's share of its spectacularly large Reagan-inflated budget. It was still a dangerous world out there, and Secretary of Defense Cheney, for one, meant to keep the nation's military on high idle. He had made it clear that all those hopelessly irenic congressmen and senators like Ted Kennedy who insisted on redirecting resources from the military into programs like job retraining and education and—my God!—universal health care were simply harebrained. "In a speech in Washington before a Princeton University student group," the *Los Angeles Times* reported a month after the fall of the Wall, "Cheney excoriated 'irresponsible' critics who suggest 'there is some kind of big peace dividend here to be cashed in and to buy all the goodies everybody on Capitol Hill can think about buying.'"

Within six months, the Hill's most powerful Democrat on the budget had conceded Cheney's point. The chairman of the House Ways and Means Committee bluntly waved off a gathering of mayors who asked that defense money be reallocated to urban programs. "There's no money. . . . The peace dividend is already going to be swallowed."

The real "peace dividend," it turned out, in a twist of sad and stunning irony, was that it became much *easier* to make war in places like the Persian Gulf without worrying about the opportunity cost for our ongoing standoff with the Soviets. "We could be so lavish with resources because the world had changed," Powell later said. To fight a war in the Gulf, for example, "we could now afford to pull divisions out of Germany that had been there for the past forty years to stop a Soviet offensive that was no longer coming."

And of course Reagan's presidential antidote for the nation's Vietnam syndrome—to simply ignore the Constitution, or go around the Congress, when you want to make war—had proved hugely successful in cutting the constraints on war in all but one particular. The only line still tying down the US war machine was the legacy of Creighton Abrams, the good old Abrams Doctrine—the idea that sending the military into war would mean, by definition, sending *the country* into war. In 1990, it was not possible to mobilize the military for action of any considerable size (as Lyndon Johnson had tragically done in Vietnam) without calling up the Guard and Reserves. The wrenching actuality of calling all those weekend warriors to active duty—active *combat* duty, active *you-could-be-killed-on-the-field-of-battle* duty—would not go unnoticed. Colin Powell had told President Bush, "Sir, call-up means pulling people out of their jobs.

It affects businesses. It means disrupting thousands of families. It's a major political decision." The Abrams Doctrine made sure that a decision in Washington, DC, to start a war rang clear in every state and every city and just about every one-horse town in America. Colin Powell was counting on it.

Not that Powell was opposed to kicking Saddam's ass, but he hoped to have public recognition, and public debate, and a real show of popular support, before the bombs started flying. When the president's pushy little chief of staff, John Sununu, had suggested they could simply leave the Reserves at home and still whip Saddam, Powell insisted. The Reserves needed to be called up, right away, and a lot of them.

The best Sununu and the White House politicals could get was an agreement to hold the official announcement of the call-up for a week or ten days. "The political experts," wrote Scowcroft, "wanted to delay the announcement until after the congressional elections." The decision with the war council had been made on October 30, the elections were November 6, and on November 8 the troops were officially called up. By the time Cheney picked up the phone and told congressional leaders that the president's massive and momentous buildup on the Kuwaiti border was under way . . . and by the time George Bush stepped up to a White House podium to make the bland statement that "I have today directed the secretary of defense to increase the size of the US forces committed to Desert Shield to ensure that the coalition has an adequate offensive military option should that be necessary to achieve our common goals," warning bells were already pealing throughout the land. The formal announcement rang clear and rang loud. It was the Abrams Doctrine at work. Not just the president, not just the military, but the country was facing up to the very real possibility of war. "After 14 weeks of proceeding virtually unchallenged at home," the *New York Times* lead political reporter wrote within days of Bush's announcement, "the United States policy in the Persian Gulf has become the focus of a national debate."

Right!

The debate got tense, and in a hurry. The 101st Congress had come to a close before the elections, and the 102nd wasn't scheduled to reconvene until the beginning of January, but that just meant there wasn't much else on the national agenda to crowd out war talk. Big-time Democrats in the Senate ran for the open and available microphones and, as Bush saw it, started playing to the headline writers. Ted Kennedy remonstrated against the president's reckless "headlong" drive toward war with Saddam. "Silence by Congress," Massachusetts's senior senator said, "is an abdication of our constitutional responsibility and an acquiescence in war." The Senate majority leader George Mitchell was tougher on the president, stating flatly that Bush "has no legal authority, none whatever," to take the country to war. "The Constitution clearly invests that great responsibility in the Congress and the Congress alone."

And it wasn't just Democrats.

Even Dick Lugar, a Republican senator, supposedly a friend to the administration, was promising to stick the congressional nose deep into the White House's war-making business. He suggested it might be prudent for the president to spend as much energy convincing the American people that a shooting war against the Iraqi Army was the right thing to do as he was spending in convincing the rest of the world. Lugar went so far as to call for a rare special session of a lame-duck Congress to vote on a resolution authorizing a war in the Persian Gulf. Meanwhile, leaders in both the House and the Senate let Bush know they would get going on oversight hearings into the president's policies in the Gulf *tout de suite,* before the new Congress convened.

As far as Bush was concerned, this aggression would not stand either.

The president called the congressional leaders into the White House and fired a warning shot. He had bent over backward to "consult" with Congress, he said, but "consultation is a two-way street. I think it is only fair that I get to hear your specific ideas in private about the tough choices we face before people go out and take public stances." He pulled out press clippings; read them back, verbatim, to his loudest antagonists; and told them that Saddam might just get the message that the United States didn't have the spine to stay the course. "This is the wrong signal to send at this time." And about all that talk of Congress having an exclusive power to declare war? Forget it. According to one report out of the meeting, the president had pulled a copy of the Constitution from his suit jacket and waved it in front of the bipartisan congressional delegation. Bush knew what the document said about war powers, he told the group, but "it also says that I'm the commander in chief."

What'd they think, he was some kind of wimp?

There were some members of Congress on both sides of the aisle who were squarely with Bush. They were with him on the old Reagan line that open public debate was a dangerous thing. Republican Senate leader Bob Dole asked, "How do we have open debate without sending the wrong signal to Saddam?" Republican congressman Henry Hyde went so far as to say that "Congress are supposed to be leaders. We should be carrying the [president's] message to the people."

But the point was, the debate in Congress had already begun. The call-up of the Reserves had assured it. There was going to be a public airing of the merits of this war, no matter what the president said.

On November 20, a few days after Bush's "I'm the commander in chief" performance, a group of forty-five House members led by Rep. Ron Dellums gathered the Capitol Hill press corps to announce that they had filed a lawsuit asking the federal district court in Washington, DC, to demand that the president send to Congress a formal declaration of war to be debated and voted on *before* American troops were sent into battle. "There is no necessity for quick action here," said one congressman. "We are not being invaded. There is no reason at all why the Constitution in this case should not be honored. And that's what this lawsuit is all about."

This was a more aggressive challenge to the president than that initial warning letter from the Speaker of the House three weeks earlier, before 200,000 more Americans had been pointed east and told to pack. Dellums and company were essentially asking a judge to tie the president's hands unless and until he got Congress on board. "Some people have said, 'Well, don't you believe that this would inconvenience the president?'" Dellums said. "The Constitution is designed to inconvenience one person from taking us to war. War is a very solemn and sobering and extraordinary act and it should not be granted to one person."

"Some people are saying you're not inconveniencing [the president]," one reporter observed. "You're undermining his ability to conduct an effective policy in the Persian Gulf."

"To do anything other than what we're suggesting here is to undermine the Constitution of the United States," Dellums countered. "This is not the president's sole prerogative."

In the Senate, the Armed Services Committee, chaired by Georgia Democrat Sam Nunn, convened hearings on military readiness and capability in the Gulf, but the hearings quickly turned to questions about the advisability of and the need for a shooting war in Kuwait. And not just whether we ought to fight a war like that, but who would get to say so. Nunn even called as a witness the sharp-eyed Vietnam vet and author James Webb, not long removed from a tour as Reagan's secretary of the Navy, who argued that Bush needed to get a declaration of war from Congress. Further, if Bush really meant to start a war of this size, his actions ought to live up to the magnitude of that decision. Stop-lossing active-duty troops was one thing, calling up the Guard and Reserves was all well and good, but to knit this into American life even further, the president needed to reinstitute the draft. The entire country needed to feel it, not just the military.

Up till that point, all the president's steps toward war had been taken unilaterally. But the sheer magnitude of his actions, the number of military personnel he'd had to involve, demanded attention and challenge. The Bush White House seemed to understand that, but to resent and resist it too. "We were confident that the Constitution was on our side when it came to the president's discretion to use force if necessary," wrote Brent Scowcroft. "If we sought congressional involvement, it would not be authority we were after, but support."

Actually, again, not to insist, but the Constitution "with studied care vested the question of war in the Legislature." But by 1990 the executive branch wasn't operating as if this was true anymore. Sure, a president going to war would be wise to engage with Congress on the issue. But that engagement was not determinative of whether we would in fact have that war—it was akin to lining up support from some foreign, sometimes-friendly ally: friends with political benefits. Better to have them on board than not, but if they didn't come along, no biggie.

Not only *didn't* the "question of war" vest in the Legislature anymore—it *shouldn't,* either. The loudest voice in the Bush White House in favor of steamrolling the national legislature was the secretary of defense, Dick Cheney. Cheney had cut his bureaucratic teeth (and exceedingly sharp they were) as White House chief of staff during the Gerald Ford presidency, back when Congress was first wielding its War Powers Resolution (stupid regulations!) and making unprecedented and unwelcome trips to the White House to stop Ford from taking the country into another war in Vietnam.

"Cheney and I dealt with this congressional backlash in the Ford White House," Cheney's mentor, Donald Rumsfeld, wrote in his autobiography. "In the early days of the Ford Administration, Bryce Harlow, the savvy White House Liaison to Congress, former Eisenhower aide, and friend, told me—and I am paraphrasing from memory: 'The steady pressure by Congress and the courts is to reduce executive authority. It is inexorable, inevitable, and historical. Resolve that when you leave the White House, leave it with the same authorities it had when you came. Do not contribute to the erosion of presidential power on your watch.' Harlow's words left an impression on me, and, I suspect, on Cheney."

Even before the congressional hearings on Saddam and Kuwait had commenced in November 1990, Secretary of Defense Cheney had shipped out to the Sunday talk-show circuit to sound the old Reagan line about the "risky proposition" of leaving national security decisions in the shaky hands of 535 members of Congress. "I take you back to September 1941, when World War II had been under way for two years," Cheney said on *Meet the Press*. "Hitler had taken Austria, Czechoslovakia, Poland, Norway, Denmark, the Netherlands, Belgium, France, and was halfway to Moscow. And the Congress, in that setting, two months before Pearl Harbor, agreed to extend the draft for twelve more months . . . by just one vote." That Saddam Hussein's misbegotten—and already-stopped-dead-in-its-tracks—adventure in the Middle East was in no way comparable to Hitler's blitzkrieg through Europe was beside Cheney's point. Cheney's point was that Congress was sure to get out that white paint . . . and run with the antelopes. Wimps.

Secretary Cheney was no more conciliatory when he went to Capitol Hill to testify at Nunn's hearings; this was not a man coming hat in hand to ask his former colleagues for permission for anything. In an exchange with Sen. Edward Kennedy, Cheney laid down a stunning new marker for executive power.

> KENNEDY: Barring an act of provocation, do you agree that the president must obtain the approval of Congress in advance before the United States attacks Iraq?

> CHENEY: Senator, I do not believe the president requires any additional authorization from the Congress before committing US forces to achieve our objectives in the Gulf. . . . There have been some two hundred times, more than two hundred times, in our history, when presidents have committed US forces, and on only five of those occasions was there a prior declaration of war. And so I am not one who would argue, in this instance, that the president's hands are tied or that he is unable, given his constitutional responsibilities as commander in chief, to carry out his responsibilities.

> KENNEDY: Well, Mr. Secretary, we're not talking about Libya [where Reagan had run a one-shot bombing raid on its leader, Muammar Qaddafi]. We're not talking about Grenada. . . . We're talking about 440,000 American troops who are over there. We're talking about a major kind of American military involvement if it becomes necessary to do so. And do I understand from your response

that you are prepared to tell the American people now
that barring provocation by Saddam Hussein, that you believe [the president], and [the president] alone, can bring
this country to war?

CHENEY: Senator, I would argue, as has every president
to my knowledge, certainly in modern times, that the
president, as commander in chief, under Title II [*sic*],
Section 2 of the US Constitution, has the authority to
commit US forces.

Despite Kennedy's disbelieving challenge to Cheney in
that hearing room, despite Dellums's lawsuit, Congress as an
institution—and congressional leadership in particular—didn't
exactly get up on their hind legs and make a full-on fight with
the president. The truth was, it looked like the leaders stepped
back and prayed the crisis would resolve itself before they had
to show up again for work in January 1991. By then, they hoped,
Saddam would have summoned the sense to get out of Kuwait
before the shooting started, relieving them of the need to be
counted for war or against it.

With Congress in a state of strategic deferral, the White
House's real political energy was spent convincing the rest of the
world. The Bush administration was busy shepherding a new
UN resolution giving Saddam a drop-dead date for leaving Kuwait: January 15, 1991. If he was still in Kuwait on that day, according to UN resolution 678, the US-led military coalition was
free to use "all necessary means" to remove him.

It was only once that resolution was passed—once that international path to war had been cleared—that the president decided he ought to at least make some gesture in the direction
of caring about Congress. They'd be back in session—a new
Congress convened—before the January 15 deadline, after all.

He couldn't tell the people that the United Nations had more sway over our military than did the elected representatives of the American people. "The Security Council," Bush wrote, "had voted to go to war . . . but the carefully negotiated UN vote also called attention to whether, having asked the United Nations, we were obliged to seek similar authority from Congress. Once again we were faced with weighing the president's inherent power to use force against the political benefits of explicit support from Congress."

The political benefits! Had President Ronald Reagan believed that the decision to wage war (or not to) resided solely in the executive branch, and not in Congress—that the legislature's role was just to cheer a president on and give a little political cover—he would never have waged his Contra adventure in secret. He did do it in secret—in violation of federal statute—and he got caught for it. To defend Reagan once he got caught, his administration cooked up the ad hoc, backfilling defense that no crime had been committed, that the legal constraint the president had taken such great secretive pains to elude didn't really exist. Congress, their argument went, actually had no power over war making—pro or con; the president could wage any war he wanted, on his own terms. It was an absurd argument. But it spewed enough of a smokescreen to save Reagan from impeachment, and after he was gone, it was convenient enough to successor presidents that it survived. It didn't have to—but it did.

And by 1990, it was this bizarre political inheritance that allowed old small-*c* conservative patrician George H. W. Bush—a man with no Fum-Poo flair at all, a man who grew up in a town where the country-club locker room was filled with men railing against the unconstitutional presidential overreach of Franklin Delano Roosevelt—to claim for himself and all presidents "inherent powers to use force" for which Congress's explicit support was useful only as a "political benefit." We had come a long way in a short time, and the strain showed on George H. W. Bush.

Ignoring the founders' loud and explicit warning that we should not allow one person to unilaterally take us to war has been demonstrably bad for this country. Turns out it's not so great for that one person, either. For all his hard-line "I'm the commander in chief" talk, Bush was tied in knots about the whole war powers business. A bracing little tour of President George H. W. Bush's private diaries and letters from his months of captivity in the Should-I-Make-War-on-Saddam hall of mirrors is instructive:

> I feel tension in the stomach and in the neck. I feel great pressure. . . . I worry, worry, worry about eroded support. . . . Some wanted me to deliver fireside chats to explain things, as Franklin Roosevelt had done. I am not good at that. . . . I think this week has been the most unpleasant, or tension filled of the Presidency. . . . If you want a friend in Washington, get a dog. . . . Nobody is particularly happy with me. . . . But some way I have got to convey to the American people that I will try my hardest, and [am] doing my best.

The president was aware of the political risks in going to war without some show of congressional support. His best ally in the Senate, Bob Dole, had publicly said that this was "make or break time" for the Bush presidency. But Dole hadn't exactly been clamoring for Congress to take any of the burden of decision on themselves. "If we in Congress want to participate, then we owe our boys and the president support for policy." *If we want to participate?* There's a choice? Bush hoped not. "Is there a way for the president to fulfill *all* his responsibilities to Congress by say-ing, a few days before any fighting was to begin, 'hostilities are imminent—period!'" Bush asked his White House counsel. "Is there something short of 'declaring' war that satisfies Congress yet doesn't risk tying the president's hands? . . . Please hand carry your reply to Brent for 'Eyes Only' transmission to me."

Bush did take the time to write a personal and private letter asking for advice from Sen. Bob Byrd, a Democrat, but a fair one, Bush thought, and a stickler for constitutional correct-ness. When Byrd told the president he was obligated to ask for a declaration of war, Bush waved it off. The president was in a muddle. He was concerned enough about Congress to ask the counsel of one of the wisest solons of the Senate, then miffed by the idea that the Senate had something to say.

Bush wrote about his war decision in his diary over and over again, in tones halfway between confession and pep talk. "I'm getting older but does that make it easier to send someone's son to die, or does that make it more difficult? All I know is that it's right . . . and I know what will happen if we let the 15th slide by and we look wimpish, or unwilling to do what we must . . . and I keep thinking of the . . . Marines and the Army guys—young, young, so very young. . . . They say I don't concentrate on do-mestic affairs, and I expect that charge is true: but how can you when you hold the life and death of a lot of young troops in your hand?"

As Bush psyched himself up for what he had decided was his grave and lone responsibility, he talked himself well beyond a president's normal resentment of congressional meddling and toward a real emotional rage that the Congress might insinuate themselves into this at all. This was getting personal. Even years later, he could still work himself into a state remembering it. "They had none of the responsibility or the worries that go with a decision to take military action yet they felt free to attack us," Bush wrote in his 1998 book, *A World Transformed*. "They did not have to contend with the morale of the forces, the difficulty of holding the coalition together, or the fact that time was running out. Above all, they had no responsibility for the lives of our soldiers, sailors, and airmen."

No responsibility? Only a president had that responsibility? To the president's mind, a war was not the country's or even the government's, but the president's alone. And woe be unto that lonely man.

> It is my decision. My decision to send these kids into battle, my decision that may affect the lives of innocence [*sic*]. It is my decision to step back and let sanctions work. Or to move forward. And in my view, help establish the New World Order. It is my decision to stand, and take the heat, or fall back and wait and hope. It is my decision that affects [the] husband, the girlfriend, or the wife that is waiting, or the mother that writes, "Take care of my son." And yet I know what I have to do.
>
> I have never felt a day like this in my life. I am very tired. I didn't sleep well and this troubles me because I must go to the nation at 9 o'clock. My lower gut hurts, nothing like when I had the bleeding ulcer. But I am aware of it, and I take a couple of Mylantas. I come over to the house about twenty of four to lie down. Before I make my calls at 5, the old shoulders tighten up. My mind is a thousand miles away. I simply can't sleep. I think of what other Presidents went through. The agony of war.

In mid-December, at the orders of the president and his secretary of defense, the United States military was conducting an air- and sea-lift operation larger and more costly than the one at the height of the Vietnam War. Nearly two hundred freighters were hauling men and matériel—trucks, jeeps, tanks, and bombs—into the Gulf in preparation for something big. And that was when Federal District Judge Harold H. Greene weighed in with his ruling in the case of *Dellums v. Bush*.

The judge's decision is worth framing:

> Article I, Section 8, Clause 11, of the Constitution grants to the Congress the power "To declare War." To the extent that this unambiguous direction requires construction or explanation, it is provided by the framers' comments that they felt it would be unwise to entrust the momentous power to involve the nation in a war to the President alone; Jefferson explained that he desired "an effectual check to the Dog of war"; James Wilson similarly expressed the expectation that this system would guard against hostilities being initiated by a single man. Even Abraham Lincoln, while a Congressman, said more than half a century later that *"no one man* should hold the power of bringing" war upon us.

The judge, in his decision, waved off as spurious Bush administration arguments that it was for the president to decide whether or not a military action constituted war.

> If the Executive had the sole power to determine that any particular offensive military operation, no matter how vast, does not constitute war-making but only an offensive military attack, the congressional power to declare war will be at the mercy of a semantic decision by the Executive. Such an "interpretation" would evade the plain language of the Constitution, and it cannot stand. . . .
> Here [in the Persian Gulf], the forces involved are of

such magnitude and significance as to present no serious
claim that war would not ensue if they became engaged
in combat, and it is therefore clear that congressional
approval is required if Congress desires to become
involved. . . .

The Court has no hesitation in concluding that an
offensive entry into Iraq by several hundred thousand
United States servicemen under the conditions described
above could be described as a "war" within the meaning of
Article I, Section 8, Clause 11, of the Constitution. To put
it another way: the Court is not prepared to read out of
the Constitution the clause granting to the Congress, and
to it alone, the authority "to declare war."

But Judge Greene also refused to issue an injunction preventing the president from taking the country to war in the Persian
Gulf. "The majority [of Congress] is the only one competent to
declare war, and therefore also the one with the ability to seek
an order from the courts to prevent anyone else, i.e., the Executive, from in effect declaring war. In short, unless the Congress
as a whole, or by a majority, is heard from, the controversy here
cannot be deemed ripe."

In other words, it was up to Congress to get off its ass and
do its job. The court wasn't going to do it for them. A minority
of a few dozen members of Congress bringing a lawsuit made
for a splendid legal argument. But to stop a war (or start one)
Congress needed to act as a whole, as an institution, by majority vote.

When Congress reconvened the first week in January, the two
leaders in the Senate, Democrat George Mitchell and Republi-

can Bob Dole, agreed that it would be best if they didn't bring up a war resolution until January 23, eight days *after* the deadline for Saddam to leave—likely after the president had given the orders for our Air Force and Navy to begin bombing Iraq. There were angry floor statements from a handful of senators, such as Tom Harkin, who cautioned patience and sanctions. "The best time to debate this issue is before this country commits itself to war and not after," said Harkin. "Our constitutional obligations are here and now."

But this was one hot potato that congressional leaders clearly did not wish to handle. One Republican senator summed it up nicely on that opening day of the 102nd Congress: "A lot of people here want it both ways. If it works, they want to be with the president. If not, they want to be against him."

The president might have seized the reins from Congress on war making, but Congress wasn't exactly fighting to seize them back. The country was split and every member of the House and Senate knew it. Polling data showed that about half the country was for a full-out military invasion in the Persian Gulf, and about half against it. Closer inspection showed ambivalence on either side of the ledger. A woman whose husband had already been deployed told a newspaper reporter in the first week of January 1991 that she was torn. "I'm not sure we have negotiated enough," she said. "I support our troops, and I certainly support my husband. And I keep to myself in my letters and our few phone calls what I really feel."

"I want to be a good citizen and support our country," a cleaning lady in Mississippi told the same reporter. "But I keep waiting for somebody to explain to me why we are over there and whether it's worth it. I still don't know, and it's been going on for months. I'm afraid we might be headed for another Vietnam."

Anecdotal evidence like that, and a mountain of polling data, made clear that calculating the politics of the Gulf War was as complicated as calculating its merits. But that made things simple for much of Congress; they were hoping to stay on the sidelines and pick a side after the fact. They were willing to cede the decision to Bush, and let him take the heat (or the greater share of the glory)—willing, in effect, to allow the country to once again drift into war without the constitutionally required debate and a formal national declaration. "Congress in recent decades has avoided its responsibility," the Pulitzer Prize–winning columnist and longtime student of the Constitution Anthony Lewis wrote the day after Mitchell and Dole kicked the can down the road. "We have come very far toward the monarchical Presidency that Hamilton and Madison and the others feared. If a President on his own can take us into a war in the gulf, George III will be entitled to smile—wherever he is. The United States has lasted this long, free and strong, by respecting the constraints of law—of the Constitution. For President Bush to disrespect them now in the name of world order would be a disaster, for him and for us."

Finally, at the eleventh hour, when war was all but inevitable anyway, the president and the Congress did the right thing in spite of themselves. Against the advice of Secretary of Defense Dick Cheney, who insisted that asking for any kind of congressional approval for a war in the Persian Gulf would set a "dangerous precedent" and "diminish the power" of the presidency, Bush made the ask . . . sort of. He didn't want a formal declaration of war, but a congressional vote supporting the UN resolution to use "all means necessary" to remove Saddam from Kuwait—in other words, to support his war. "Such action would send the clearest possible message to Saddam Hussein that he must withdraw without condition or delay from Kuwait," Bush wrote in his letter to Congress on January 8, 1991. "I am determined to do whatever is necessary to protect America's security. I ask Congress to join with me in this task. I can think of no better way than for Congress to express its support for the President at this critical time."

So in the few days before the UN deadline for Saddam to leave Kuwait (or else), Congress got down to business and formally considered the wisdom of unleashing a massive half-a-million-Americans-on-the-ground war in the Persian Gulf. With the president deriding their work as nothing more than a decision about whether or not to *express support* for him, our elected representatives nevertheless fought out the decision to go to war on the floor of the House and the floor of the Senate, in the wells of democracy, before the shooting started. And it wasn't all just preening and posturing and pandering. It was real, and heartfelt, and raucous, and public.

> *There is broad agreement in the Senate that Iraq must fully and unconditionally withdraw its forces from Kuwait. The issue is how best to achieve that goal.*

> *Without a credible military threat, our alternative is sanctions followed by nothing at all. This is why I cannot vote for sanctions alone. This is why I cannot vote to deprive the president of the credible threat of force.*

> *Saddam Hussein . . . seeks control over one of the world's vital resources, and he ultimately seeks to make himself the unchallenged anti-Western dictator of the Middle East.*

> *We are not in an international crisis. Nothing large happened. A nasty little country invaded a littler, but just as nasty, country.*

Solidarity, we need it now, not division, but solidarity.

I reject the argument that says Congress must support the president, right or wrong. We have our own responsibility to do what is right, and I believe that war today is wrong. At this historic moment, it may well be that only Congress can stop this senseless march toward war.

I think it's time for Congress to help rather than hinder the president. I think it's time for the Congress to join with the president and get behind him and our young men and women over there sitting in the sand and show that we're willing to back the use of force.

If we do nothing, and Saddam pays no price for swallowing up the country of Kuwait, destroying people's property, torturing, raping, and killing innocent men and women and children, we are as guilty as he is.

War is about fire and steel and people dying. If the sons and daughters of all of us, of the president, the vice president, the Cabinet were all over there in the Persian Gulf right now, right up on the front line and were going to be part of that first assault wave that would go on into Kuwait, I think we'd be taking more time. I think we'd be working harder on the sanctions policy. I think we'd be trying to squeeze Saddam Hussein in every other way that we could, short of a shooting war.

If we fail to act, there will be inevitably a succession of dictators, of Saddam Husseins—of which around this globe there are an abundance, either in reality or would-be. And those dictators will see a green light, a green light for aggression, a green light for annexation of its weaker neighbors. And, indeed, over time a threat to the stability of this entire globe.

When the talking was over, virtually every member of Congress stood up and was counted as being for a war in the Persian Gulf or against it. It was a narrow margin—the Senate was 52–47—but Congress (which is to say the nation) voted to go to war.

Agree or disagree with the outcome, the system had worked. Our Congress had its clangorous and open debate and then took sides. We decided to go to war, as a country. This in itself was kind of a miracle, given how dismissive the Bush White House was of Congress's responsibility for such decisions, and congressional leaders' inclination to shirk those responsibilities. What forced this national debate was not humble respect for the Constitution or the founders' intent to make any decision to go to war difficult, deliberate, wrenching, and collective. No, what forced us to do the right thing was the last surviving structural barrier to war making—the Abrams Doctrine. The sheer need to call up a huge number of troops to mount any military operation of any significance anywhere in the world. Even in the face of radically reimagined presidential power and the precedent of secret war and congressional irrelevance, the call-up had fixed the country's eyes on the real possibility of war, had made it all but impossible for the president to conduct any serious war business alone, and had ultimately forced Congress to shoulder its burden. By the time of the George H. W. Bush presidency, the Abrams Doctrine was doing a lot of work in keeping the country from drifting too easily into war.

Which is why we probably should have had a real debate—or at least thought twice—before we got rid of that, too.

Chapter 7

Doing More with
Less (Hassle)

IT WAS THE TODDLERS WHO DID IT . . . TEETHING, SLOBBERING,
paste-eating, ungovernable, ever-dependent tots. In the decade
that followed the Gulf War, preschool kids ended up being among
the most effective shock troops in the assault on the last remaining constraints keeping us from going to war all the time. The little darlings were terribly dear. Not dear as in cuddly, but dear as
in expensive. They demanded resources. A Pentagon study in 1995
figured it cost $6,200 per toddler, per year, to provide day care for
the youngest military dependents. And there were 575,000 preschool children in US military households around the world. As
an employer, the military had to accept all those dependents as its
responsibility; they were an enormous chapped-bottom drag.

The demographics of our Army, Navy, Air Force, and Marine
Corps had changed drastically since the Vietnam War. By the
mid-1990s, twenty years after we had gotten rid of the draft, the
all-volunteer military was steadier, more professional, more able,
more educated; it was also more reflective of the civilian world
at large. The number of women in uniform, for example, had increased exponentially. Well over half of the nation's servicemen

and -women were married. And like the rest of the country, which by the mid-'90s had been enjoying relative peace and ample prosperity, the military was part of a national wave of fecundity.

But as in the country at large, having kids didn't automatically give military families an *Ozzie and Harriet* makeover. The number of single parents raising children alone had trended up on military bases as it had all over. Two of every three soldiers had spouses who worked full-time outside the home. And so something like 80 percent of the preschoolers on the military's dependent list needed full-time day care so Mom and Dad could keep the family afloat. Not only that, but military parents had come to expect a reasonable safety net for their children. "Military people stay in the service because they like being part of something special," said the chairman of the Joint Chiefs, John M. Shalikashvili, in May 1995. "They won't stay long, however, if families aren't treated well."

Long experience taught that open-ended deployment could be crushing to military families: instances of child abuse, substance abuse, divorce, and check kiting at commissaries all increased. It didn't take the broad survey by researchers at the US Army Research Institute for Behavioral Sciences to convince commanders that "family separation" was a main reason for enlisted troops and officers alike to leave the service.

"Sir," one Air Force sergeant stationed in Germany told a Pentagon researcher, "we are ready to go anywhere as long as you take care of our families."

The House and Senate had passed legislation that set up all sorts of standards for how the military was supposed to handle its tots, but then they badly underfunded the provision of those services. Much of the money needed to make up the gap came from base commanders raiding their tiny pots of nonappropriated funds, leaving unmarried soldiers to bitch and moan that the kiddies were stealing the money intended to keep up bowling alleys, golf courses, and other recreational goodies. If the best hope for commanders was robbing from the base bowling alley, the Pentagon's stated aim of meeting 80 percent of the military-family child-care demand by 1999 (up from a mere 52 percent in 1995) was clearly beyond reach.

And these goals took into account only the troops on active duty. What about all those Guard members and reservists? In the Gulf War, more than a quarter million had been called up; 105,000 had been shipped to the Saudi desert for months. And thirty-one days into active-duty deployment, the benefits kicked in for those soldiers: health care, housing allowances, employer reimbursements, tuition credits . . . day care!

This was a tremendous headache to the Pentagon planners. The operative budgetary mandate in the 1990s was to reprioritize the shrinking defense budget to get back to the important business of weapons procurement and modernization. In the ten years after 1985, the procurement budget had dropped from $126 billion to $39 billion and represented a paltry 18 percent of total defense expenditures. Sure, the active-duty force had been pared by nearly 30 percent and a few bases had been closed, but that didn't come close to solving the problem. How were we supposed to ensure our Last-Superpower-on-Earth superiority when just the overhead cost of keeping our standing army milling around was swallowing between 40 and 50 percent of the Pentagon's annual cash allotment? The budget gurus still couldn't find the money for really great new bombs and invisible planes and impenetrable tanks, not to mention some sprucing up of the greatest and most expensive unusable arsenal the universe had ever known—our nukes. "In other words," yet another Pentagon-sponsored task force lamented in 1996, "Department of Defense support infrastructure has remained largely impervious to downsizing."

There was only one glimmer of hope for peeling away some of this impervious-to-downsizing overhead. It was a technocratic little solution that had morphed in just a few scant years—and without much forethought—from a slightly distasteful option of last resort to the last viable remedy: Outsourcing. Privatization. Civilian Augmentation. In other words, can't we get someone in here who doesn't come with day-care costs? "Without such an initiative," said the Pentagon Task Force study, "DoD may not be able to procure the new weapons systems and technological edge needed to ensure the continuing military preeminence of the United States in the coming century."

In fact, the privatization idea became so alluring to the military in the mid-'90s that they even tried it on day care itself. The Navy funded pilot programs to use private contractors to provide day care in Norfolk, Virginia, and at Pearl Harbor in Hawaii. The private sector was always better at controlling costs, wasn't it?

In dozens of studies commissioned and funded by the Pentagon or the separate branches of services in the early '90s, it was generally taken as an article of faith that the private sector did things cheaper. Those task forces, after all, were manned by a rotating phalanx of corporate executives (many retired military) from companies like Boeing and Westinghouse and General Electric and Perot Systems and Bear Stearns and Military Personnel Resources Inc. (a generic-sounding name, but one worth remembering), salted with some active-duty generals and maybe a few think tankers. After small-scale private-contractor deployments to accompany US military missions in the early

1990s in places like Haiti, Somalia, and Rwanda, the Pentagon was looking to go big. The 1996 Defense Science Board Task Force on Outsourcing and Privatization, to take the most important example, didn't waste a lot of energy weighing the question of private versus public cost consciousness, they just went for the hard sell:

> The Task Force believes that all Department of Defense support functions should be contracted out to private vendors except those functions which are inherently governmental, are directly involved in warfighting, or for which no adequate private sector capability exists or can be expected to be established. . . . The Task Force is convinced that an aggressive Department of Defense outsourcing initiative will improve the quality of support services at significantly reduced costs . . . could generate savings of up to $7 to $12 billion annually by fiscal year 2002—resources which then would be available for equipment modernization.
>
> The private sector is the primary source of creativity, innovation, and efficiency in our society, and is more likely than government organizations to provide cost-effective support to the Nation's military forces.

The grand-scale cotillion debut for the privateers would be the Balkans. Private for-profit companies had provided food service, garbage collection, and water bearing for previous missions, but in Bosnia they'd do almost everything, and in huge numbers. When twenty thousand US soldiers were sent to help keep a fragile peace among the Serbs, Bosniaks, and Croats, who had been fighting a bloody three-way war in the former Yugoslavia, an equal number of private company employees went with. They were employees of DynCorp and

Brown & Root Services Corporation (whose parent company, Halliburton, was run by former secretary of defense Dick Cheney), corporations that were themselves under contract with the United States Department of Defense. Brown & Root employees built the barracks where US soldiers bunked, made sure they were fed, their clothes and bedding laundered, their recreational needs seen to, their mail delivered, their e-mail working. DynCorp's biggest contract was from the State Department, to provide a private police force to support the larger UN mission and to train the local constabulary in Western law enforcement. But DynCorp also had a smaller contract with Defense for things like maintaining US military aircraft in Bosnia.

Brown & Root proved wanting in the "innovation" department when it came to the procurement of construction materials for the barracks. It turned out they were flying sheets of plywood into Bosnia from the United States, thus transforming each $14 sheet into an $85.98 sheet. Not that this hurt their bottom line. The company did show itself to be remarkably agile (if not timely) in fiscal reporting; overruns had raised the payout on their Army contract from $350 million to $461 million. One of the big drivers in the cost overrun was their "Management and Administration" line item, which came in $69 million over budget, an impressive 80 percent overrun. It apparently took a lot of layers of Brown & Root management and administration to turn a $14 sheet of plywood into an $86 sheet of plywood.

Brown & Root might not have been all that cost-effective, but it did fulfill its contractual obligations. The soldiers at the thirty-four base camps the company serviced in Bosnia, Croatia, and Hungary were generally well pleased with the PXs stocked with American grocery items, and the cafeterias' twenty-four-hour food options. "Sandwiches, soups, and beverages are always available," the General Accounting Office crowed a few years into the big Balkan contract. "Unit officials in Bosnia said that the quantity and quality of the food is so good that personnel are gaining weight." Oh, good!

For a full appreciation of the "innovation and creativity" that a private American company was able to bring to bear in Bosnia, DynCorp is worth considering. In the field of contractor support of overseas US military operations, DynCorp's reputation for ingenuity was already separating it from the pack. Consider, for instance, the portrait painted by the employees of the aircraft maintenance hangar that DynCorp operated at Camp Comanche in Dubrave, Bosnia. Ben Johnston, a helicopter mechanic who retired from the military into a much higher paycheck for doing the same job under the DynCorp contract, was pretty quickly disturbed by what he saw. As he recounted to a reporter from *Insight* magazine:

> There was this one guy who would hide parts so we would have to wait for parts. They'd [DynCorp foremen] have us replace windows in helicopters that weren't bad just to get paid. They had one kid over there who was right out of high school and he didn't even know the names and purposes of the basic tools. Soldiers that are paid $18,000 a year know more than this kid, but this is the way they [DynCorp] grease their pockets. What they say in Bosnia is that DynCorp just needs a warm body—that's the DynCorp slogan. Even if you don't do an eight-hour day, they'll sign you in for it because that's how they bill the government. It's a total fraud. . . .
>
> It was a rougher crowd than I'd ever dealt with. It's not like I don't drink or anything, but DynCorp employees

would come to work drunk. A DynCorp van would pick us up every morning and you could smell the alcohol on them.

And picture this scene: a fellow DynCorp maintenance man, a trencherman, nearly four hundred pounds by Johnston's estimate, at work on a Black Hawk helicopter. He "would stick cheeseburgers in his pockets and eat them while he worked," Johnston said. "He would literally fall asleep every five minutes. One time he fell asleep with a torch in his hand and burned a hole through the plastic on an aircraft."

"The bottom line is that DynCorp has taken what used to be a real positive program that has very high visibility with every Army unit in the world and turned it into a bag of worms," the site supervisor told the same *Insight* reporter.

And yet general corporate malfeasance and pedestrian bilking was not what truly bothered Johnston; what truly bothered him was the slimiest bag of worms in the DynCorp locker: it was a common practice among the contract workers at Comanche to buy themselves live-in sex slaves from the local Serbian mafia. The men boasted about it openly around the hangar and invited coworkers home to meet their new "girls." Some of these girls were said to be as young as twelve. By the time Johnston was hip to what was going on, a few sex slavers in the Camp Comanche crew had already been caught by local cops, but it hadn't changed anything. The Army asked DynCorp to remove the workers whose crimes had been uncovered, and DynCorp management hustled the men out of Bosnia within forty-eight hours and then back to the States, asserting its "zero-tolerance policy" for this sort of criminal behavior.

The manager of DynCorp's European operations seemed certain that the company's quick and decisive action was a feather in its cap with their favorite new client, the US Army. "We were able to turn this into a marketing success," he bragged, as the company took pains to make sure the unsightly news never became public.

A DynCorp manager sent to suss out the damage the sex-trafficking scandal had done to the company's reputation found the Army supervisors mainly worried about the quality of the work being done. Whatever the morons on the DynCorp payroll were doing off-hours was a DynCorp problem. Outsourcing maintenance meant outsourcing the headaches that come with maintenance workers too, right? Besides, the Army lawyers had told military investigators that neither Bosnian law nor US law applied to the contractors, so the Department of Defense had no authority to prosecute any crimes private contract workers committed over there, and therefore no responsibility for them either. Thank God.

And so nothing changed. A few of their colleagues had been shipped out, but DynCorp workers on the Comanche crew still bought sex slaves and talked openly about it on the shop floor. One starred in a sex tape on which two young girls were heard to plead with him to leave them alone. DynCorp management looked the other way. When one of the DynCorp police monitors working for the United Nations insisted on investigating the rampant sex-trafficking in the Balkans, she was reassigned to a desk job, and when she refused to back off, she was fired without cause. At the Comanche hangar, DynCorp employees bragged, according to Johnston, about "how good it was to have a sex slave at home," and about selling them back to Serbian mafia bosses at a discount when they got tired of the same girl night after night.

According to a later UN investigation, one worker at Dyn-Corp's Camp Comanche readily admitted to buying a young woman at a nightclub run by a Serbian mob boss named De Beli ("the Fat Boy"). The worker told the US Army investigators that he bought the Moldovan teenager for $740. And the Fat Boy had thrown in an Uzi as a parting gift. This girl was pretty typical of the sex-trafficking victims in Bosnia. She'd left home on the promise of a job as a waitress in Italy and then found herself sold into prostitution in Hungary and later in Bosnia. That relationship was fairly tame among the foreign nationals buying sex slaves in Bosnia. The Moldovan girl said she woke up at his house every day with a new toy and 20 deutschemarks on her pillow. The DynCorp guy even gave her back her passport before he dumped her and left the country.

The most egregious example, as far as Johnston was concerned, was that Comanche worker who was prone to falling asleep with a burning blowtorch. He "owned a girl who couldn't have been more than fourteen years old. It's a sick sight anyway to see a grown man [sexually involved] with a child, but to see some forty-five-year-old man who weighs four hundred pounds with a little girl, it makes you sick."

Johnston's Bosnian-born wife also met a few of the young girls. "They didn't like to talk a lot," she said. "They were very sad."

"You could see them [the sex slaves] right out the window [of my house]," Johnston said. "Playing with other children. A lot of them are so young, they would play with other kids, and you could see them riding bikes and stuff like that."

DynCorp, thank you for small miracles, didn't get any day-care contracts, but the company did real damage in the Balkans. "The Bosnians think we're all trash," Johnston said. "It's a shame. When I was there as a soldier they loved us, but DynCorp employees have changed how they think about us. I tried to tell them that this is not how all Americans act, but it's hard to convince them when you see what they're seeing. The fact is, DynCorp is the worst diplomat you could possibly have over there."

"Although a system of contractors for hire might seem reasonable to supplement and support U.S. military presence," wrote Kathryn Bolkovac, the DynCorp police monitor who was fired, "the outcome has been the creation of a band of mercenaries—a secretive, unregulated, well-paid, under-the-radar force that is larger than the U.S. Army."

So how did we get to the place where private American citizens representing us—men whose salaries were paid by the US government—could cut this greasy, lawless swath through the Balkans with no real consequences for the criminals, or for DynCorp itself? The company's zero-tolerance policy continued to be little more than a marketing slogan. In 2004, a videotape of the company's contract workers raping local underage girls had reportedly surfaced near a DynCorp facility in Colombia. And in 2010, DynCorp employees at a police training facility in Kunduz, Afghanistan, were believed to have procured drugs and prepubescent boys for the gratification of some prominent local men. A cable to US State Department officials from our ambassador to Afghanistan is suggestive of just how little things had changed in ten years. "An investigation is on-going, disciplinary actions were taken against DynCorp leaders in Afghanistan, we are also aware of proposals for new procedures, such as stationing a military officer at [Regional Training Centers], that have been introduced for consideration. (Note: Placing military officers to oversee contractor operations at RTCs is not legally possible under the current DynCorp contract.) Beyond remedial actions taken, we still hope the matter will not be blown out of proportion."

This slide to full-on, consequences-be-damned privatization of military functions—in all its unaccountable gory glory—wasn't inevitable: it didn't have to happen this way. And it wasn't inexorable either; you can trace it to specific decisions, made for specific, logical reasons. But this is how snafus happen—there isn't enough debate, there isn't enough chivalry toward the virtues of the old system we're killing for efficiency's sake. And then bad things happen.

To understand how we got to DynCorp and the prepubescent boys in Kunduz and the sex slaves in the Balkans, it helps to revisit the red-letter day of August 2, 1990. That was the day Saddam Hussein chose to invade Kuwait. That was also the day the Pentagon had circled on its calendar for the rollout of the George H. W. Bush administration's big new deep thoughts about reengineering American military power to fit a post-Soviet world.

Secretary of Defense Dick Cheney and Chairman of the Joint Chiefs Colin Powell had been scrambling for months to head off what they were convinced was a rash congressional assault on the nation's defense budget. The Pentagon imagined enemies at the gate. Talk on Capitol Hill was all about the "peace dividend": the Soviet Union was slain. We'd won the Cold War. It was time to do what we did after every big war: draw down the number of troops, pare the defense budget, reroute tax dollars to domestic spending. Powell decided to get out front with his own plan for downsizing. He'd been proposing to Cheney for months a manpower reduction of 25 percent, which—even factoring in a big jump in research and development of new weapons technology—allowed for some minimal but calculable give-backs. "I wanted to offer something our allies could rally around and give our critics something to shoot at rather than having military reorganization schemes shoved down our throat," Powell later wrote.

Cheney was a latecomer to the idea that the military budget could be at all whittled. His friends in the old Team B Soviet-hysteria business were still preaching wild-eyed tales of the USSR coming back and maybe stronger—like Jason in the *Friday the 13th* movies. But by August 2, 1990, Cheney was on board. The president would give a speech that day laying out America's new national security strategy. Then a delegation from the Pentagon would brief Congress (in secret) on the details of this bold new plan to demobilize and restructure the US military machine for a post–Cold War world.

When August 2 rolled around, though, Saddam stole the day's headlines by rolling his 700 tanks and 100,000 soldiers into Kuwait. August 2 wasn't going to be a big deep-thought day for anyone. "Cheney, Paul Wolfowitz, and I went to supersecure Room S-407 in the Capitol to pitch the [new plan] to leaders of the Defense Department's congressional oversight committees," Powell wrote of the August 2 briefing. "But all we heard was, yeah, sure, right. But what's going on in Kuwait?"

Who wanted to pay attention to policy and planning for the next century when there was a real fight brewing right now in the Persian Gulf?

The shooting war that followed did the US Armed Forces more public relations good than a dozen presidential speeches or a hundred congressional briefings. Our military dazzled. The First Gulf War was all Powell could have hoped for: a clear mission, explicit public support, and an overwhelming show of force. It was fast—the ground assault lasted just a hundred hours, the troops were home less than five months later. It was relatively bloodless for the away team—fewer than two hundred American soldiers were killed in action. It was cost-effective—happy allies reimbursed the United States for all but $8 billion spent. And it was, withal, a riveting display of our military capability, almost like it was designed for TV. Americans, and much of the world, watched a Technicolor air-strike extravaganza every night. The skeptics were forced to stand down; our military had proved beyond doubt or discussion that we were the Last Superpower Still Standing.

By the end of the Gulf War, there wasn't much room for kumbaya talk about George H. W. Bush's New World Order, where the rule of law would replace the rule of the jungle and lions would lie down with lambs. Turns out our new operating metaphor was that there were lots of lions now, everywhere, but they were still cubs. Our job was to make sure they didn't grow up to be fierce, capable predators. All that stuff about the Gulf War being a path to world peace took a backseat to more politically rousing rhetoric about . . . *danger.*

Saddam became Exhibit A, filed under Post–Cold War Planet, Possible Snags: "America must possess forces able to respond to threats in whatever corner of the globe they may occur," Bush said in his speech the day after Saddam invaded Kuwait. "Even in a world where democracy and freedom have made great gains, threats remain. Terrorism, hostage-taking, renegade regimes and unpredictable rulers, new sources of instability—all require a strong and engaged America. The brutal aggression launched last night against Kuwait illustrates my central thesis: Notwithstanding the alteration in the Soviet threat, the world remains a dangerous place with serious threats to important US interests."

That sort of tough talk certainly put the bounce back in Dick Cheney's step. He'd had to give up on having the Soviets as a real enemy, but he and deputies like Paul Wolfowitz and Scooter Libby went to work constructing a rationale for refitting the US military for this new New World Peril. "If we choose wisely today, we can do well something America has always done badly before," Cheney would say, "we can draw down our military force at a responsible rate that will not end up endangering our security."

The basic idea was that in this dangerous world, where threats to our national security could rear up in the Middle East, or the Korean Peninsula, or even in the Americas, we had to be ready to move quickly, and maybe into more than one place at a time. Think of it as a two-fisted game of intercontinental Whac-A-Mole. "Highly ready and rapidly deployable power projection forces," Cheney wrote, "including forcible entry forces, remain key means of precluding challengers."

If, in 1990, the new mission for the US military was stopping the emergence of any challenger anywhere in the world, the mission sure wasn't shrinking, but budget pressures meant the active-duty force would have to. Cheney and company hit on what seemed like a simple and rational way to squeeze dollars without squeezing military capability: do more with less. Take the Gulf War, for example. So many of the soldiers shipped to the Persian Gulf were simply there to handle the care and feeding of the fighting troops. Did the cooks at the base in Saudi Arabia need to be US Army? The maintenance workers? The electricians? The plumbers? Did it require a US-trained soldier to wash sheets and towels and skivvies? Couldn't someone else do that? Not a bad idea, on the face of it.

Cheney started by reordering the architectural bureaucracy of the US military. He changed the so-called four pillars of military capability (readiness, sustainability, modernization, and force structure) to—*voilà!*—six pillars. Modernization became two pillars now—one for science and technology and one for systems acquisition (in other words, the pillar that was *buying stuff from defense contractors* became, instead: *buying stuff from defense contractors A*, and *buying stuff from defense contractors B*). Cheney also invented a sixth pillar—and this was genius—called infrastructure and overhead. As if there was no infrastructure and overhead already in weapons acquisition or force readiness or any other part of the military. Cheney pretended that infrastructure and overhead could be sequestered in one part of the budget and cut, alone, without affecting anything else. "The Department must vigorously pursue reductions and management efficiencies in defense infrastructure and overhead," Cheney, Wolfowitz, and Libby et al. wrote as they were on their way out of office. And how would this vigorous pursuit of reductions be executed? What they left in place for the business school wannabes of the next administration was a little something called the Logistics Civilian Augmentation Program (a defense program name that for once made sense: civilians *augmenting* the military).

The first private contractor under this program was signed on in 1992, during the last months of Dick Cheney's tenure as secretary of defense. It was a company called Brown & Root Services Corporation. Four years later, while the contract was still in place, Cheney was making a very comfortable living as CEO of Brown & Root's parent corporation, Halliburton. And after *Vice President* Cheney helped push us into wars in Afghanistan and Iraq, the value of those contracts kept Halliburton stock bouncing happily along. You can read all the conspiracy you want to into that, but focusing on Cheney's bank accounts misses the forest for the trees. In utterly nonconspiratorial point

of fact, the merits of that big Halliburton contract—known by
its acronym, LOGCAP—seemed so obvious to all concerned that
the military's congressional overseers never seriously discussed
the possible downsides of handing over pieces of military budget
line items to private contractors.

LOGCAP soon became the darling of technocrats on both
sides of the political aisle. The program that began under the
first President Bush grew enormously under President Bill Clinton. Tiny cohorts of civilian augmenters had been deployed
alongside US troops before, "but it wasn't until the U.S. led
NATO forces into Bosnia in 1995," wrote *BusinessWeek*, "that
the entire private military industry came of age."

The Clinton administration leaned hard on LOGCAP. Vice
President Al Gore, who was vigorously reinventing government
to be more responsive and empowering federal employees to find
cost savings and generally imposing the kind of management efficiencies that get the profs at Harvard Business School all hot
and bothered, held up the Pentagon's LOGCAP program as a
poster child for good governance. "Outsourcing or privatization
of key support functions, with the strong prospect of lowering
costs and improving performance, is under way under the leadership of the Deputy Secretary of Defense," trumpeted Gore's
1996 report on the streamlining of the Defense Department.

Some sections read like brochure copy for Cheney's Halliburton: "LOGCAP has provided the Army with a highly flexible
contractual means of providing quality of life services to troops
deployed in some of the harshest environments in the world,
without impacting its combat capability."

It's like they thought it was magic; you half expected the pages
of that Al Gore report to shake loose a little glitter, a smiley face
sticker or two.

In Clinton's eight years in office—massive cost overruns and sex-slave scandals notwithstanding—the military's program of privatization exploded. In 1992, the US Department of Defense did a few hundred million dollars' worth of business with private contractors. By the time Clinton left office, the Department of Defense had executed more than three thousand contracts valued at about $300 *billion*. In fact, Defense had been contracting private vendors with such eager rapidity that nobody at the Pentagon could actually tot up the number of private workers who were on the military's payroll (once removed). Maybe it was 125,000 people. Maybe closer to 600,000. Not quite sure.

They were unable to tell Congress or anybody else exactly how much was being doled out for training, security, or food services. But the Pentagon did have some other numbers to share that sounded good. Consider the savings, they told congressional committees: skilled local laborers hired to do plumbing or electrical work on overseas bases, for instance, were paid at least ten dollars an hour less than a soldier might be. And a company like KBR (Brown & Root had merged with another company to become Kellogg, Brown & Root, or KBR) could pay $1.12 an hour to an unskilled Croatian laborer, where an American soldier might cost $16 an hour, and leave the government on the hook for all those "quality of life" benefits like medical care and dental care and day care. Didn't take a degree in finance to see the value in that.

The Clinton years saw some spectacular mission creep in outsourcing, too. By the time Clinton left office, Department of Defense privatization was a damn sight more than the effort to get twenty-four-hour Oscar Mayer products and cornflakes and Gatorade into PXs on forward military bases in Bosnia. The military had also outsourced pieces of information technology, data processing, payroll, mapping, aerial surveillance—even intelligence gathering.

Private American companies were providing military expertise and weapons training to countries like Saudi Arabia and Kuwait. One particular beneficiary was a private company founded by a gaggle of recently retired US Army generals, Military Professional Resources Incorporated (MPRI), "with a recognition that there is a great national resource in the retired military community," as one of the principals said. "And if that talent could be brought together we could provide various military expertise in a variety of ways to our government." Less modestly, MPRI described itself as "the greatest corporate assemblage of military expertise in the world."

In 2000, MPRI (its many talents in tow) was bought for $40 million by a company called L-3, which envisioned a bright future for it. The company profile noted "changing political climates have led to increased demand for certain services . . . these programs tend to expand." At that time MPRI was already training America's future officer corps, having taken charge of key jobs in ROTC programs at more than two hundred universities. So pleased with MPRI were Clinton's guys at Defense that they had basically handed the privateers the keys to what should be a public kingdom. In 1997, when the Pentagon wanted to overhaul its doctrine for working with private contractors, it outsourced the writing of that doctrine to a private contractor, MPRI.

It was like the old Baltimore pol/saloon owner who was asked if he should recuse himself on a pending question about how to regulate saloons:

Why would I do that?

The conflict of interest with the legislation regulating saloons.

I don't see how that conflicts with my interests at all. I'm in that business myself.

Private contractors in general, and MPRI in particular, had not demonstrated that they had improved the dollar cost of doing

US military business. In fact, the sort of huge cost overruns the government had encountered on Brown & Root's original Balkan contract were the norm on even the most straightforward contracts. The Army, according to a 1997 investigation by the US General Accounting Office, "did not implement a systematic method of inspections to monitor contract performance. As a result, they could not ensure that the contractor performed work in accordance with contract provisions, used the minimum number of resources to meet the Army's requirements, and furnished the appropriate level of support."

In other words, nobody was sure exactly what we were getting for our money. Whatever the aggregate weight gain among the soldiers stationed in Tuzla or Slavonski Brod, nobody could tell if private contractors were more cost-effective, or more effective in general, than the military would have been, doing its own work. The soldiers flying the DynCorp-serviced helicopters that came out of the little chamber of horrors at Camp Comanche were certainly no safer. Neither was the local population, for that matter.

Meanwhile, all through the Clinton years, the stench at the center of the privatization experiment was obscured by all the Al Gore–created systems-efficiency nosegays about the flexibility and the streamlining and the sewage and solid-waste disposals and transportation grids and the generally empowering quality-of-life services at work in the fields of civilian augmentation and outsourcing. And so nobody in the Clinton administration ever really apprehended the acute and lasting problem of LOGCAP and the thousands of other small privatization ploys they unleashed; the acute and lasting problem was that they cut that mooring line tying our wars to our politics, the line that tied the decision to go to war to public debate about that decision. The idea of the Abrams Doctrine—and Jefferson's citizen-soldiers—was to make it so we can't make war without causing a big civilian hullabaloo. Privatization made it all easy, and quiet.

Like Reagan, President Bill Clinton had come to appreciate the merits of shifting ever-greater slices of difficult-to-sell foreign policy missions into the private sector. Unlike Reagan, who had secretly and illegally privatized military and fund-raising operations in support of the Contras, Clinton's "outsourcing" allowed him to do much of what he wanted on the books, legally, as a matter of policy, but without the public much noticing. Take, for example, the Balkans.

Commander in Chief Clinton had inherited this disaster when he came into office in 1993. The bloodbath had begun in the George Herbert Walker Bush years, when, in the euphoria of the Soviet breakup, the state of Yugoslavia started spinning off its component parts with all the centrifugal force that ethnic and religious differences can muster. Roman Catholic Slovenia declared its independence, as did Roman Catholic Croatia, as did the ethnoreligiously mixed state of Bosnia. Bosnia's population was part Muslim, part Eastern Orthodox Christian (Serbs), and part Catholic (mostly Croats). Slobodan Milošević, incensed at having lost much of the Yugoslav federation he had just taken over, stirred his Serbian followers into a fury of paranoid ethnic and religious hatred, seized control of the Yugoslavian Army (JNA) and its arsenal, and began a series of punishing attacks on these new, internationally recognized sovereign countries.

The worst Serbian rampage was in Bosnia, where the JNA and bands of Serbian paramilitary thugs cut a vicious swath beginning in April 1992. The Serbs killed more than twenty-five thousand Muslims, along with many Bosnian Christians who tried to protect them; they burned out entire villages, tortured and killed Muslim leaders and intellectuals, and raped more than twenty thousand women and girls. All told, a million and a half Muslims fled their homes during the Serbian blitz. The Serbian strongman on the ground in Bosnia called it "ethnic shifting." A US State Department Human Rights Report called it "ethnic cleansing," and said that the killing "dwarfs anything seen in Europe since Nazi times." Others called it flat-out genocide. The Serbs were undeterred by the world's condemnation. They continued to shell civilians in the capital of Sarajevo, cluster-bombed other urban Muslim and Croat areas, and even shot down a plane carrying relief supplies into Bosnia. The Bosnian president lamented the "threat of extinction."

But the Bush administration had its hands full and was determined to steer clear of this European war. Their shiniest new hero, Gen. Colin Powell, reportedly called Bosnia a "nonstrategic interest." He wrote in a *New York Times* op-ed, "The crisis in Bosnia is especially complex . . . one with deep ethnic and religious roots that go back a thousand years. The solution must ultimately be a political one." Bush's secretary of state, James Baker, put it succinctly: "We don't have a dog in this fight."

Clinton had talked tough on Bosnia during the 1992 campaign. He said as president he would likely lift the UN-imposed arms embargo and help arm the Croatians and the Bosnians to fight the Serbs themselves. He also said he would order bombing runs on Serb artillery positions near Sarajevo and use military force to make sure relief supplies got to the Bosnian refugees. "I specifically would not foreclose the option of the use of force on that issue, because I'm horrified by what I've seen."

"We lay great hopes in the new administration," Bosnia's foreign minister said a few days after Clinton's election. "We hope they will fully understand the importance of the American role

in halting the tragedy." Holocaust survivor Elie Wiesel button-
holed Clinton at a public event a few months into his presidency
and implored him to do something to stop this unfolding European disaster. And Clinton really wanted to do something, really *wanted* to fix this nightmare in the Balkans.

But by the time the president bent himself to selling to the
American people the notion of using American power to halt
the Serbian-run massacre in Bosnia, he was already taking hard
knocks in the public arena. A series of air strikes, critics sniffed,
was a hopeless tactic suggested by a national security naïf. Sen.
John McCain, a hero pilot and the country's most famous Vietnam prisoner of war, was leading the charge against. "Can you
guarantee me that no American will be killed?" he asked a fellow senator who was supporting the use of air power.

In public, McCain was even more forceful. "Air strikes would
frankly not affect the situation, unless—and this is a huge
unless—we are prepared to commit ground troops in a pro-
longed military operation in Yugoslavia. And frankly, the polls
show, by two to one margins, the American people even oppose
air strikes. . . . I will not place the lives of young Americans, men
and women, at risk without having a plan that has every possibility of succeeding, a way in, a way to beneficially affect the situation, and a way out, and we do not have that." Clinton's plan,
said McCain, "has a hauntingly familiar ring to me. It was the
same rationale we used to start the bombing of North Vietnam.
That's the way we got our fist into a tar baby that took us many
years to get out of and twenty years to recover from."

McCain was carrying a lot of water for the Pentagon in those
days. Popular myth to the contrary, the American institution
often least interested in going to war is the US military; it is
especially wary of a war civilian leaders promise will be limited.
"The use of force was controversial," wrote Nancy Soderberg,

Clinton's deputy assistant for national security affairs, "and the strongest opponent was the Pentagon and Powell."

The holdover chairman of the Joint Chiefs of Staff, Gen. Colin Powell, seemed to be aware that he was already a few points *ahead* of President Clinton in the earliest 1996 election polls, and that triple the number of Americans trusted General Powell in the arena of foreign policy than trusted the president. And he frankly judged Clinton as a bit too much of an on-the-one-hand-on-the-other-hand academic. Long years on the national security watch had given the general a much stronger stomach than the new president when it came to absorbing the daily press accounts of prison camp survivors, or of homeless and starving Muslim and Croat refugees, or of the victims of Serbian artillery, snipers, and paramilitary knife-wielding thugs. Polite, slightly condescending, and occasionally testy was how Soderberg described Powell's demeanor when he was engaged in steering Clinton and his national security team away from the "limited war" scenario of bombing runs followed by . . . more bombing runs. "Powell argued repeatedly that any such action would be tantamount to going to war with Serbia," Soderberg wrote. "'Don't fall in love with air power because it hasn't worked,' [he said]. To Powell, air power would not change Serb behavior, 'only troops on the ground could do that.'"

"Time and again he led us up the hill of possibilities and dropped us off on the other side with the practical equivalent of 'No can do,'" Clinton's ambassador to the United Nations Madeleine Albright wrote in her memoir. "After hearing this for the umpteenth time, I asked in exasperation, 'What are you saving this superb military for, Colin, if we can't use it?'"

"I thought I would have an aneurysm," Powell wrote of that moment.

"The Pentagon," wrote Soderberg, "dragged its feet developing the military plans for Bosnia and raised numerous objections. . . . Senior military leaders were quick to point out that any such deployment would require a call-up of reserves, which would be politically unpopular, especially for a new president wanting to focus on domestic issues so early in his term."

Meanwhile, some in the press were throwing down the gauntlet. "Nobody in Clinton's administration has yet explained, simply and plainly, what America's interests and objectives in the Balkans are," the *Economist* editorialized. "[President Clinton] will have to do better than say that he has thought things over carefully. He will have to tell a puzzled people, with no great desire to put its children in harm's way, why he is doing precisely that. It is, by a long way, the greatest test yet of whether he is up to the job."

With his public approval ratings already sinking under the weight of policy fumbles like gays in the military and a failing health-care initiative, Clinton decided to take a pass on his Balkans test. In this game of chicken with the Pentagon and mouthpieces like McCain, Clinton blinked. Clinton managed to commit the US military to a fairly impotent "no-fly zone" operation, and applauded the UN-formed "safe zones" in the Balkans, but other than that he sat back and watched while Milošević and Serb warlords continued to grind down the Croats and the Bosnians, and then taunt the West. The Serbs waved off calls for peace plans or other diplomatic overtures. "Bosnia never existed," said one of Milošević's deputies, "and it will never." The nastiest general in the Serbian Army, Ratko Mladić, who would kill seven thousand Muslim men and boys (civilians all) in Srebenica, warned that if the Americans and their allies ever did try to stop them, "they would leave their bones in Bosnia. . . . If [the West] bombs me, I'll bomb London. There are Serbs in London. There are Serbs in Washington."

Even with a villain like Mladić to help his case, President Clinton never really expended much effort on the politically costly task of convincing the American public of the need to arm the Bosnians or Croatians, or the need to unleash American air power on Milošević and the Serbs, or the need to put US boots on the ground. Instead, he found a way to do something without the necessity of making any vigorous public argument for it, and without much involving his own balky Pentagon. Thank you, MPRI!

It happened like this: In 1994, a little more than a year into Clinton's presidency, the Croatian minister of defense asked Washington if he might, in spite of the UN arms embargo, get some help—like, say, weapons or training or a leg up in gaining admission to NATO. The Pentagon referred the minister (a native Croatian with a successful Canadian pizza business; well-spoken and serious, he was) to an outfit down the road in Alexandria, Virginia, called Military Personnel Resources Incorporated. A few months later, MPRI signed a contract with the Croatian government—sanctioned in advance by the US Departments of Defense and State—called the Democratic Transition Assistance Program. By early 1995, a cadre of former US generals, including a former Army chief of staff and a former head of US Army, Europe, together with retired line officers and NCOs, began "training [Croatian] officers in basic leadership skills and an understanding of where they fit into a democratic society," according to an MPRI spokesman. "We teach general management, training management. We teach how to do planning, programming, the budgeting process, which is new to them."

By the time MPRI's "democratic transition assistance" work in Croatia got under way, the Clinton administration had already given a tacit go-ahead to other countries (particularly Iran!) to arm the Bosnians too. For allowing the flow of arms to

Bosnia through its ports and across its airspace, the Croatians got a cut that added up to about 30 percent of the Iranian weapons shipments. While under the tutelage of MPRI, the Croats also bought a billion dollars' worth of tanks and assault helicopters from the old Warsaw powers. And then they put them to good use.

In August 1995, about half a year after MPRI took up their instruction at the Petar Zrisnki Military Academy in Croatia, the Croats launched an offensive called Operation Storm. The objective was to take back a former Croatian region called Krajina, which the Serb Army had violently seized a few years earlier. Within a week, the Croat Army had routed the Serbs, surprising everyone in the Balkans, and the world. "The lightning five-pronged offensive, integrating air power, artillery and rapid infantry movements, and relying on intense maneuvers to unhinge Serbian command and control networks, bore many hallmarks of U.S. Army doctrine," a reporter in Krajina wrote at the time. "It was a textbook operation," said a British colonel in charge of UN troops in Krajina, "though not a [Yugoslav Army] textbook. Whoever wrote that plan of attack could have gone to any NATO staff college in North America or Western Europe and scored an A-plus."

Suspicions for training up the Croatian Army into a lethal, Western-style fighting force naturally fell on MPRI, but the contract generals took pains to remind anybody who asked that the company was just there to provide "democratic transition assistance" and not to plan battles or game out wars. Clinton didn't appear to care one way or another about MPRI's actual role in Operation Storm. He was giddy with the result. "I was rooting for the Croatians," the president wrote in his autobiography. "It was the first defeat for the Serbs in four years, and it changed both the balance of power on the ground and the psychology of all the parties. One Western diplomat in Croatia was quoted as saying, 'There was almost a signal of support from Washington. The Americans have been spoiling for a chance to hit the Serbs, and they are using Croatia as their proxy to do the deed for them.'" Clinton apparently agreed with the diplomat's assessment enough to quote him, and proudly.

After four years of assuming Western impotence, if not outright approval, Milošević finally felt the noose tightening. Within weeks of the Croat victory at Krajina, in the face of ever more energetic NATO air strikes, and with the prospect of facing a newly armed (American-trained and -supported) coalition of Bosnians and Croatians, the Serb leader knuckled under. He came to the negotiating table to sign a deal that ended his genocidal four-year rampage.

So it was soon after the peace accords were signed that those twenty thousand American peacekeepers—who would be joined by twenty thousand private citizens under contract to provide support services—arrived in Bosnia and Croatia as part of an international force to keep Milošević and his Serbian military under heel. And did Clinton have a hard time selling that manpower commitment to the American people? He did not. He was helped greatly by—what else? Outsourcing. Clinton had only had to make a minimal call-up of Guard members and Reserves. "An Army planner told us they could have asked the national command authority to increase the force ceiling and reserve call-up authority," according to a US government audit of the Bosnian operation. "However, because they had LOGCAP as an option, it was not necessary to seek these increases to meet support needs."

It was also not necessary for a skittish and unsure president to put himself on the line seeking a real show of public support for *our* mission. And Congress didn't take a stand one way or the other. The president simply shipped American troops off to a possible war zone and both houses of Congress offered a mealy vote of almost-approval, expressing reservations about the president's policy but agreeing to support "the men and women of the United States Armed Forces who are carrying out their missions in support of peace in Bosnia and Herzegovina with professional excellence, dedicated patriotism and exemplary bravery." The Clinton administration got this not-quite-approval approval largely because it assured Congress that the mission would be short and limited.

More than three years later, there were *still* thousands of American troops in Bosnia. And when Milošević's Serbian Army started menacing a new target in former Yugoslavia, Kosovo, Clinton had a game plan at the ready. NATO started up another bombing campaign and the president prepared to deploy an entirely new contingent of US soldiers to keep the peace in yet another former Yugoslavian state. "How could the U.S. military find a way to provide the logistics for its forces, without calling up reserves or the National Guard, while at the same time helping to deal with the humanitarian crisis that the war had provoked?" asked Peter W. Singer in his book *Corporate Warriors*. "Simple: the U.S. military would pass the work on to someone else. . . . Instead of having to call up roughly 9,000 reservists, Brown & Root Services was hired."

Cheney's little "augmentation" program had proved a godsend to the Clinton administration. "It is often necessary to use LOGCAP in these missions," noted the Government Accounting Office report on Bosnia in 1997, "because of the political sensitivity of activating guard and reserve forces."

That political sensitivity is there for a reason. Mounting an overseas military operation should force a national gut-check about wars that presidents might otherwise rush us into. It lessens the possibility of stranding our military in conflicts the country doesn't support or, worse, doesn't care about. Having a work-around for that political sensitivity must have felt like genius to those who wanted war without the hassle, but even in the short run, that work-around had clear unintended consequences. Not only was there little public debate about the merits of a major American deployment, there was also less pressure to bring the mission to a quick conclusion. American peacekeeping troops were in the Balkans for more than eight years, without the general public much noticing. Even at the time of the initial deployment, little more than a third of the country was closely following the story; only a fifth understood the details of the US contribution to the international peacekeeping force. The American public, according to a Pew Research Center poll, was much more interested in a recent blizzard and a weekend-long federal government shutdown. Eight years into the Balkan mission, the American public was even less engaged.

"Deploying LOGCAP or other contractors instead of military personnel can alleviate the political and social pressures that have come to be a fact of life in the U.S. whenever military forces are deployed," wrote Lt. Col. Steven Woods in his Army War College study about the effects of LOGCAP. "While there has been little to no public reaction to the deaths of five DynCorp employees killed in Latin America or the two American support contractors from Tapestry Solutions attacked (and one killed) in Kuwait . . . U.S. forces had to be withdrawn from Somalia after public outcry following the deaths of U.S. soldiers in Mogadishu. . . .

"Additionally, military force structure often has a force cap, usually for political reasons. Force caps impose a ceiling on the number of soldiers that can be deployed into a defined area. Contractors expand this limit." To infinity and beyond, in other words, with a pay-to-play pop-up army.

By the time Bill Clinton left office in 2001, an Operation Other Than War, as Pentagon forces called them, could go on indefinitely, sort of on autopilot—without real political costs or consequences, or much civilian notice. We'd gotten used to it.

By 2001, the ability of a president to start and wage military operations without (or even in spite of) Congress was established precedent.

By 2001, even the peacetime US military budget was well over half the size of all other military budgets in the world combined.

By 2001, the spirit of the Abrams Doctrine—that the disruption of civilian life is the price of admission for war—was pretty much kaput.

By 2001, we'd freed ourselves of all those hassles, all those restraints tying us down.

Chapter 8

"One Hell of a Killing Machine"

THE HOUBARA BUSTARD IS NOT A PARTICULARLY LARGE OR regal bird. It looks a little like what you might get if you bred a common pheasant with an ostrich—like a miniature ostrich with a shorter neck and legs, or maybe a pheasant on steroids, with a stretched neck, sprinter's legs, and a much more impressive wingspan. But the little fella has recently provided crucial assistance in making America's war in Afghanistan (and its spillover in Pakistan) the longest-running military hot show in our nation's history.

In May 2011, Pakistan got its nose out of joint when US Special Forces sprung a surprise mission on a compound in Abbottabad and offed the most infamous terrorist on the planet, without giving a heads-up to the host government. The Pakistani military and intelligence service found itself having to explain how the target, Osama bin Laden, could have been living in tranquility just a few miles down the road from Pakistan's most important military academy, in a neighborhood crawling with current and retired military officers. Was Pakistani intelligence that incompetent, or were they protecting bin Laden? And then they had to explain how a US strike force and its very big helicopters could fly into Abbottabad, spend nearly an hour on the ground, and then leave the country with bin Laden's carcass in tow without being detected, let alone stopped.

While President Obama and the rest of America took a celebratory victory lap, the Pakistanis found the entire episode hugely shaming—but not so much on the bin-Laden-in-our-backyard count. They really fixated on the lack of respect accorded their nation by the United States. "American troops coming across the border and taking action in one of our towns . . . is not acceptable to the people of Pakistan," former president Pervez Musharraf said the day after the raid. "It is a violation of our sovereignty." Worse, word quickly leaked out that President Obama had not only ordered that the Pakistani military and its intelligence service be kept in the dark while the mission was being planned and executed, he had his team ready to do battle with any Pakistani military forces that tried to stop the operation once in progress.

The Pakistani parliament called the country's military and intelligence chieftains into a rare (and marathon) closed-door session, where the generals had a spot of trouble in covering their respective lapses, but they did deftly deflect much of the civilian ire: the United States, they reminded everyone, was the bad guy here. The generals had little trouble encouraging parliament to formally demand that, henceforth, the United States would ensure that "Pakistan's national interests were fully respected." Ally *schmally*—the Pakistani people deserved some respect. To add some bite to this declaration of sovereignty, the generals suggested a good first step would be forcing the United States to shut down the secret program the CIA had been running out of an airbase in a remote corner of Pakistan called Balochistan. Unfortunately, in publicizing their demand that

the CIA leave that airbase, the generals also revealed to surprised Pakistani legislators . . . *that the CIA had been using that
airbase*. This was cause for an uproar in parliament, but the fact
that the CIA had been flying armed drones out of the airfield
known as Shamsi came as much less of a surprise to the citizens
of the areas those drones were targeting—the tribal regions.

The CIA's rather dumpy-looking high-tech unmanned aircraft had been used mainly for surveillance in the early stages
of the war in Afghanistan. But they could also be armed with
Hellfire missiles. Very occasionally from 2004 to 2007, and
more frequently in 2008, the Bush administration used drones
to launch airborne attacks on suspected terrorists in Pakistan.
When the Obama administration took over in 2009, the number
of drone attacks spiked; the next year the 2009 numbers more
than doubled. The Obama administration refused as a matter of policy to officially acknowledge the CIA's drone attacks,
but in the days following a big get, they announced that some
key Al-Qaeda or Haqqani Network leader "was killed," as if the
event were an act of providence or, like a rainbow, a remarkable
atmospheric happening.

Meanwhile, in North and South Waziristan, the presence of
the drones has become a hated fact of life—the locals reportedly call them "wasps." So this was a very popular move in Pakistan, telling the CIA to get the hell out of Shamsi, that there
would be no more lethal American drones launched from Pakistani soil . . . or else. Or else what? Well, Pakistan's air marshal
reminded the Obama administration, the F-16 jets the United
States had sold the Pakistani Air Force could knock the drones
out of the sky. Team Obama did not flinch. These drone attacks
had become the centerpiece of Obama's recalibration of America's Global War on Terror, even if we didn't call it that anymore.
The strikes had proved Democrats could be as serious about

killing bad guys as Republicans were. In fact, the successes had been among the few bright spots on a fairly bleak political landscape for a young, inexperienced, first-term president. The Obama administration had no intention of pulling up stakes in Shamsi. "That base is neither vacated nor being vacated" was the anonymous but official word from Washington. It was a Mexican standoff in Balochistan.

Here's where the Houbara bustard provided a little wiggle room in what otherwise looked like a very knotty situation. This tiny forgotten strip of land that held the airbase in Shamsi, it turned out, did not actually belong to Pakistan; it had been quietly signed over to the United Arab Emirates twenty years earlier, in a show of friendship. You see, Balochistan, aside from being full of spectacular Garden of Eden natural wonders, is among the few wintering grounds of the Houbara bustard, a bird held in high esteem among hunters from the UAE and Saudi Arabia and Qatar. Falconry is the sport of Arab kings, and the poor bustard had long been the preferred prey for falconers. So Emirati royalty were really pleased to have this special foothold in Balochistan, and right away built themselves a sizeable landing strip for easy access to this surprisingly sought-after corner of the world.

"The sheiks tell me it is the ultimate challenge for the falcon," a chieftain in Balochistan told *New Yorker* writer Mary Anne Weaver back around the time the Emiratis built the Shamsi airstrip. "The falcon is the fastest bird on earth, and the houbara is also fast, both on the ground and in the air. It is also a clever, wary bird, with a number of tricks." Among these tricks, the chieftain continued, is an ability to ink-jet "a dark-green slime violently from its vent. Its force is so strong that it can spread for three feet, and it can temporarily blind the falcon, or glue its feathers together, making it unable to fly." The belief also persisted that the meat of the bustard was an aphrodisiac. Not hard to see why the bustard had been sought and consumed with such sustained effort that the bird was nearly extinct on the Arabian Peninsula.

Cold War politics had added degrees of difficulty for the sportsmen as well. The fall of the shah in 1979 made bustard hunting problematic for Sunni Arabs in Shiite Iran, as had the near-constant state of war in Afghanistan. So Balochistan emerged as *the* destination spot for latter-day Arab Nimrods. For the last twenty years or so, Emirati sheiks and Saudi princes and the more general run of ambitious Arab dignitaries had jockeyed for the best allotments in the last good place on earth to hunt the bustard. (When Pakistan's foreign office bestowed upon the Emirati poobahs an allotment once held by the Saudis, the Saudis withheld oil supplies from Pakistan and money for flood relief.) Arab royalty of various stripes show up every year with, according to Weaver's description, pop-up tent cities, hundreds of servants, satellite dishes for better communication, and hunting vehicles tricked out with sophisticated laptops, infrared spotlights, and bustard-seeking radar. Maybe not sporting, but certainly effective.

Officials at Pakistan's Ministry of Environment warned over and over about their ever-dwindling bustard population, but they were powerless to keep the Arab potentates to their bag limit of one hundred birds a year. "They never respect code of conduct," said one ministry man. "What can the Wildlife Department do if the crown prince of Saudi Arabia, the president of the UAE or emir of Qatar go into a region that is prohibited for hunting and cross their bag limit?" Not much, apparently, if Pakistan still wanted cheap oil and dirhams and riyals for flood relief, or jet fighters and tanks.

The Emiratis had made one concession that slightly crimped

their style in the bustard-hunting department. In the weeks after the 9/11 attacks in 2001—when everybody wanted to pitch in—they had agreed, with the consent of Pakistani president Musharraf, to let the Americans use Shamsi as a base to supply US troops fighting the Taliban just across the border in Afghanistan . . . and maybe for a few special and classified operations. In the ten years that followed, as the CIA (and its many private contractors) began operating lethal attack drones out of Shamsi, the remote top secret base remained off-limits to Pakistan's own Air Force. So when the shit hit the fan (when the slime hit the falcon) in the aftermath of the bin Laden raid, thanks to the Houbara bustard, everybody had an out: the United States could make it plain that the CIA was not vacating Shamsi, and Pakistan could still save face. Pakistani government officials could say—and did!—Hey, we just checked our land records and it turns out this little strip of Balochistan is not, legally speaking, Pakistan-controlled territory after all. We gave it to the Emiratis for bustard hunting! So, sorry, but there's nothing we can do to stop the part of America's secret drone war operating out of Shamsi. But we do condemn it in the strongest possible language.

The UAE meanwhile went on record saying they'd only *built* the airstrip. Emirati sheiks and others used it for "recreational purposes." What "recreation" the CIA was pursuing there, the Emiratis couldn't say. Shamsi, they assured the world, "was never operated or controlled by the UAE."

And so we still had our drone base in Shamsi, and no skittish ally had to take the blame for having handed it over to us. Even after the bin Laden raid and the Pakistani freak-out, America stepped up the already furious pace of the drone attacks, executing twenty-one multiple-kill sorties in the next two months (as many as three in one day), though nobody in the US government would say where the unmanned flights originated. "A U.S. military official, who also spoke on condition of anonymity because of the sensitivity of the subject, said there are presently no U.S. military personnel at Shamsi," the Associated Press reported. "But he could not speak for the CIA or contractors used by any other U.S. agencies. The CIA rarely discusses the covert drone program."

When reports surfaced that all US operatives finally packed up and left Shamsi about six months later, at the end of 2011, the official word from our government was still . . . no comment. "If the agency did have such a [covert drone] program," the Obama administration's counterterrorism czar told a forum at the president's alma mater, Harvard Law School, in the fall of 2011, "I'm sure it would be done with the utmost care, precision, in accordance with the law and our values." Wink-wink. The audience chortled knowingly.

"While we don't discuss the details of our counterterrorism operations," a CIA spokeswoman told the *Washington Post*, "the fact that they are a top priority and effective is precisely what the American people expect."

By the time the weird Shamsi who's-on-first disavowal filtered out to the public, there had already been a good bit of reporting on the CIA drones. Thanks to reporters like Jane Mayer at *The New Yorker*, James Risen and Mark Mazzetti at the *New York Times*, and Greg Miller and Julie Tate at the *Washington Post*, the outlines of the program were a fairly open secret. In 2011, the United States had hundreds of armed drones, a few in the air at all times, many of them attached to the CIA, and many of those based at hidden airfields, where America is not permitted by the host country to keep permanent combat troops on the ground. No problem: the drones there were guarded, maintained, and loaded with bombs by, you guessed it, private contractors from companies like the one that used to be called Blackwater, until they committed enough murder and mayhem and overbilling in America's post-9/11 wars that they had to change their name *twice*, first to Xe (pronounced "ze," but let's all pronounce it "she," just to annoy them) and then to the comparatively drab Academi. Blackwater ops also provided assistance on the ground with intelligence-gathering and targeting for the drone sorties.

When one of those Blackwater-armed drones takes off with a specific target location programmed into its hard drive, it is operated remotely by a CIA-paid "pilot" on-site, in a setup that looks like a rich teenager's video-game lair: a big computer tower (a Dell, according to some reporting), a couple of keyboards, a bunch of monitors, a roller-ball mouse (gotta guard against carpal tunnel syndrome), a board of switches on a virtual flight console, and, of course, a joystick. Once the drone is airborne and on its way to the target, the local pilot turns control over to a fellow pilot at a much niftier video-game room at the CIA headquarters in Langley, Virginia. The "pilot," sitting in air-conditioned comfort in suburban Virginia, homes the drone in on its quarry somewhere in, say, North Waziristan. Watching the live video feed from the drone's infrared heat–sensitive cameras on big to-die-for-on-Super-Bowl-Sunday flat-screen monitors, the pilot and a team of CIA analysts start to make what then CIA chief Leon Panetta liked to call "life-and-death decisions." Maybe not sporting, but certainly effective.

The CIA's joystick jockey and his copilots, according to Mayer, "can turn the plane, zoom in on the landscape below, and decide whether to lock on to a target. A stream of additional 'signal' intelligence, sent to Langley by the National Security

Agency, provides electronic means of corroborating that a target has been correctly identified. The White House has delegated trigger authority to C.I.A. officials, including the head of the Counter-Terrorist Center, whose identity remains veiled from the public because the agency has placed him under cover."

By design, everything the CIA does is at least partially occluded from public view, but there's a bit more reportable detail about the drones we do admit to, the ones operated by the US military. The Air Force joystick operators show up at their virtual consoles in actual flight suits; they call the video feed there Death TV, and they have a name for the Pakistanis on the ground who make a run for it when they see the drone approach: "squirters."

The military drone warriors have also insisted they adhere to strict rules of engagement. "Some people are approved for killing on sight," Mayer wrote in *The New Yorker*. "For others additional permission is needed. A target's location enters the equation, too. If a school, or hospital, or mosque is within the likely blast radius of the missile, that, too, is weighted by a computer algorithm before a lethal strike is authorized." The algorithm apparently provides the acceptable number of innocent civilian "squirters" for any given high-value "squirter."

The CIA's Counterterrorism Center remains buttoned-up about its clandestine drone program. Nobody knows if their "pilots" dress themselves up in flight suits too. If they are constrained by any rules or civilian-casualty-ratio algorithms, they aren't saying. But we do know that one out of every five CIA analysts is now assigned to the mission of hunting terrorism suspects, and that the agency has upgraded "targeting" to an official and nicely euphemistic in-house career track. The CIA's fundamental mission is still supposedly spying—providing information about the world to the president. So it used to be when the agency missed something truly significant—like, say, the fall of the Soviet Union—there was lamentation and hand wringing about what exactly we had them for anyway, if they couldn't see something like that coming. Now the CIA can be caught totally unaware by something like the world-transforming Arab Spring movement, and . . . who cares! We're just psyched we got bin Laden.

The transformation of America's spy service into a new, out-of-uniform (and 100 percent deniable) branch of the military is a big decision for us as a country, but for our new assassin corps—long saddled with the effete managerial identity of "the intelligence community"—it's been like a shot of testosterone. They have trigger authority! They are the Assassins of the Air! "You've taken an agency that was chugging along and turned it into one hell of a killing machine," an anonymous (they're always anonymous) former intelligence official exclaimed to the *Washington Post* before thinking better of it. "Instead say, 'one hell of an operational tool.'"

"We are killing these sons of bitches faster than they can grow them now," the CIA counterterrorism chief reportedly boasted. Flight suits or no, they have become a bona fide, full-fledged, and very busy US military resource, by another name. Those *Washington Post* reporters summed up their investigation of the secret drone war like this: "The CIA now functions as a military force beyond the accountability that the United States has historically demanded of its armed services. The CIA doesn't officially acknowledge the drone program, let alone provide public explanation about who shoots and who dies, and by what rules."

The CIA has always used force. The agency was only about kindergarten age when they arranged the overthrow of the government of Iran, for crying out loud. And then on to mining the harbors in Nicaragua! But the covert action mission of the CIA has become something different now: the CIA is now a de facto branch of the military, with its own troops and its own robotic air force. President Obama chose for his second CIA director a man with no background whatsoever in civilian intelligence. No matter. Retired general David Petraeus had spent the previous four years running the US military in Iraq and Afghanistan, which apparently made him the perfect candidate for the job. Post-9/11, the CIA is a military force that wages war on America's behalf. And it has the handy feature of being able to do so in places where we are not supposed to be at war. Having a secret military force with no visible chain of command, or recognizable rules of behavior or engagement, has become a most useful thing.

The secrecy extends to the CIA's budget. In the ten years after the 9/11 attacks, the civilian spy budget doubled, but we taxpayers aren't allowed to know what the various spy agencies are doing with our ever-more-generous contributions. We are told, after the fact, that the federal government spends around $55 billion a year on civilian intelligence (that's not counting $27 billion for military intelligence), but what do we spend that on? Dunno. We've only been allowed to know the total dollar figure for the US intelligence so-called black budget since 2007. The idea that they'll ever let us know its line items seems laughable; the 2007 press release noting with some resentment that the overall budget number would now be public also made clear that this was all we were getting: "Beyond the disclosure of the top-line figure, there will be no other disclosures."

That attitude works for specific operations as well as it works for the overall enterprise. When pressed in 2009 by Pakistani reporters about "relentless" drone strikes in the Waziristans killing civilian bystanders, Secretary of State Hillary Clinton demonstrated the political benefit of using the CIA as trigger pullers. She just stonewalled. "I'm not going to comment on any particular tactic or technology."

The CIA is obligated to brief the handful of souls on the House and Senate Intelligence Committees about their actions, but the briefees are legally required to keep their traps shut about anything they hear inside the closed-door sessions in ultrasecure rooms S-407 and HVC-304. They can't even share it with fellow senators or House members. This can sometimes lead to an almost comic pantomime of what oversight is supposed to be. In 2010, two senators on the Intelligence Committee decided they were so upset by something they'd been briefed on that they had to alert the public. Senators Ron Wyden and Mark Udall did send up the alarm that they'd been briefed on something very disturbing; they just couldn't say what it was. The press tried to report on their concerns, but it was difficult. The *New York Times* gamely described the senators' worries about "some other kind of activity" and "some kind of unspecified domestic surveillance," but they couldn't explain further. "Unspecified" and "other" aren't exactly the kinds of details that get the public's heart pounding. Those senators may have been trying to ring alarm bells by going to the press, but those bells were pretty muffled. Our intel agencies are now well and truly integrated into how we wage war, but intel agencies don't kowtow to lowly congressmen. You can know it, Mr. Wyden, but you can't say a word. Sleep tight.

Of course, even that meager level of pseudo-sharing makes many a senior spook uncomfortable. So thank goodness for private contractors. Outfits like the She formerly known as Blackwater are not legally required to show up at HVC-304 and S-407 and tell how many Hellfire missiles they loaded on drones today, or where they did it. In 2011, the *New York Times* reported that private contractors accounted for about a quarter of the US intelligence jobs. And if you don't trust the *Times,* here's what the director of national intelligence had to say in October of that year. The director wasn't against lowering the number of contractors, but he insisted that private contractors would remain an integral and crucial part of our national spy game. "If all the contractors failed to come to work tomorrow," he said, "the intelligence community would stop."

Oh, and hey, if private contracts don't provide sufficient insulation from public oversight, if the White House is queasy about turning over to Congress the civilian-to-bad-guy casualty-ratio algorithms used by the CIA and its for-profit civilian augmentees, *not a problem*! The executive branch has a work-around for that, too. For operations the White House deems too sensitive or too politically combustible for congressional ears, there is always Joint Special Operations Command.

JSOC was created out of the embarrassments of post-Vietnam military operations: the botched attempt to rescue the Iran hostages, the bombing of the Marine barracks in Lebanon, and the unholy operational mess of the invasion of Grenada. We needed some elite badass soldiers in every branch, it was decided, whose various talents could be brought to bear, in concert, on difficult problems. JSOC has the use of elite, secretive units from all branches of the military, including the celebrated Navy SEAL Team 6, the Army's Delta Force, and the Air Force's Special Tactics Squadron. JSOC squads are sort of like Hasbro's old Vietnam-era G.I. Joe Adventure Team come to life. ("Five rugged men with lifelike hair, outfitted for action, they'll dare anything, and risk everything!") Remember, the Adventure Team had the "flocked" hair, the beards, the Kung Fu Grip, the too-racy-for-regulation uniforms, the "Devil of the Deep" fantail watercraft, the "secret mission to Spy Island." These were no regular Joes. They were clearly not bound by convention. They made their own rules.

By 2001, JSOC had run occasional and secret and daring operations at real-life Spy Islands in the Persian Gulf, Panama, Kuwait, El Salvador, Somalia, Haiti, and the Balkans. But the George W. Bush White House was the first to realize the full potential of Special Ops. Defense Secretary Rumsfeld and Vice President Cheney made them the equivalent of Reagan's private-war-on-Nicaragua NSC—a thousand Ollie Norths (only more skilled and much more governable) at the ready. As Jeremy Scahill reported in *The Nation* at the end of 2009, "Special Forces turned into a virtual stand-alone operation that acted outside the military chain of command and in direct coordination with the White House."

Unlike the Reagan White House, Team Bush didn't wait around until after the fact to provide a justification for this move. The Bush lawyers (lots of them had worked for Meese) wrote up all the legal findings *before* the White House started sending Special Ops off with secret orders in their pockets. Essentially, the Bush administration claimed the Special Ops guys could do most anything they wanted in the War on Terror, anywhere the president chose to send them, and without telling anyone.

This is the sort of executive prerogative presidents in general appreciate, and President Obama has not been the exception to that rule. JSOC reportedly runs its own terrorist-targeting and drone-flying operations, with the help of contractors. "Contractors and especially JSOC personnel working under a classified mandate are not [overseen by Congress], so they just don't care," an intelligence source told Scahill. "If there's one person they're going after and there's thirty-four people in the building, thirty-five people are going to die. That's the mentality. . . . They're not accountable to anybody and they know that."

While America has been fighting two of its longest-ever boots-on-the-ground wars in the decade following 9/11, and fighting them simultaneously, less than one percent of the adult US population has been called upon to strap on those boots. "Not since the peacetime years between World War I and World War II," according to a 2011 Pew Research Center study, "has a smaller share of Americans served in the armed forces." Half of the American public says it has not been even marginally affected by ten years of constant war. We've never in our long history been further from the ideal of the citizen-soldier, from the idea that America would find it impossible to go to war without disrupting domestic civilian life.

The reason the founders chafed at the idea of an American standing army and vested the power of war making in the cumbersome legislature was not to disadvantage us against future enemies, but to disincline us toward war as a general matter. Their great advice was that we should structure ourselves as a country in a way that deliberately raised the price of admission to any war. With citizen-soldiers, with the certainty of a vigorous political debate over the use of a military subject to politicians' control, the idea was for us to feel it—uncomfortably—every second we were at war. But after a generation or two of shedding the deliberate political encumbrances to war that they left us— of dropping Congress from the equation altogether, of superempowering the presidency with total war-making power and with secret new war-making resources that answer to no one but him, of insulating the public from not only the cost of war but sometimes even the knowledge that it's happening—war making has become almost an autonomous function of the American state. It never stops.

The war in Afghanistan was an all but foregone conclusion after 9/11. The Taliban overthrow was engineered by CIA operatives, Special Forces, and a smallish contingent of US troops. It took a few weeks, but then we decided we should stay on and save Afghanistan from itself. Starting the war in Iraq took deceit and trickery on the part of the Bush administration (and severe chickenshittery on the part of the Congress). But once we had both those wars under way, what's more telling—what's less about specific politicians and temporal politics and more about us as a country—is how freaking long it's taken to end them. Regardless of the culpability of the Paul Wolfowitzes and Donald Rumsfelds and Dick Cheneys in starting the Iraq War, there's a national culpability for the fact that we have, without any real debate or thought, settled into a way of waging war that ensures minimal political pushback.

No matter how long the troops slog through the muck, no matter how many deployments they endure, the American public can no longer really be touched by war. Need twenty thousand more soldiers for the surge in Iraq? Military commanders simply extended the combat tours from twelve months to fifteen, no guarantee about how long a rest you'd get between deployments—and this in spite of what the military bosses already knew about the toll on the minuscule slice of American society that would shoulder this burden. "We've done these mental-health assessment team studies for six years now— between nine and twelve [months] is where a lot of the stress problems really manifest themselves, where the family problems really manifest themselves," former Army chief of staff George Casey said recently. "The human mind and body weren't made to do repeated combat deployments without substantial time to recover." The suicide rate among active-duty servicemen doubled in the first five years of the Afghanistan War and then kept rising. In the past decade, the US Army lost more soldiers to suicide than to enemy fire in Afghanistan.

Civilian life has rolled on virtually uninterrupted. If you're not in a military family, you've barely even felt it. The country has perfected the art of frictionless war. America's wars thrum away like Muzak in the background here in the United States, kind of annoying when you tune in, but easy enough to tune out. Three years? Five? Ten? What's the difference? And where are we fighting, anyway? We're shooting missiles into Pakistan all the time. Does that count? Are we allowed to know?

In a statement on the House floor in February 2007, arguing against a reduction in US troop levels in Iraq, Congressman Phil Gingrey of Georgia said, "What indeed are we going to save our troops for? Working the rope lines at Fourth of July parades? Helping senior citizens across the street?" The rhetorical answer to his rhetorical question is of course that America should not save the troops for any such peaceable nonsense—they're there to be used, in combat.

And not just the full-on active-duty military, mind you. We'd found a way to do smaller missions like Rwanda, Haiti, and Somalia without reserve troops—even the Balkans, with some help from our friends at DynCorp and Halliburton. But the Iraq War (and the Iraq War at the same time as the Afghanistan War) was of a different magnitude. The administration had hoped it wouldn't be. Bush's war council had hopefully supposed that Iraq would be quick work. "It could last six days, six weeks," Rumsfeld said the month before the invasion. "I doubt six months." Yeah, no.

As the war dragged on, the initial Bush administration decision to leave the reserves at home became untenable. So they deployed them—and how. In the third year of the war, at one point in 2005 more than half the soldiers in Iraq were from the National Guard. This was a first in American history, but it was a necessity. Thanks to the good old Abrams Doctrine, it remains true that we can't do big wars with active-duty forces alone: two-thirds or more of our military's transportation, engineer, medical, military police, and logistics corps is in the Reserves. But a funny thing about the Reserves now, and about the Abrams Doctrine: through ten years of fighting in Afghanistan and Iraq, the connection's gone bad in the whole idea of the *citizen-soldier*. That hyphen's doing way more work than it used to. The Guardsmen and reservists have been called to duty so often in the last ten years that it's hard to distinguish between regular and reserve forces. Maybe our neighbors in the Guard and Reserves were having their lives turned upside down in the last ten years, maybe they were wounded and killed in staggering numbers in Iraq and Afghanistan, but we got used to it.

The Abrams Doctrine only functions as a constraint on war making to the extent that we're shocked by Americans being called away from their regular lives to join combat. Through sheer repetition, sheer volume, though, those call-ups eventually just stopped being shocking. The post-9/11 deployment pace has put Guardsmen and reservists and their families squarely on the soldier side of the citizen-soldier ideal. Calling them up no longer ensures a big national debate about the merits of a given war. The Abrams Doctrine still forces us to use the reserves if we want to fight a big war, but that's ceased to be a check against wars the American public doesn't want to fight.

We're using everybody in uniform, right up to the limit, and price has been no object. In this past decade, the United States took what was already the world's most robust military budget and supersized it (and also funded a slew of permanent

and highly operational intelligence agencies, and special adventure teams and privately owned contract-warrior companies). By 2011, the total federal R&D budget for alternative
energy sources—derided by the right as a huge Obama-era
boondoggle—was about $3 billion a year. Meanwhile, the de-
fense R&D budget was $77 billion a year—derided by no one,
ever. If you added up what every other country spent on its military in 2001, the US military budget was about half that total;
by 2005, those two numbers were equal. In other words, the
United States spent as much on national defense as every other
country in the world combined. And the Pentagon can now
spend those dollars in a way that insulates the decision makers
from the political consequences of making life uncomfortable
for the voting public.

When the Pentagon farms out soldiers' work to contractors,
it not only puts extra bodies in the field, it puts a different type
of body in the field; the American public doesn't mourn contractor deaths the way we do the deaths of our soldiers. We rarely
even hear about them. Private companies are under no obligation to report when their employees are killed while, say, providing armed security to tractor-trailer convoys running supplies
into Iraq. In the 1991 Gulf War, the United States employed one
private contract worker for every one hundred American soldiers on the ground; in the Clinton-era Balkans, it neared one
to one—about 20,000 privateers tops. In early 2011, there were
45,000 US soldiers stationed inside Iraq, and 65,000 private
contract workers there.

Thanks to the skyrocketing use of privateers, and thanks to
our new quasi-military institutions empowered to make war
while keeping the details of that war making (and often even the
simple fact of that war making) hidden from us, and thanks to
public relations triumphs like the Bush administration sparing

us the sight of the flag-draped caskets of dead American soldiers deplaning week after week at Dover Air Force Base, thanks to all that and more, the American public has been delicately insulated from the actuality of our ongoing wars. While a tiny fraction of men and women fighting our wars are deploying again and again, civilian life remains pretty much isolated in cost-free complacency.

And about those costs . . .

In June 2001, George W. Bush signed into law a massive, budget-busting tax cut that would add about $2 trillion to the deficit over the next decade. Three months later, the 9/11 attacks happened. US troops (and the CIA) were at war in Afghanistan within weeks, but we decided to keep the tax cuts in place anyway. Less than two years later we'd shipped troops off to a second and simultaneous war, in Iraq. Weeks after that invasion, Bush signed another huge round of tax cuts. We also started massively scaling up on the secret intel side of things. *Washington Post* reporters Dana Priest and William M. Arkin, in their seminal 2010 investigative series, detailed more than three thousand government organizations and private companies in ten thousand separate locations at work on counterterrorism. In just less than ten years, the US federal government had deputized 854,000 people with top secret security clearances, invented or reorganized nearly three hundred government agencies, and built office space equivalent to twenty-two US Capitols to create what Priest and Arkin call Top Secret America. The country never debated the need for this vast new superstructure, and still doesn't, mostly because we've never been asked to cover the massive new expense. We just added the cost to the growing deficit, like we have the trillion or two in recent war spending.

This deferred-payment plan has been one of the few bipartisan points of agreement in the last decade. After Bush's pre–Afghanistan War tax cuts, and the second round after the Iraq invasion, his successor followed suit. In 2010, President Obama added thirty thousand more soldiers to Afghanistan, extended the military stay there until 2014, ordered up a few hundred more drones for the CIA, and then—yes—extended those Bush tax cuts.

When civilians are not asked to pay any price, it's easy to be at war—not just to intervene in a foreign land in the first place, but to keep on fighting there. The justifications for staying at war don't have to be particularly rational or cogently argued when so few Americans are making the sacrifice that it takes to stay. When we invaded Iraq in 2003, the first official justification from the White House was that we had to secure Saddam's dangerous piles of weapons of mass destruction. ("We don't want the smoking gun to be a mushroom cloud" was the Bush administration line.) There was plenty of evidence at the time that this threat was bullpucky, and that was proven as soon as we got there. So then we decided we were really there to get rid of Saddam. It took three weeks for Baghdad to fall, and he was caught in his hidey-hole by December.

So why stay after that, for a whole second year? For a third, fourth, sixth . . . eighth? Our official stated reason for staying in Iraq after Saddam was in his grave was a moving target: we were restoring order, we were protecting Iraqi women, we were keeping the Shiites and the Sunnis and the Kurds from killing one another, we were there until the Shiites and the Sunnis and the Kurds learned how to share power in their new government, we were there to defeat the terrorists, we were trying to reform Iraq as a beacon of Jeffersonian democracy in the Middle East (There would be elections! We would have an ally!), we were there to make sure Iran didn't undercut our fledgling democracy and make Iraq *its* Crazy Muslim Theocrat ally. As time went on, it didn't much matter what the president said. Eventually the Bushies quit trying to be creative and just settled on the accusation that leaving would be cowardly. The entire justification for being at war—"Withdrawal is not an option," the Senate majority leader offered three years into the Iraq escapade, "surrender is not a solution"—fit neatly on a bumper sticker. As Ford said, we don't cut and run.

The Bush administration did start to feel some heat about three years into the war: the Republicans lost control of both houses of Congress in 2006 and polls showed as much as two-thirds of the voting public opposed the continuation of the war in Iraq. The White House turned for help to the one national institution of sufficient size and public esteem to provide necessary political cover—the military. If the country didn't trust the president anymore on the war or on foreign policy, the president would get out of the way and let the "commanders on the ground" take the lead. And they wouldn't simply be in charge of prosecuting the war, they'd be commander-in-chiefing it too.

Bush charged the military with more than just coming up with a plan for how to win the war; he charged them with creating something he never really had: a vision of what a win would look like. And if the military brass was becoming the foreign policy maker in the Middle East, the Pentagon—can-do central—had just the man for the job. He was regarded in most circles as the smartest general we had, David Petraeus, a PhD in international relations from Princeton. And the smartest man in the Army decided the military wasn't going to simply win a war, it was going to win a country.

General Petraeus had already authored a textbook on how the military would execute this maximalist mission. *Field*

Manual 3-24 was a can-do treatise on how to fight wars that were both indefinite and expandable, a full-on twenty-first-century rewrite of US military doctrine. The new doctrine—counterinsurgency—was basically a plan to double down in Iraq. The US military could do it, if the rest of America could just relax. The general judged his new plan a much easier sell now than it would have been back in the early days of his military career, when the public was so . . . *engaged.* "Vietnam was an extremely painful reaffirmation that when it comes to intervention, time and patience are not American virtues in abundant supply," General Petraeus had written while working on his PhD. He turned out to be right, about the selling part anyway. *Field Manual 3-24* was such a hit in Washington policy circles that the University of Chicago Press decided to publish it for the general public under a more marketable title: *The U.S. Army/ Marine Corps Counterinsurgency Field Manual.* You can read the reviews at Amazon: "a nifty volume" . . . "the most important piece of doctrine written in the past 20 years" . . . "has helped make Counterinsurgency part of the zeitgeist . . . In short, this is not your parents' military field manual."

Counterinsurgency Petraeus-style turns out to be a very intellectually satisfying theory. The study is full of examples of insurgencies and counterinsurgencies from modern history. Perhaps if Napoleon had had the principles of *Field Manual 3-24* at hand in Spain in 1808, the study implies, all of Europe and much of the rest of the world would be speaking French and enjoying rich food and fine wine without gaining weight. Counterinsurgency doctrine is elegant and fulfilling as an academic exercise, particularly for liberals: the story of how a public entity (that is, the military) does everything the right way, anticipating and meeting a population's every need, and thereby wins. The idea is that the Iraqis will love us in the end, and want to be like us, as long as our military applies the correct principles. Americans had already absorbed the belief that our military was our most able institution, the one we could depend on, the one that could do anything we asked; counterinsurgency doctrine went further, arguing that the military not only could do anything, it should do *everything*. If there was a big national mission outside our borders, the military owned it.

For this new doctrine to work, however, our soldiers were going to be asked to do a lot more than fire their weapons at bad guys, or clear a city block in Baghdad. The new field manual quotes a classic counterinsurgency expert: "To confine soldiers to purely military functions while urgent and vital tasks have to be done, and nobody else is available to undertake them, would be senseless. The soldier must then be prepared to become . . . a social worker, a civil engineer, a schoolteacher, a nurse, a boy scout." Deposing a corrupt dictator, finding the proper local leadership, establishing public utilities or judicial systems, running prisons, directing traffic, hooking up sewage pipes, providing medical care was now all the work of the 82nd Airborne. "Arguably," says *Field Manual 3-24*, "the decisive battle is for the people's minds."

It's hard not to be sympathetic to the entire enterprise. There are no Americans more impressive or more capable than the post-9/11 generation of Iraq and Afghanistan soldiers and veterans. But they are not superhuman. They cannot do the impossible. The general problem with the entire benighted theory of counterinsurgency is that there are no examples in modern history in which a counterinsurgency in a foreign country has been successful. None! The nearest example we have is in Indochina, where we pretty decisively lost the battle for the South

Vietnamese "hearts and minds." And it seems highly unlikely that Napoleon could have overcome Spanish resistance in 1808 by understanding that the population there was "accustomed to hardship, suspicious of foreigners and constantly involved in skirmishes with security forces." In fact, you'd have to go back to the Roman Empire to find an army that ran success-ful counterinsurgency operations. The Romans applied rather different methods from those suggested in *Field Manual 3-24*. They generally involved the Old Testament tactics of killing the able-bodied males and enslaving the women and children. There wasn't much social work involved.

But in a can-do institution like the US military, if Washing-ton asks for a way to "win" something like the years-long occupa-tion of Iraq, then win we shall. With infinite resources anything is possible: open checkbook, swivel wrist. "I have always felt that success in Iraq was achievable," Army chief of staff George Casey assured a gathering of the national press in the summer of 2007. "It will take patience and it will take will. And the terror-ists are out to undermine our will, our national will to prosecute this. But as complex and as difficult and as confusing as you may find Iraq—it is—we can succeed there. And we will succeed there if we demonstrate patience and will. . . . [The Iraqis] have an educated population. They have oil wealth. They have water. They have some of the most fertile land that I've ever seen. In a decade or so this will be a remarkable country—if we stick with it. It's imminently doable." A decade or so . . . if we stick with it? At that point we were already four years in. This should be a fourteen-year war?

"It would be fine with me," Sen. John McCain said while cam-paigning for president not long after the counterinsurgency doctrine–inspired surge began, if the US military stayed in Iraq a hundred years. Or maybe a thousand, he said, or even a million, as long as the Iraqi government wanted us there, and as long as there were no casualties, which would prove the Iraqis really liked us. The million-year-war proposal didn't persuade the American public to back Senator McCain. He lost badly to Illinois senator Barack Obama in the 2008 presidential election. But even for President Obama, a man who made a name for himself as an avowed opponent of the Iraq War, getting out was not easy. In year nine of the war, Obama finally got the Iraqi government to provide the fig leaf of insisting upon our departure.

A few days after we agreed to leave, the Pentagon announced it would be stationing as-yet-undetermined thousands of troops in Kuwait, just across the border, where we could jump into Iraq in case the security situation deteriorated in our absence. Don't forget to make room for the Predator and Reaper drones in there too. And don't forget the thousands of private American contractors who could stick around inside Iraq and help out with US foreign policy by proxy, without fear of congressional interference.

The Guard and Reserves were ready at a moment's notice too. "We're in a situation now where the soldiers we have recruited . . . want to serve, and if we don't continue to challenge them and maintain that combat edge, we think we're going to see soldiers leave us because what we recruited them for and what we promised them, we weren't able to deliver on," the acting director of the National Guard said in 2011. "This country made a huge investment [in the reserve component] to this point, and we think they'll get short-changed if we don't take advantage of this operational reserve."

The military commissioned a study in 2011 of the Guard and Reserve in the post-Iraq and post-Afghanistan era. The lead author told the *Army Times:* "Why would you want to take that progress and put it on the shelf and let it atrophy? You want to use it. . . ."

With the World's Greatest Privately Augmented Standing Army in place, we are, as Jefferson feared, constantly scanning the horizon for "a speck of war." When Gen. George Casey returned from his job as the honcho of the Iraq War in 2007 to take over as Army chief of staff, one of the first things he did was send his transition team out to take a wide-angle view of the world his Army faced. Then he shared the findings with the national press. "I said, 'Go talk to people who think about the future. Ask them what they think the world is going to look like in 2020.' And they did. They went to universities. They went to think tanks. They went around to the intelligence agencies. They went around the government. And they came back and they said, 'You know, we're surprised at the almost unanimity that the next decades that we face here will be ones of what they call persistent conflict.'" The Army was going to have to grow, he said.

In his farewell-to-the-Army speech in 2011, when he was moving over to the CIA, David Petraeus implored the nation to keep hold of the can-do-everything counterinsurgency doctrine. "We will need to maintain the full-spectrum capability that we have developed over this last decade of conflict in Iraq, Afghanistan, and elsewhere," the general said. "But again I know that that fact is widely recognized."

In 2011, new secretary of defense Leon Panetta was running around Capitol Hill with his hair on fire saying cuts in the annual increase of the Pentagon budget would "hollow out" the military. "This is not as if we've come out of a major war and everything is fine," Panetta said, lamenting "rising powers . . . rapidly modernizing their militaries and investing in capabilities to deny our forces freedom of movement in vital regions." He's right. But the reason those foreign powers were rising in the first place is not necessarily because of their military strength but because of their economies—something this country had largely neglected in our decade of hot war.

However much blood and treasure we shoveled into the Hindu Kush and the deserts of Al Anbar Province after 9/11, we can look back at that expenditure now from a position of grave, grave weakness. Unless three-ton V-hulled armored MRAP trucks and flying killer robots are going to provide the basis of America's new manufacturing base for the twenty-first century, we've built ourselves—to the exclusion of all other priorities—a military superstructure we can't use for anything other than war and that we can no longer afford. And it's going to be really hard to take this thing apart. Even the manifestly hilariously dangerously stupid parts of it we can't take apart. Have you heard the one about the wing fungus?

Chapter 9

An $8 Trillion Fungus Among Us

SAY YOU'RE A HIGH SCHOOL SENIOR IN 2007. WE'RE FOUR YEARS into Iraq, and six years into Afghanistan. If you're feeling a call to patriotic duty, a sense of adventure, thinking about the training opportunities offered by a career in the US Armed Forces, where do you tell that recruiter that you'd like to end up? Probably not in a missile silo in Minot, North Dakota. In the post-9/11 era, who'd want the job of sitting through the nuclear winter on the high plains, running maintenance on the thirty-five B-52s, guarding the "silos" that housed 150 giant and largely untested intercontinental ballistic missiles (ICBMs), babysitting the hundreds of smaller nuclear warheads stored in sod-topped bunkers like canned fruit shelved in a tornado shelter? The munitions maintenance team and the weapons handlers and the tow crews in Minot could call those bunkers "igloos," but giving stuff funny names didn't make life there any more fun.

"Our younger airmen, once they've reached that decision point, if they have been stationed in one of our northern bases where the environment's a little bit tougher, they tend to leave the service," an Air Force general told the Senate. Those who didn't leave the service didn't stick around the tending-the-nukes life for long. In 2007, an Airman assigned to a nuclear bomber wing could look around and note that more than eight in ten members of her wing's security force were rookies. One senior officer in the Air Force's nuclear enterprise admitted that standing alert duty in missile silos is not considered "deployed," and "if you are not a 'deployer,' you do not get promoted."

The Air Force pleaded for more missileers, but "deployments in support of regional conventional operations [i.e., Iraq and Afghanistan] decrease manpower available to the nuclear mission." But even without Iraq and Afghanistan siphoning off military talent, would anyone expect that ambitious young airmen would be clamoring for silo duty?

"We need a nuclear career field," concluded a Pentagon blue-ribbon task force on the nation's nuclear mission in 2008. Sixty years into America's nuclear superpower age, sixty years as the only nation to have ever used a nuclear weapon against an enemy in wartime, sixty years of hair-trigger nuclear alert, and we don't have a nuclear career field? We used to have one, but it's been eclipsed by changing times, changing wars.

That Pentagon report noted that "many Airmen were skeptical of hearing repeated pronouncements that the nuclear mission is 'number one' ... No one explains to junior Air Force personnel why ICBMs are important." But no matter what they might figure out to say about ICBMs being important, the Air Force's actions spoke louder. Ask the staff sergeant who got written up for failing a Storage Access and Missile Safe Status Check inspection but still retained his position as a nuclear weapons handler. Status check? The airmen handling weapons capable of unleashing Armageddon were stuck on low.

So was the whole nuclear enterprise. It wasn't just the personnel; it was the aging hardware, too. Consider page thirteen of a

recently declassified 2007 report on the care and feeding of our
nation's nuclear weapons at Barksdale Air Force Base in Shreve-
port, Louisiana:

RECOMMENDED IMPROVEMENT AREAS:

- Numerous air launched cruise missiles had fungus on
  leading edge of wings

- Forward missile antenna sealant delaminated

- Corrosion on numerous H1388 storage and shipping
  containers

While our nuclear-armed cruise missiles were growing
leading-edge wing fungus in the subtropical moisture of Louisiana, other US military flying hardware was having rather
the opposite problem: in the words of *Defense Industry Daily*,
they "were about to fly their wings off—and not just as a figure
of speech." In 2006, the Air Force embarked on an emergency
(and expensive, at $7 million a pop) upgrade of the nation's fleet
of C-130 aircraft. After heavy service moving cargo and flying combat missions as retrofitted gunships, the huge planes'
wing-boxes were failing. Wing-boxes are what keep the wings
attached to the fuselage.

So take your pick of your maintenance priorities, Taxpayer: wings falling off enormous gunships in the Middle East
and central Asia from constant use in the longest simultane-
ous land wars in US history, or sedentary nuclear missiles in
Shreveport growing fungus. At least we can easily tally the
twenty-first-century benefits where the C-130s were concerned;
those airplanes have moved a bucketload of troops—along with
"beans, boots, Band-Aids, and bullets"—to the various war
zones we've kept humming since 2001. Operationally speaking,

that workhorse fleet of no-frills, have-a-seat-on-your-helmet airplanes has been tremendously effective and cost-efficient.

The nuclear thing is harder to figure.

The United States, according to a 1998 study by the Brookings Institution, spent nearly eight *trillion* in today's dollars on nukes in the last half of the twentieth century, which represents something like a third of our total military spending in the Cold War. Just the nuke budget was more than that half-century's federal spending on Medicare, education, social services, disaster relief, scientific research (of the non-nuclear stripe), environmental protection, food safety inspectors, highway maintenance, cops, prosecutors, judges, and prisons . . . combined. The only programs that got more taxpayer dollars were Social Security and non-nuclear defense spending.

What do we have to show for that steady, decades-long mushroom cloud of a spending spree? Well, congratulations: we've got ourselves a humongous nuclear weaponry complex. Still, today. Yes, the Nevada Test Site is now a museum, and the FBI converted J. Edgar Hoover's fallout shelter into a *Silence of the Lambs*–style psychological-profiling unit, but as atomic-kitschy as it all seems, the bottom line is this: twenty-four hours a day, 365 days a twenty-first-century year, we've still got thousands of nuclear missiles armed, manned, and ready to go, pointed at the Soviet Union. *Er* . . . Russia. Whatever. At the places that still have thousands of live nuclear weapons pointed at us.

Warheads, and the missiles that carry them, and all the nuts and bolts that support them from shelter to bomber wing and back again have been on the shelf for way too long. The nukes and their auxiliary equipment were generally designed to have a life span of about ten to twenty years. Constant manufacturing and modernization were the assumptions back in the glory days, especially with Team B's armchair instigators kicking up all that magic fear dust. But by the start of the Barack Obama presidency, some of that hardware had been in service for forty or even fifty years.

Bad enough that missiles were growing wing fungus and storage containers were rusting through, but at least those problems were mostly solvable with Lysol and Rustoleum. For the more serious nuclear maintenance issues, we had by then started shoveling money into something called the Stockpile Life Extension Program, which—even if you avoid the temptation to call it SchLEP—is still essentially a program of artificial hips, pacemakers, and penile implants for aging nukes. How'd you like to be responsible for operating on a half-century-old nuclear bomb?

These were fixes that required real, hard-won technical nuclear expertise—expertise we unfortunately also seemed to be aging out of. Fuzes, for example, were failing, and there was nobody around who could *fix* them: "Initial attempts to refurbish Mk21 fuzes were unsuccessful," admitted an Air Force general, "in large part due to their level of sophistication and complexity." The fuze that previous generations of American engineers had invented to trigger a nuclear explosion (or to prevent one) were apparently too complicated for today's generation of American engineers. The old guys, who had designed and understood this stuff, had died off, and no one thought to have them pass on what they knew while they still could.

Then there was the W76 problem. W76s were nuclear bombs based mostly on the Navy's Trident submarines. By refurbishing them, we thought we might get another twenty or thirty years out of them before they needed replacing. The problem with refurbishing the W76s—with taking them apart, gussying them up, and putting them back together—is that we had forgotten how to make these things anymore. One part of the bomb had the code name "Fogbank." Fogbank's job was to ensure that the hydrogen in the bomb reached a high enough energy level to explode on cue. But no one could remember how to make Fogbank. It was apparently dependent on some rare and highly classified X-Men-like material conjured by US scientists and engineers in the 1970s, but no one today remembers the exact formula for making it. Very embarrassing.

The Department of Energy was not going to take this lying down; they promised the Navy, "We did it before, so we can do it again." I like that can-do spirit! But sadly, no. It took more than a year just to rebuild the long-dismantled Fogbank manufacturing plant at the Oak Ridge nuclear lab, and from there, while a bunch of aging W76 warheads lay opened up like patients on an operating table, government scientists and engineers tried to whip up new life-extending batches of Fogbank. But even after years of trying, even after the Fogbank production program went to "Code Blue" high priority, the technicians were never able to reproduce a single cauldron of Fogbank possessed of its former potency. The Department of Energy, according to an official government report, "had lost knowledge of how to manufacture the material because it had kept few records of the process when the material was made in the 1980s and almost all staff with expertise on production had retired or left the agency." The experts were gone. And nobody had bothered to write anything down!

Maybe this should have been a sign. When all the scientists and engineers are dead, or senile, or at least just fishing, and the know-how is gone with them, isn't it fair to say that a destroy-the-world-thousands-of-times-over nuclear weapons program has run its course?

It's not worth (at least here) querying the sanity of how we got all these nukes in the first place. There was a logic to it. In the Cold War, with the Soviet Union pointing Armageddon-making bombs in our direction, we answered in kind. The deterrent force of our nukes—you move to wipe us out, you're going down with us—was rational, although kind of bizarre. The perfectly acronymed doctrine of Mutually Assured Destruction (MAD) required that we have whatever the Russians had, plus better, plus one. And the same for them toward us. Last superpower with a bullet in the chamber wins. At one remarkable moment in the completely MAD Atomic Age of the 1960s we possessed more than 31,000 armed nuclear warheads, scattered around the globe aboard submarines, in underground missile silos, or strapped on the underside of bomber wings. And most of the warheads in this sea-land-air triad were a simple key-turn away from launch. We had to be ready to fire those suckers in a hurry.

If your desire is to discourage (in the biggest way possible) imminent thermonuclear war with the Soviets, MAD at least theoretically justified keeping that many missiles ready to fly on the shortest possible notice. Once the Soviet Union dissolved, though, what was the remaining justification for our keeping an arsenal of that size on hair-trigger alert?

How about the fact that it is not a simple thing to walk away from a sixty-year, eight-trillion-dollar investment? Eight-trillion-dollar habits die hard. In 2005, Gen. Lance Lord, described as a "man with missile in his DNA," said in a speech to a Washington think tank, "As the wing commander at F. E. Warren, routinely I was asked, 'How does winning the Cold War change your mission?'" His answer: "It doesn't." Institutions have inertia. When the original justification for a huge investment goes away, the huge investment finds another reason to live. It's not just the military; it's true of pretty much all organizations. The more money and work and time it takes to build something, the more power it accrues, and the more effort it takes to make it go away.

But in the case of the nuclear arms race, what built it wasn't just money (*tons* of money), work, and time, it was also a grab-you-by-the-throat existential urgency. To convince ourselves we needed a nationwide web of hair-trigger-alert nuclear weapons capable of destroying the earth thousands of times over, we had to commit ourselves to a beautifully apocalyptic theory of how we would not just possess but also *use* these weapons. We *would* push the button, maybe even hundreds of times. We'd do it because we'd need to—because an enemy was in the act of doing the same or worse to us.

After the Cold War, without the realistic threat of a massive, multistrike nuclear assault by the USSR, our bristling-with-nukes posture made no sense. If we wanted to keep this huge web of nukes in place, we needed a post-Soviet scenario for how and why we'd ever want to push the button, maybe even hundreds of times.

Cue the American spirit of invention. In that same no-change-in-my-mission speech in 2005, General Lord ventured a new idea for why his Wyoming missileers should keep going to work every day tending their ICBMs: "The triad no longer means ICBMs, bombers, and submarines. The new triad consists of offensive strike, defensive capabilities, and highlights the revitalization of the defense infrastructure to meet emerging threats." When military planners start talking about new paradigms and using nukes for *offensive* strikes, don't look for the budget requests to go down.

If we're in the business of thinking up constructive new uses for all these nukes, let's think big. After all, it's not just us and the USSR anymore. The UK, France, China, Pakistan, and India have nukes too. Oh, and Israel, but that's supposed to be a secret.

Apartheid-era South Africa had them—yikes—but decided to get rid of them, as did the former Soviet states of Belarus, Kazakhstan, and Ukraine. Brazil and Argentina could very well have had them, but they agreed to be part of a nuclear-weapons-free Latin America instead.

Then there are the wannabes. On October 9, 2006, North Korea tested a nuclear device. The CIA director reportedly called the test a failure, but it sure didn't feel like a failure internationally. Kim Jong Il, then the "Supreme Leader" of North Korea, wanted to join the most depressing club ever—the so-called nuclear club—and the prospect of his getting even close to that achievement was a real kick in the teeth. It was one thing to marvel at state-run news reports that Kim Jong Il hit holes-in-one every time he golfed and that his birth was heralded by a double rainbow and a new star in the sky; it was another to imagine that same guy having the power to level part of the planet at the touch of a button.

But as the world recoiled in collective horror at the idea of a nuclear-armed weirdo Dear Leader, the response of American conservatives to the North Korean nuclear test revealed the fact that mainstream Washington discussion about nukes had become pretty weird too. A week and a half after the North Korean nuclear test, conservative Charles Krauthammer argued in the *Washington Post* that the best response would be for the United States to persuade Japan to develop nukes as well.

Japan. Nukes. Japan?! Nukes?!

Krauthammer argued that if Japan were to say it was developing nuclear weapons in response to North Korea having them, China would so dislike that idea that the Chinese would force North Korea back in the box. Of course, back in reality, there was also the possibility that the Chinese would respond to the threat of a nuclear-armed Japan not by disarming their ally,

North Korea, but by *up*-arming it. And why would they stop at North Korea—how about Burma? Indonesia? East Timor? Kazakhstan used to have nukes under the USSR—maybe they'd like them again?

On the other hand, if you buy the principle that adding nuclear capability to "good" countries somehow reduces the threat of nukes in "bad" countries, then why stop at Japan? Why not South Korea, too? Why not Taiwan, the Philippines, Thailand, or Vietnam? Since Burma has such a disastrously bad government, maybe the United States should insist that every country that borders Burma get nuclear weapons just to be on the safe side. If so, let's all welcome Bangladesh and Laos to the atomic age. Hey, Somalia sucks too—how about nukes for our ally Kenya? Or Djibouti? Does Djibouti have enough room for a fleet of nuclear-armed B-52 Stratofortresses?

Something's gone haywire in our politics if nonproliferation is still nominally the policy of the United States of America but a proposal like Krauthammer's isn't cause for a national spit-take. And it wasn't. "Maybe Japan should give it more thought," mused an editorialist in the *Oklahoman* while admitting, "understandably, that's a touchy subject in Japan."

Meanwhile, lurking in the background as we conjure up new excuses to spread nukes around the world, is the unattractive aging process of our own stack of nuclear weapons.

"It is becoming apparent that any number of serious problems may be waiting around the corner," the commander of the Air Force Nuclear Weapons Center said in 2011. Then he quoted one of his predecessors: "Nuclear weapons, even when sitting on a shelf, are chemistry experiments. They are constantly changing from chemical reactions inside of them." The military knows the potential of this nuclear woodpile they're responsible for, not just its deliberate capacity as weaponry but its potential to be a catastrophic mess, too. So one must assume there are a lot of precautions and fail-safes and quintuple-checks and whatnot. One must assume that everyone working around these weapons takes extra-special precautions to make sure nothing *ever* goes wrong. The history of the program, one would think, would bear that out. Nope.

In 1980, stray fuel vapors in an ICBM silo set off an explosion that blew off the 740-ton steel-and-concrete door covering the missile. The nuclear warhead was thrown more than six hundred feet toward the Ozarks. One airman was killed and twenty-one were injured. The warhead itself did not explode (praise be) or break apart and leak plutonium all over Damascus, Arkansas. So we got lucky there. The cause of that explosion was an Air Force maintenance worker who accidentally dropped a socket wrench into the darkness of the silo. The socket wrench punched a hole in the missile's fuel tank, which loosed the combustible vapors. A socket wrench did all that.

For much more of our nation's nuclear history than you'd think, we designed our nuclear systems in a way that invited peril. Through almost all of the 1960s, it was someone's genius idea that American bombers armed with live nuclear weapons should be in the air at all times, twenty-four hours a day, seven days a week, 365 days a year. The idea was that if the Soviet Union decided to annihilate the United States and succeeded in doing so, these poor pilots—somewhere over the earth—would lose radio contact with home, figure out that their country was a cinder, and, for the sake of the memory of what used to be the United States of America, make a beeline for anything Russian and drop their bombs. It would be one last "America from beyond the grave" nuclear attack on the Soviet bastards. This wasn't some cockamamie idea for a science-fiction novel or a *Dr. Strangelove* sequel; it was an approved strategy, and the bombers really did fly those missions for years.

B-52 Stratofortresses and their siblings, the B-52H high-altitude Stratofortresses, which were then in the healthful blush of youth, were supposed to be up there flying around the clock. Remember, this was an era when even television stood down for six or eight hours a night. Not our bombers. The Strategic Air Command kept a dozen or more of its bombers in the air *at all times*. A third of the SAC fleet was fully weaponized and ready for takeoff at a moment's notice *at all times*. And not only would there be a dozen or so of these 160-foot-long, 185,000-pound behemoths in the air at any given moment, but each individual plane would be flying for twenty-four hours straight, fully loaded with live nuclear weapons, fully combat-ready. They called the operation "Chrome Dome." They also called these flights "training missions," on the theory that this would somehow mitigate public or international outcry if something went wrong.

Of course, there was no way those B-52s could stay aloft for twenty-four hours at a stretch, given the way they devoured fuel. So in addition to being armed with multiple ready-to-release nuclear bombs, flying twenty-four-hour missions, they also had to refuel in midair, sometimes twice a day, every single day, 365 days a year.

What could possibly go wrong?

On January 17, 1966, a B-52 armed with four live hydrogen bombs smashed into a KC-135 tanker during a midair refueling. Conveniently enough, the way the flight patterns worked for these Chrome Dome missions, these two planes were 29,000 feet over a coastal region of Andalusian Spain while this refueling was taking place. (The tanker had taken off from an American air base in Spain called—I kid you not—Morón.) When the bomber came down, four of the live nuclear bombs came down along with it. One of them landed in a tomato field and did not blow up. One of them dropped into the Mediterranean and was found after much effort, two and a half months later, 2,600 feet down. They used a submarine.

The other two nuclear bombs blew up in the Spanish countryside. There obviously was not a nuclear blast in Spain in 1966, but these two nuclear bombs did explode. They were essentially massive dirty bombs. The conventional explosives that form part of the fuze in these nukes blew the bombs apart and scattered radioactive particles and bomb fragments all over Palomares, Spain. *Whoopsie!*

The United States arranged for 1,400 tons of radioactive Spanish earth to be removed from Spain. They shipped it to lucky, lucky Aiken, South Carolina, and kept it all as quiet as they could. And forty years later, while the United States continued to subsidize the Palomareans in their trips to Madrid for annual health checkups, and the local farmers continued to complain about depressed tomato and watermelon sales in the decades since the contamination, the incident was largely forgotten. Palomares, Spain, had become a kind of a tourist area. In 2004, they were starting the digging on a luxury condo-and-golf-course development and discovered the land there was still, as Gen. Curtis LeMay used to say, "a little bit hot." So the Spanish government confiscated all the radioactive land it could find. And after a heartfelt request from the Spanish government, the United States agreed to pay $2 million to facilitate the removal of more of Spain's accidentally overheated land.

A one-off, right?

Wrong. Just before the Palomares accident, another American plane carrying a nuclear weapon was on board an aircraft carrier called the USS *Ticonderoga*. Now, we were never supposed to have nuclear weapons anywhere near the Vietnam conflict, but . . . we did. And the *Ticonderoga* was apparently sailing its nuclear-armed way from Vietnam, where we weren't supposed to have nuclear weapons, to Japan, where we really, really, really were not supposed to have nuclear weapons for obvious historical and political reasons. And then something very bad happened. One of these fighter jets, armed with a nuclear bomb, had been hoisted up on the elevator from the lower deck when it slid right off the elevator platform, off the flight deck, and into the sea, where it sank to a depth of more than three miles—pilot, plane, nuclear bomb, and all. And it's still down there. *Whoopsie!*

A few years after the sliding-off-the-aircraft-carrier thing and the midair crash over Palomares, in 1968 it happened again: another B-52 on one of these Chrome Dome always-have-the-nukes-in-the-air missions crashed in Greenland, near an Air Force base there called Thule (*thoo*-lee). The B-52, again with four nuclear bombs on board, suffered a fire in the cockpit, and the pilots attempted to bring down the plane at an airstrip in Thule. They missed. The B-52 crash-landed on the ice and the nuclear bombs on board exploded: again, not nuclear explosions but massive dirty-bomb explosions that scattered highly radioactive particles everywhere. The people who saw it happen say that "the ice burned black." *Whoopsie!*

Local Greenlanders were called out to help with the cleanup. The Air Force personnel on the decontamination job had lots of special protective gear. The Danes . . . not so much. Aided by this underdressed Danish "civilian augmentation," the Air Force collected 500 million gallons of radioactive ice, and you don't want to know about the cancer rates of that Danish cleanup crew.

The Pentagon said forty years ago that all four nuclear bombs exploded in that Greenland crash and were subsequently destroyed, which was almost true. But not quite. Using recently declassified documents and film, the BBC reported in 2008 that three bombs exploded, but the fourth was never found. The fourth bomb is thought to have melted through the sea ice and sunk to the bottom of the ocean. Our military looked for it for a long time but figured that if they couldn't find it, then no bad guys could either. Maybe after a few more decades of global ice melt, its location will reveal itself to us.

There's also a large plutonium-packed bomb still stuck in a swampy field in Faro, North Carolina. In 1961 a busted fuel line caused a fire and then an explosion in a fully loaded nuclear B-52 during a predawn "training flight," causing the plane's right wing to more or less fall off, making it hard to fly. The crew managed to bail out before the explosion, and then the plane's nukes separated from the plane in the general breakup of the falling aircraft. What happened to those two bombs keeps me up at night sometimes. One of the bombs had a parachute on it, and that one had a soft landing—or as soft a landing as a twelve-foot-long, five-ton missile can have. Strategic Air Command found it just off Shackleford Road, its nose burrowed eighteen inches into the ground, its parachute tangled in a tree overhead, its frangible bomb casing deformed but largely intact. That bomb, the bomb by the tree, had six fuzes on it designed to prevent an accidental full nuclear detonation. The first five of the six fuzes had failed. The last one held.

The second hydrogen bomb on board that plane did not have the benefit of an open parachute. When it hit a marshy field in Faro, it was traveling at more than seven hundred miles per hour, by knowledgeable estimate, and buried itself more than twenty feet deep in the swamp. A woman living nearby remembered the impact "lit up the sky like daylight." *Whoopsie!*

A farmer named C. T. Davis owned that field, and he said that when the military came out to look for the lost bomb—heading straight for the right spot, thanks to an enormous crater—they said they were looking for an ejection seat that they had lost. A very valuable ejection seat. But the field was so muddy, so quicksandy, that they started to lose their excavating equipment into the crater before they could get the bomb out of the hole. So they decided to just leave it there, and got an easement from the Davis family that said nobody could ever dig deeper than five feet on that piece of land. If you're ever in the neighborhood and want to play with your metal detector, you can find the exact spot on Google Earth. It's just immediately west of Big Daddy's Road.

Overall, the United States admits to having lost track of eleven nuclear bombs over the years. I don't know about other countries, but that's what we admit to. And we're regarded as top-drawer, safety-wise. We're known to go the extra mile, like in 1984, when a computer malfunction nearly triggered the launch of a Minuteman III ICBM, and some resourceful missileer parked an armored car on top of the silo in a heroic effort to prevent the accidental opening salvo of World War III. These things all happened back in the good old days, when we were really minding the store.

Here's what happened more recently, since our awesome nuclear responsibilities slipped a bit from the forefront of our national consciousness: On August 29, 2007, at around 8:20 a.m., a weapons-handling team entered one of those Minot igloos (#1857, to be precise) to retrieve the first of two pylons, each with six twenty-one-foot-long cruise missiles attached. This had become a familiar drill in the previous few months, ever since the secretary of defense had ordered four hundred of these aging missiles off-line. The Minot team had already successfully shipped about half of them to be mothballed at Barksdale Air Force Base in Louisiana. The crewmembers' familiarity with the task may have been why they didn't much bother with the safety checklist.

The first pylon in question, GZ377, had two letter-sized "Tac-Ferry" signs attached to it, signaling that it had been prepped for the flight, or tactical ferry, to Barksdale. That meant that the silver nuclear warheads had been removed and replaced with harmless dummy weights. Nobody on the weapons crew followed the mandated procedure of shining a flashlight into a postage-stamp-sized, diamond-shaped window on the missile to verify that no nukes were on board. Nor did the tow-rig driver shine his light into that little window—as his Technical Order required him to—before hooking the pylon to his trailer. The driver later said he was "under the impression that this package for sure was TacFerry." For sure.

The second missile pylon on the schedule sheet, GZ203, was stored just down the way in igloo 1854. The handlers were in and out of igloo 1854 in twenty-two minutes, not enough time to do the most cursory of checks. The junior member of the team was apparently told not to bother with the whole flashlight thing—not that he really knew what that meant, because he was new on the job and had never performed any such check. The second tow driver, as far as anyone could see, also failed to check the little window for signs of nuclear warheads aboard. In fact, one member of the team said he did not see anyone even carrying a flashlight that day, much less putting one to use.

Oh, and one more thing: the second pylon displayed no Tac-Ferry signs, but this did not raise any red flags for the team. Nobody called a higher-ranking officer to ask why GZ203 lacked a TacFerry placard or checked the computer database to verify the status of the pylon. So nobody on the team got the information that a few weeks earlier an officer at Minot had made a switch and ordered an older pylon prepped for shipment instead. She put it on the official schedule. Problem was, nobody ever checked the updated official schedule. So the prepped pylon with its dummy warheads sat undisturbed in its igloo that morning, while the tow driver carrying the unplacarded GZ203 pulled onto Bomber Boulevard, completely unaware that he was hauling six real operational nukes.

In the eight hours it took to attach the two pylons to a forty-five-year-old B-52H Stratofortress, no member of the loading crew noticed the warheads aboard, or the fact that one of the pylons was not marked for shipment. The six nuclear bombs strapped to the Stratofortress then sat on the runway unguarded except for a chain-link fence from five o'clock that afternoon until early the next morning, when an aircrew from the 2nd Bomb Wing out of Barksdale arrived to prep for flight. Happily, there was a member of the flight crew, the instructor radar navigator, whose job it was to check and see what exactly his aircraft was carrying before the bomber could take off.

But the navigator had apparently been infected with the general feeling about this mission of decommissioning old missiles; as one of his fellow airmen put it, "We're only ferrying carcasses from Point A to Point B." Others told investigators, without a hint of shame, that they weren't sure that verifying meant, like, actually physically checking something. And so it was that "the Instructor Radar Navigator only did a 'spot check' on one missile, and only on the right pylon loaded with nuclear-inert payloads," according to the report of an after-incident investigation. "If the IRN had accomplished a full and complete weapons preflight, the IRN should have discovered the nuclear warheads." He did not.

The bomber, named, interestingly, *Doom 99*, departed North

Dakota on schedule on the morning of August 30, 2007. "The takeoff from Minot," noted the after-incident report, "was uneventful." The flight itself was notable: it was the first time in forty years a nuclear-armed bomber had traversed US airspace without clearance. Six nuclear warheads—each one capable of Hiroshima-size damage times ten—were unwittingly flown 1,400 miles, from up around the US–Canadian border to within a few hundred miles of the Gulf of Mexico, within plutonium-spittin' distance of Sioux Falls and Sioux City and Omaha and Kansas City and Tulsa. The instructor pilot on *Doom 99* was not qualified for a nuclear mission. In fact, she later told investigators, she had never physically touched a nuclear weapon.

Happily, the nukes did get back to land without incident. They then sat unguarded on the runway at Barksdale Air Force Base in Louisiana for another nine hours before the ground crew there discovered that its command had accidentally acquired six new nuclear warheads, and they decided they'd better get them in a safe place, under guard. All told, six nuclear warheads were misplaced for a day and a half.

Here was the good news, according to the testimony of Air Force generals at the Senate Armed Services Committee on the occasion of presenting findings from the blue-ribbon review of the incident: "During the incident there was never any unsafe condition, and the incident was promptly reported to our national leadership including the Secretary of Defense and the President. These weapons were secure and always in the hands of America's Airmen."

"General," the chairman of that Senate committee responded, "I'm a little taken aback by your statement that warheads were—there was never a safety issue and they were always under the control of American pilots. Did the pilots know they had nuclear weapons on board?"

"Sir, they did not."

"So when you say they were under the control of the pilots, not knowing that you have nuclear weapons on board makes a difference, doesn't it?"

"Yes sir, it does. The intent behind that statement is to make it clear that they never migrated off the aircraft anywhere else."

Migrated?

As for whether or not an accident involving *Doom 99* could have occasioned a spread of plutonium from the warheads, one of the generals at the hearing was forced to plead ignorance. "I'm a logistician, not a technician. But knowing the knowledge of how a system is developed, and that's part of the reliability of the system, is that there is no inadvertent detonation of the system."

"I'm not talking about detonation," the chairman said. "I'm talking about could the plutonium be released inadvertently if this weapon were smashed into the ground from fifteen thousand feet."

"That piece," said the general, "I would not know."

It was left to the senator to remind the Air Force that the United States was still cleaning up pieces of Spain forty years after the Palomares accident.

One of the first things the Air Force did in the aftermath of the Minot-to-Barksdale debacle was to institute no-warning inspections, and the first one they ran was on the 2nd Bomb Wing. Thirty-one inspectors (including six civilian augmentees) were detailed to assess the Barksdale nuclear team, and they spent ten months' worth of man-days doing it. (That was the assessment that turned up the wing fungus.) Barksdale's first inspector-assigned task was to stick a pylon full of cruise missiles onto a Stratofortress bomber and ready the bomber for a combat mission. The first try failed because the $450,000 bomb hoists kept malfunctioning and the electrical generators crapped out three times. After fourteen hours and two separate "mating/demating" operations, the loading crew decided to give up and start from scratch. The second try was delayed when the loading team parked the weapons bay over uneven pavement and the bomb hoist could not gain proper purchase, and then delayed again when the bomb hoist "boogie wheel" failed. The second mating attempt was aborted after fifteen hours. On the fourth attempt—after only a minor lift-arm malfunction—the Barksdale technicians managed to generate a combat-ready mission.

The 2nd Bomb Wing received a rating of Excellent from the inspectors in the following areas:

- Weapons Maintenance Technical Operations

- Storage and Maintenance Facilities

- Motor Vehicle Operations

- Safety

They had to settle for a Satisfactory in Loading and Mating. The inspectors did give extra-credit points to the loading and mating team for gamely fighting through the failure of six weapons load trailers, five power generators, a power-controller-unit trailer malfunction, and a range of unfortunate tire-pressure issues. "The weapons loading community overcame numerous equipment malfunctions," the inspectors reported. They also commented favorably on the loading community's "strong two-person concept adherence," its "cohesive squadron teamwork," and its "highly effective communication." The inspectors did ding the loading and mating team for not prepositioning chocks to keep the loading trailers from accidentally bashing into the bomber, and suggested that they get some foam cutouts in the weapons expediter truck to keep the enabling switches and data cartridge safe during transport. But they gave Team Barksdale a thumbs-up for successfully preparing one bombing run . . . after three failed attempts . . . at somewhere past the thirty-hour mark.

"It's very, very difficult to believe they could receive a passing grade on any kind of inspection when they were unable to generate a single successful nuclear sortie until the fourth attempt," one weapons expert told the pseudonymous blogger (and former airman) "Nate Hale," after reading the report that Hale had jimmied free from the Pentagon through a Freedom of Information Act request.

Hale quoted a second retired Air Force weaponeer, who was more to the point: "Tell me this is a joke."

Still and all, the Air Force and the Pentagon decided the whole Minot-to-Barksdale mishap could be a lemons-into-lemonade moment. Apparently we needed some renewed attention to our nuclear-handling skills—we just hadn't known it. That seemed all the more true when, a few months later, we discovered that we had erroneously shipped to Taiwan four nose-cone fuzes designed to trigger nuclear explosions in lieu of the helicopter battery packs Taiwan had requested, and that it had taken a year and a half to discover the accidental switcheroo. So the Air Force and the Pentagon embarked on some serious soul-searching, which took the form of a mess of incident investigations and blue-ribbon reviews and task-force studies to see how our atomic hair trigger was faring in the twenty-first century.

When all the investigations and reviews and task-force studies were completed, the consensus was clear: they all found erosion and degradation and a general web of sloth and anxiety within our nation's nuclear mission. The root cause? Lack of self-esteem. The men and women handling the nukes were suffering a debilitating lack of pride. Their promotion rates, it was noted, were well behind the service average. We had to remind them in big ways and small that they were important to us, that the "pursuit of the nuclear zero-defect culture" and "generating a culture of nuclear excellence" wasn't just hot air. What the program needed was resources: better pay, new layers of high-level managers dedicated to the nuclear mission, upgraded computer systems for tracking all the nuclear nuts and bolts, a commitment to more (and more serious) nuclear-training exercises, and of course, you know, a bigger program to upgrade and modernize the hardware. Money! "Definitely," the logistician Air Force general told the Senate's key nuclear oversight committee, "a re-look at recapitalizing that."

Do I hear nine trillion?

Even though there's been a lot of blue-ribbon hand-wringing about how best to sustain and rejuvenate our big, leaky, can't-quite-keep-track-of-our-warheads nuclear-bomb infrastructure, our worries about it haven't caused us to re-ask the big question of *why* we still have it. Given the manifest difficulties of maintaining our apocalyptic nuclear stockpile, how many nuclear bombs does the United States need to complete every conceivable military mission in which we'd use them?

An attack with one of the nuclear weapons we've got now would cause an explosion about ten times the size of the one at Hiroshima. Can you imagine us setting off two such bombs now? How about five of them? Fifteen? Fifty? What do we imagine would be on the list of fifty targets for those fifty American nuclear blasts, each ten times the size of Hiroshima?

Our current arsenal of nukes is about 5,000 weapons. Of

those, between 2,000 and 2,500 are deployed and ready to use—about the same number as Russia has ready. Thanks to the New START treaty negotiated in President Obama's first year in office, that number is slated to eventually go down to 1,500 in both countries. But to get the Senate to agree to the deal with Russia reducing our total number of ready-to-launch nukes, President Obama also agreed to a huge new increase in the size of America's nuclear weapons infrastructure. Fewer weapons, but *more* money. A lot more. To secure the two-thirds vote necessary in the Senate to ratify the treaty, the initial Obama administration plan was to commit an extra $185 billion over ten years to our nukes—a nearly 10 percent annual increase. This was in 2009 and 2010, at a time when our economy was cratering and Republicans were insisting that the rest of the budget be slashed. "This might be," noted one nuclear expert, "what's necessary to buy the votes for ratification."

Actually, it wasn't enough. Republicans in the Senate thought this treaty-ratification fight was a good chance to monetize the nuclear-bomb infrastructure going forward. They evinced furrow-browed concern that the Obamanauts were not serious and might allow the whole reinvestment in nukes idea to "peter out." Six months later, the Obama folks came back with more goodies. They added another whopping 10 percent to the next annual budget request, reiterated their promise to keep nuclear subs continuously patrolling both the Atlantic and the Pacific, and to stand ready—in a phrase that seemed to have migrated from the previous administration—to "surge additional submarines in a crisis." They agreed to spend whatever it took to keep the ICBMs and the B-52s ready to fly for another full generation.

Settle in, Missileers, it's gonna be at least another few decades.

The Obama administration said it was even ready to fund

a new nuclear-capable remote-controlled long-range nuclear bomber. How did eighty to one hundred nuclear-armed drones sound? Nuclear-armed flying robots. On remote control. What could possibly go wrong? "The most robust, sustained commitment to modernizing our nuclear deterrent since the end of the Cold War" was what the head of the National Nuclear Security Administration called Obama's treaty-ratification goodie bag. "My predecessor put it best, saying he 'would have killed' for budgets like this."

A couple of months after the Grand Bargain that bought the START treaty ratification, in 2011 a team of Air Force generals was back on Capitol Hill to share with a handful of senators the wonderful strides they had made in the three years since all that bad press that surrounded the six lost nukes; they were happy to explain just exactly what America was getting for the extra $650 million Congress had appropriated to shore up our nuclear program in the wake of Minot-to-Barksdale. For instance, there were the new posts manned by the generals testifying that day. ("The positions Lt. Gen. Kowalski, Maj. Gen. Chambers, and Brig. Gen. Harencak now hold were all established as a result of that mistake," the subcommittee chairman noted by way of introduction.) The generals assured the congressional oversight committee that the Air Force's relatively new oversight bureau, the Nuclear Weapons Center, was being spectacularly collaborative. The Pentagon had even invented a new someone with whom the Nuclear Weapons Center could exercise teamwork. "One of our most vital collaborations is with the newly created office of the Program Executive Officer (PEO) for Strategic Systems. The PEO . . . has assumed the responsibility for the development and acquisition of future systems and for modernization efforts while [the Nuclear Weapons Center] focuses on day-to-day operations and sustainment." The Nuclear Weapons Center commander assured Congress that they were also being more proactive and forward-looking! They'd find problems before they hit the crisis stage; they'd train their personnel properly and give them working equipment and tools. (Let's hope somebody thought of safety leashes for the socket wrenches.) They'd already merged databases so we'd no longer accidentally ship nuclear parts to warehouses in Taiwan or less-friendly countries. Oh, and they were determined to fix that problem with the sophisticated and complex Mk21 fuzes. They'd work that out.

Sadly, only two senators showed up for the hearing: the subcommittee's chairman and its ranking member. And even those guys didn't feel that we had too many nuclear doodads to keep track of. This was not what was keeping them up at night. In fact, Republican senator Jeff Sessions of Alabama was mostly worried that the new nuclear arms reduction treaty was like some bureaucratic seductress beckoning us toward dangerous cuts in our nuclear forces. For the senator's money, the president seemed awfully eager to actually comply with this new treaty.

Sessions wanted the generals to know he was going to make sure their new positions were safe and sound, that he was going to see to it that there was plenty of arsenal to keep them all busy for a very long time. "Last month, along with forty of my colleagues," Senator Sessions told the military men, "I sent a letter to the president regarding our desire to be consulted on any further reduction plans to the nuclear stockpile. The New START treaty was only signed a few weeks ago, yet the administration is moving forward in my opinion at a pace that justifies the phrase 'reckless,' pursuing more reductions at an expedited and potentially destabilizing pace."

Yeah, slimming down the stockpile of our thousands of nuclear weapons, that would be reckless. That would be unsafe.

Epilogue

You Build It, You Own It

If the military drifts away from
its people in this country, that
is a catastrophic outcome we as
a country can't tolerate.

—Adm. Mike Mullen, chairman of the
Joint Chiefs of Staff, 2007-2011

HAVING GROWN UP IN THE SUBURBS IN CALIFORNIA, WHEN I
moved to rural New England I was surprised by how much
god-awful work it takes to keep a still-life landscape looking un-
changed. Leave stuff alone and it blows up. Not metaphorically, literally: if you leave wet hay in a silo, the decomposition of the plant
material can make the hay (and your silo) catch fire. And when the
trick isn't keeping things dry, it's keeping things wet. The logging
company I buy firewood from turns its sprinklers on big piles of
logs (hey, that's my firewood!) to stop them from spontaneously
combusting on cold days. Rot's the problem there too—simple, inexorable decay. Rot makes heat, and if there's dying wood in the

middle of that big pile, cold air hitting that rot-generated heat can create a chimney effect. If that channels enough heat over the dry layers of wood in there, then *kablooey:* your firewood pile has just turned itself into a bonfire without virtue of a match. It catches fire just from sitting there too long, unattended.

Our place in Hampshire County looked like a horror-movie haunted house when we moved in—broke-down busted, over-grown, spongy stairs, clapboards gaping like black teeth. It looked like that because it had been abandoned for . . . one winter. One long winter untended rendered the place virtually uninhabitable. In our beautiful, unforgiving little hamlet, we developed a shorthand for explaining what had caused the need for a repair of some kind: "The earth took it back."

It is unsettling to realize that the earth takes back even nu-clear missiles, that they're growing wing fungus down in Shreve-port. But stuff left sitting around, unused, still needs attention; there's a cost and a duty that attend to everything we own. If we built it, we're responsible for it, unless we take it down and take it apart. Maybe it's a variation on Colin Powell's cautionary "Pot-tery Barn Rule"—you not only own it if you break it, you own it if you build it too. If you've *ever* built it, you own it. And after two centuries of a standing army, and two generations of mas-sive military buildup—the defense budget doubling and then doubling again—we've built ourselves a whole lot of national se-curity state. We haven't made a habit of taking this stuff down, ever, of taking it apart. And we haven't made a habit of consider-ing the consequences of just letting it roll along unchecked.

That's not to say that some of it isn't amazing. A fact that's underappreciated in the civilian world but very well appre-ciated in our military is that the US Armed Forces right now are absolutely stunning in their lethality. Deploy, deploy,

deploy . . . practice, practice, practice. The US military was the best and best-equipped fighting force on earth even before 9/11. Now, after a solid decade of war, they're almost unrecognizably better. Early worries such as how much gear we were burning through in Iraq were solved the way we always solve problems like that now: we doubled the military's procurement budget between 2000 and 2010.

Consider also the state of the reserves. Thanks to the unprecedented deployment pace of the post-9/11 wars, gone are the days of the weekend warriors and the three-weeks-a-year training at some run-down outpost in the States. "For years, [reserve] soldiers would walk out the door on Fridays and say, 'I've got to go play Army this weekend,'" the adjutant general of the Utah National Guard told a reporter from the *Salt Lake Tribune*. "I don't think that's the case anymore. We are the military to most citizens today. If you think of a uniform, you're probably thinking of a Guardsman or a Reservist, who is your neighbor." Probably your very physically fit neighbor. As a first sergeant who joined the National Guard in 1986 told the same paper, "There were a lot of overweight soldiers in the Guard back then who stuck around forever and talked big." Not anymore. Not with the way we use the Guard and Reserves now, he explained: "You can't [be overweight] if you have to put on body armor."

America's reservists have been in top gear or on high idle for ten years now, and their bosses say they want to keep them that way. "If we're going to train to that level," says the general in charge of the Army Reserves, "then my position is we've got to use them."

Contrast that with LBJ explaining in 1965 that he didn't want to call up the reserves because that would be "too dramatic"—it would be a shock to the nation's system to tap the Guard and Reserves, even with eighty thousand US troops already deployed in Vietnam. Peacetime and civilian life used to be the norm for reservists; war, the unsettling aberration. Now that's reversed.

As the gap has closed between regular active-duty forces and the reserves, the gap between those fighters and the rest of us has never been wider. One of the stranger political developments of the post-9/11 era was the backlash against efforts to close that gap. On Wednesday, April 28, 2004, about a month after the first anniversary of the Iraq War, Ted Koppel announced that on Friday, April 30, his program, *Nightline*, would honor Americans killed in Iraq by showing their faces and reading all of their names. It would be a televised memorial to those who had died in a year of war. There are, of course, war memorials to fallen heroes in every town and hamlet in America, but critics pounced on Koppel as though he'd proposed mugging the wounded at Walter Reed rather than airing a solemn memorial to the dead. His critics accused him of undermining the war effort, of being unpatriotic. The pro-war *Washington Post* accused Koppel of mounting a cynical ratings stunt, headlining its news article on the subject "On *Nightline*, a Grim Sweeps Roll Call." The conservative Sinclair Broadcast Group immediately announced they'd boycott *Nightline* on all of their stations that were ABC affiliates.

Koppel said he was surprised by the controversy. But the controversy itself showed that something had changed about how a war abroad was being viewed at home. The simple and actual fact of American lives lost in the post-9/11 wars was not just a shared source of grief and national honor but had become something to be kept at a distance; casualties, for a time at least, became bad politics.

From 2003 to 2008, the Bush administration exercised a tight hold on imagery about the cost of the wars. Not only were news photographers banned from the solemn transfer ceremonies for flag-draped caskets at Dover Air Base, but the president and vice president did not attend military funerals. Even when families of fallen soldiers wanted to invite the media to cover a funeral or the return of remains, the government maneuvered as best it could to prevent such coverage. The Pentagon ultimately even effectively banned images of wounded troops in Iraq when it quietly changed its rules to require that news agencies get signed consent forms from soldiers photographed after they were wounded.

With tax cuts in wartime, with no sense of collective national sacrifice on behalf of the war effort, with less than 1 percent of the American population taking up arms to fight, with US casualties politically and literally shielded from public view, the cumulative effect was to normalize our national wartime. We've become a nation "at peace with being at war," in the words of the *New York Times* media critic David Carr.

And as the country learned to be untroubled by the fact that we had troops at war, troops coming home from those wars learned to look out for themselves. "It's like AIDS was thirty years ago," Iraq veteran Paul Rieckhoff told me in 2011. "It's a huge crisis for us, but no one else in the country thinks they're us. No one even thinks they're *like* us." Shortly after his return from Baghdad in 2004, Rieckhoff founded Iraq and Afghanistan Veterans of America, the first and largest group of veterans of our post-9/11 wars. IAVA's slogan is "We've Got Your Back"—with the implication that it might not feel like anyone else does. Online, they've organized a "Community of Veterans" social media site, essentially a version of Facebook for Iraq and Afghanistan veterans only. Their 2010 public service announcement, titled "Alone," won the advertising industry's Ogilvy Award for its disorienting turn-Norman-Rockwell-on-his-head depiction of a soldier's lonely homecoming, until he finds other Iraq and Afghanistan veterans.

Another PSA, called "Camo," shows empty street scenes, and a newly returned veteran at home, sitting at his computer; the voice-over says, "You may feel like you're all alone," and then the seemingly empty streets are revealed to be camouflaging other veterans, hiding in plain sight. The visual trick gives way to the emotional payoff of the ad—the palpable relief of the once-isolated soldier who finds other veterans to connect with.

A 2011 Pew poll found that 84 percent of post-9/11 veterans felt the public didn't understand the problems faced by service members and their families. It also found that more than two-thirds of Americans believe the disproportionate burden shouldered by those who have served is "just part of being in the military." Iraq and Afghanistan veterans are nearly twice as likely as veterans of other wars to say they found readjusting to civilian life to be difficult. The distance between the lived experience of Iraq and Afghanistan veterans and the rest of the country since 9/11 ought to unsettle all of us, not just veterans.

As we've pushed military experience further and further away from civilian life, we've also pushed decision making about the use of the military further and further away from political debate.

"We don't have any enemies in Congress," a senior defense official told me in 2011. "We have to fight Congress to cut programs, not keep them." And those are basically the only fights the Pentagon ever loses. To paraphrase Ronald Reagan plagiarizing Sen. James F. Byrnes talking smack about government bureaucracy, if you want to achieve immortality, see what you can do about getting yourself turned into a Pentagon program. You may eventually grow wing fungus, but you'll never die. The nuclear weapons complex, the counterinsurgency nation-building apparatus,

$20 billion worth of mine-resistant, ambush-protected ve-
hicles with V-shaped hulls to disperse the energy from bombs
underneath—we built 'em, we own 'em, and we're looking for
ways to use 'em. "The Army has only recently started to plan to
incorporate MRAPs into its force structure to take advantage
of this investment," a recent think-tank study found, "instead of
mothballing them as they withdraw from Iraq." Maybe we could
park them on top of malfunctioning missile silos. The tasks we
assign to our service members are hard enough without asking
them to get their work done in the world's largest organization,
dragging around decades' worth of clattering battle rattle in the
form of defunct and deathless programs.

We all have an interest in America having an outstanding
military, but that aim is not helped by exempting the military
from the competition for resources. With no check on its growth
and no rival for its political influence, the superfunded, su-
perempowered national security state has become a leviathan.

The artificial primacy of defense among our national priorities is a constant unearned windfall for some, but it's privation
for the rest of America; it steals from what we could be and
can do. In Econ 101, they teach that the big-picture fight over
national priorities is guns versus butter. Now it's butter versus
margarine—guns get a pass.

Overall, we're weaker for it, and at enormous cost.

As the national security state has metastasized, decisions
to use force have become painless and slick, almost automatic.
The disincentives to war deliberately built into our American
system of government—particularly the citizen-soldier, and
leaving the power to declare war with Congress instead of the
president—we've worked around them. We ought to see that
constitutional inheritance as a national treasure, yet we've di-
vested ourselves of it without much of a debate.

It's not done and forever, though. We can go back. Policy decisions matter. Our institutions matter. The structure of government matters. They can all be changed. We saw that happen over the last forty years. There were specific decisions made in time that set us on our current war-is-normal course. If specific decisions in time landed us where we are today, we can unmake those specific decisions. We can walk them back. We could at least start with a to-do list.

- Going to war, being at war, should be painful for the entire country, from the start. Henceforth, when we ship the troops off to battle, let's pay for it. War costs money. Lots and lots of money. Whenever we start a new one, we should raise the money to pay for it, contemporaneously. Taxes, war bonds, what-have-you. "Freedom isn't free" shouldn't be a bumper sticker—it should be policy.

- Let's do away with the secret military. If we are going to use drones to vaporize people in Pakistan and Yemen and Somalia, the Air Force should operate those drones, and pull the trigger. And we should know about it. If the CIA is doing military missions, the agency needs to be as accountable as the military is, and the same goes for the policy makers giving them their orders. The chain of command should never be obscured by state secrets. Special Forces can be unconstrained and clandestine to the bad guys, but not to Congress.

- Let's quit asking the military to do things best left to our State Department, or the Peace Corps or FEMA. And let's please stop expecting military leaders to make judgments and decisions about policy. If presidential candidates talk about "deferring to military commanders" as to whether or not to bomb Iran, stand up and point at them and holler until they understand how backward they've got it. That's got to stop. It's no favor to the military, and it's an affront to the Constitution.

- Our Guard and Reserves need to be the Guard and Reserves again, which is to say the institutions that weave civilian life and military life together. The life of a National Guardsman or Guardswoman should be mostly a peacetime, civilian life. When we ship these men and women off to war, civilian communities all over America should feel that loss.

- Let's wind back the privatization of war and the military's dependence on contractors for what used to be military functions. Our troops need to peel their own potatoes again, drive their own supply trucks, build their own barracks, guard their own generals. Enough with the LOGCAP boondoggle. Private contractors are not cheaper, and they are certainly not indispensable. We operated without them for a long, long time, and did just fine, thank you very much. And when private contractors on our payroll commit illegal acts, like statutory rape, or murder, or outright fraud, they should be prosecuted, not given more contracts.

- If all those Team B cranks in the hawk nest want to indulge in exhaustive paranoia, they can knock themselves out. But the rest of us should try to keep it together. We can cede their point that the world is a threatening place. We can cede their point that the US military is a remarkable and worthy fighting force. But we ought to realize by now (see Korea, see Vietnam, see Afghanistan, see Iraq, see Iran) that deploying the US military, or dealing billions of dollars a year of arms to our ally of the moment that can serve as a regional rival to our enemy of the moment, is not always the best way to make threats go away. Our military and weapons prowess is a fantastic and perfectly weighted hammer, but that doesn't make every international problem a nail.

- Let's ensure that our nuclear infrastructure shrinks to fit our country's realistic nuclear mission. Let's decide exactly what we mean to deter with our nukes, and expend just exactly what we need to do that. There's a cost to keeping these chemistry experiments lying around for decades. Let's up the way-too-slow decommissioning process and shrink our nuclear inventory before another pylon of live missiles goes walkies.

- And finally, there's the Gordian knot of executive power. It needs a sword something fierce. The glory of war success will always attach itself to the president, so presidents are always going to be prey to the temptation to make war. That's a generic truth of power, and all the more reason to take decision making about war out of the hands of the executive. It is not one man's responsibility. The "imperial presidency" malarkey that was invented to save Ronald Reagan's neck in Iran-Contra, and that played as high art throughout the career of Richard Cheney, is a radical departure from previous views of presidential power, and it should be taught and understood that way. This isn't a partisan thing—constitutionalists left and right have equal reason to worry over the lost constraint on the executive. Republicans and Democrats alike have options to vote people into Congress who are determined to stop with the chickenshittery and assert the legislature's constitutional prerogatives on war and peace. It would make a difference and help reel us back toward balance and normalcy.

None of this is impossible. This isn't bigger than us. Decisions about national security are ours to make. And the good news is that this isn't rocket science—we don't need to reinvent Fogbank. We just need to revive that old idea of America as a deliberately peaceable nation. That's not simply our inheritance, it's our responsibility.

Notes on Sources

The source notes that follow are not intended to be comprehensive. They're meant to give you a sense of where I went digging, and where you might follow up yourself if you're interested in learning more. You will have found many citations in the body of the book, but it would have been jarring to keep stopping for specific attribution, especially when a fact has two or three or four sources; where there are conflicts I have used my best judgment.

One general note in dealing with presidents in particular: whenever possible, I have tried to rely on their own words. The less recent ones—Johnson, Nixon, Reagan, Bush the elder, and Clinton—already have accessible libraries full of diaries and documents and speech texts and audiotapes and even video. If you're interested in chasing down specific notes or utterances of a president of that era, having a date and key word in mind is often enough to find what you're looking for online.

When I was unable to get an official transcription of an important press conference or hearing, I found that newspapers like the *New York Times* had often provided its readers a pretty full account (or even a transcription) the day after.

Prologue: Is It Too Late to Descope This?

Hampshire County, Massachusetts, and Wazir Akbar Khān in Kabul are places I have seen with my own eyes. The debacle of the water treatment plant in Fallujah is detailed in official government reports made by the Special Inspector General for Iraq Reconstruction. The 2010 *Washington Post* series "Top Secret America" by Dana Priest and

William M. Arkin is a seminal account of our shoveling good money after bad into the vague and very profitable intel and "security" industries after 9/11. The series is available online at washingtonpost.com with a lot of supporting documentation and interactive resources—it's worth every prize it won and more.

Chapter 1: G.I. Joe, Ho Chi Minh, and the American Art of Fighting About Fighting

Direct quotes from Thomas Jefferson, James Madison, Alexander Hamilton, and Abraham Lincoln have been taken from letters, speeches, or writings that can all be found at the Library of Congress. Sources there include the Thomas Jefferson Papers, the James Madison Papers, the Abraham Lincoln Papers, *Annals of Congress*, and *The Records of the Federal Convention of 1787*, in *Farrand's Records*, vol 2. Hamilton's Federalist Paper #8 is central to the argument in this chapter.

For troop numbers across the years I have relied on the *Records of the American Expeditionary Forces (World War I)*, available at the National Archives, and official statistics compiled and published by the US Department of Defense. Also helpful was the US Army Center for Military History's *American Military History*, vol. 2, *The United States Army in a Global Era, 1917–2003*.

Instrumental to my understanding of Gen. Creighton Abrams was the work of Lewis Sorley, most especially his book *Thunderbolt: General Creighton Abrams and the Army of His Times*. Robert Timberg's *The Nightingale's Song* provided important insight on the breach between civilian and soldier that cracked open during the Vietnam War. Also helpful was Neil Sheehan's *A Bright Shining Lie: John Paul Vann and America in Vietnam*.

Lyndon B. Johnson's taped conversation with Sen. Richard Russell on July 26, 1965, is available at the University of Virginia's Miller Center, Presidential Recordings Program. It's accessible online, and well worth listening to, even just for fun. (The same archive also includes the amazing tape of LBJ ordering pants to be delivered to the White House—someone should have made that into a ringtone by now.) Also available there is the April 18, 1971, recording of Nixon discussing Abrams with Henry Kissinger.

The specifics of the Senate Foreign Relations Committee's visit to President Gerald Ford's White House are found in Memorandum of Conversation, Monday, April 14, 1975, declassified in 1992 and available online at the Gerald R. Ford Presidential Digital Library. Other details come from *A Time to Heal: The Autobiography of Gerald R. Ford*.

Chapter 2: A Nation at Peace Everywhere in the World

In understanding Ronald Reagan's life and politics I was greatly aided by Edmund Morris's authorized biography, *Dutch: A Memoir of Ronald Reagan*, as well as Lou Cannon's books, including *Governor Reagan: His Rise to Power; Reagan;* and *President Reagan: The Role of a Lifetime*. Particularly helpful on Reagan's experience in World War II was *Ronald Reagan in Hollywood: Movies and Politics*, by Stephen Vaughn. I also drew from Reagan's autobiography, *An American Life*.

Contemporaneous coverage by the *New York Times* and *Time* magazine provided nice color to the story of the 1976 Republican presidential primaries.

On the politics of the Panama Canal in the late 1970s, I benefited from and highly recommend Adam Clymer's *Drawing the Line at the Big Ditch: The Panama Canal Treaties and the Rise of the Right*. Also helpful was William F. Buckley's *The Reagan I Knew*. The text of Reagan's "To Restore America" speech is available at the Reagan Presidential Foundation and Library Archives. *Reagan, In His Own Hand: The Writings of Ronald Reagan That Reveal His Revolutionary Vision for America* was a useful source not only for the text of Reagan's radio broadcasts, but for his own thinking.

For Reagan's Fum-Poo experience, *Rear Gunner* and *Winning Your Wings*, among others, are watchable via YouTube.

The text of President Jimmy Carter's 1979 speech "Crisis of Confidence" is available at the University of Virginia's Miller Center.

The text quoted from "A Soldier's Faith" is found in *An Address by Oliver Wendell Holmes Delivered on Memorial Day, May 30, 1895, at a Meeting Called by the Graduating Class of Harvard University* (Boston: Little, Brown and Company, 1895). Louis Menand's insightful book *The Metaphysical Club: A Story of Ideas in America* was of great help in understanding Oliver Wendell Holmes Jr. and the way he was shaped by his experiences in the Civil War.

Chapter 3: Let 'Er Fly

The John Travolta Army recruiting ad is available on YouTube, as are the "Be All That You Can Be" commercials—putting them side by side makes for a dissonant but interesting comparison. *The U.S. Army's Transition to the All-Volunteer Force, 1968–1974*, by Robert K. Griffith Jr.; *I Want You! The Evolution of the All-Volunteer Force*, by Bernard Rostker; and "The Army in the Marketplace: Recruiting an All-Volunteer Force" (*Journal of American History* 4, vol. 1, June 2007) by Beth Bailey provided good color on recruiting and advertising.

Edmund Morris and Lou Cannon were again helpful in understanding Reagan's first presidential term, as was Steven F. Hayward's *The Age of Reagan: The Conservative Counterrevolution, 1980–1989*. I am indebted to Richard Reeves, especially, for his book *President Reagan: Triumph of Imagination*. His reporting provided much detail on Martin Treptow, David Stockman, and Alexander Haig, among others. David Sirota's book *Back to Our Future: How the 1980s Explain the World We Live in Now—Our Culture, Our Politics, Our Everything* is a great reference for anybody who wants to understand that strange time.

If you have a few days to spare, you can view the entirety of Ronald Reagan's testimony in the John Poindexter criminal trial via YouTube. Nicholas Goncharoff testified about Lenin to the United States Senate Subcommittee to Investigate the Administration of the Internal Security Act and Other Internal Security Laws on July 15, 1954.

For information and analysis of Team B, I relied on its own words in *Intelligence Community Experiment in Competitive Analysis. Soviet Strategic Objectives: An Alternative View. Report of Team "B"* (US Central Intelligence Agency, 1976). I was also informed by Anne Hessing

Cahn's *Killing Détente* and her 1993 article (with John Prado) "Team B: The Trillion Dollar Experiment" in the *Bulletin of Atomic Scientists;* as well as former CIA analyst Willard C. Matthias's candid book *America's Strategic Blunders: Intelligence Analysis and National Security, 1936–1991.*

The 1980s-era editions of *Soviet Military Power* make for sometimes terrifying and sometimes humorous reading, but read them with a counterpoint guide at hand: Tom Gervasi's *Soviet Military Power: The Pentagon's Propaganda Document, Annotated and Corrected.*

Chapter 4: Isle of Spice

More than you'd guess has been written about the very quick and very jumbled combat operations in Grenada. For the soldiers' views of both the planning and the execution of the invasion I was aided by the memoirs of Capt. Robert Gormly, Col. John T. Carney, and command master CPO Dennis Chalker; journalistic accounts from Orr Kelly, as well as a richly detailed section of Rick Atkinson's *The Long Gray Line: The American Journey of West Point's Class of 1966;* and by *The Rucksack War,* something of an official history—great for timeline—by Edgar F. Raines Jr. Raines also wrote "The Interagency Process and the Decision to Intervene in Grenada," which is more compelling reading than the title might suggest.

US-Grenada Relations: Revolution and Intervention in the Backyard, by Gary Williams, was helpful in seeing the wider story. Also a worthwhile read is Eastern Caribbean Regional Security Policy (NSC-NSDD-105), National Security Decision Directives, Reagan Administration, available online or from the Ronald Reagan Library.

The domestic political scene was well covered by major newspapers and magazines at the time, and I benefited from that coverage, but I was also aided by Tip O'Neill's autobiography, *Man of the House,* and Reagan's own autobiography, as well as his White House diaries, which are available in the Reagan Presidential Foundation and Library archives as well as in the book *The Reagan Diaries.*

Goldwater's dust-up with the Reagan administration—and Casey in particular—was well documented in newspapers of the day.

Chapter 5: Stupid Regulations

To understand Ronald Reagan's thinking during the Iran-Contra operation (and its aftermath) I relied on his own words, gleaning what I could from his White House diaries, his testimony in the Poindexter trial, notes from internal White House meetings, and texts of his contemporaneous speeches and press conferences. The "Report of the Congressional Committees Investigating the Iran/Contra Affair" (including Representative Dick Cheney's minority report) provided much detail on the affair, but the "Final Report of the Independent Counsel for Iran/Contra Matters," authored by prosecutor Lawrence Walsh, is the definitive source. Walsh also wrote a pretty good book, *Firewall: The Iran-Contra Conspiracy and Cover-up*.

I was able to access the minutes from the June 25, 1984, National Security Planning Group meeting at the National Security Archive website at George Washington University. The National Security Archive is a wonderful resource in general—dogged, aggressive, fair, and with mad organizational skills that would please even the most persnickety Virgo.

Aside from the aforementioned books about Reagan, *Landslide: The Unmaking of the President, 1984–1988,* by Jane Mayer and Doyle McManus, and Robert Timberg's *The Nightingale's Song* were great sources.

On the question of Ed Meese and executive power, it's worth anybody's time to read Charlie Savage's landmark book *Takeover: The Return of the Imperial Presidency and the Subversion of American Democracy.* And thanks to the *New York Times* for publishing verbatim the remarkable exchange between Attorney General Ed Meese and Sen. Daniel Inouye I've excerpted in this chapter.

Chapter 6: Mylanta, 'Tis of Thee

I relied as much as I could on the contemporaneous notes and diaries and the memories of the key players in the run-up to the First Gulf War. *All the Best, George Bush: My Life in Letters and Other Writings,* along with *A World Transformed,* which the former president wrote with Brent Scowcroft, provided the backbone of the chapter. Chairman of the Joint Chiefs Colin Powell, Secretary of Defense Dick Cheney, and

Gen. Norman Schwarzkopf each wrote autobiographies. And Karen DeYoung's biography *Soldier: The Life of Colin Powell* is helpful for anyone who wants to understand the general's thinking. There was a lot of good DC-based journalism around that time, but R. W. Apple's reporting on Washington on the verge of war was particularly sharp and uncompromising. Michael R. Gordon was already doing great work covering military matters.

C-SPAN has the video of the Ron Dellums press conference on the occasion of announcing his lawsuit. The PBS series *Frontline* has a useful reference website on the First Gulf War.

Chapter 7: Doing More with Less (Hassle)

The October 1995 "Report of the Defense Science Board: Task Force on Quality of Life" and the August 1996 "Report of the Defense Science Board: Task Force on Outsourcing and Privatization" were useful guides to the fiscal situation and thinking at the Pentagon in the 1990s. Anthony Bianco and Stephanie Anderson Forest did farsighted and smart reporting on the rise of private military contractors in *BusinessWeek*.

The United States General Accounting Office (GAO) reports on LOGCAP operations published in February 1997 and September 2000 provided details into both the benefits and costs of civilian augmentation in the Balkans.

The best reporting on the DynCorp sex-trafficking problems was done by Kelly Patricia O'Meara in the *Washington Times* magazine *Insight* and by Robert Capps in *Salon*. A November 2002 report by Human Rights Watch, "Hopes Betrayed: Trafficking of Women and Girls to Post-Conflict Bosnia and Herzegovina for Forced Prostitution," is a harrowing portrait of that world. Kathryn Bolkovac's memoir of her experiences in Bosnia, *The Whistleblower: Sex Trafficking, Military Contractors, and One Woman's Fight for Justice*, was a useful guide to the culture inside DynCorp.

Again, I drew largely from the memoirs of Dick Cheney and Colin Powell, as well as Karen DeYoung's biography of Powell, to understand their thinking about the budget realities at the Pentagon during the

George Herbert Walker Bush administration. *Rise of the Vulcans,* by James Mann, provided further detail. "Defense Strategy for the 1990s: The Regional Defense Strategy," published in January 1993, and authored by Cheney, was useful reading, as was the Clinton administration's "National Performance Review. Report on Reinventing the Department of Defense," published in September 1996.

Corporate Warriors: The Rise of the Privatized Military Industry by P. W. Singer provides great information about MPRI and other private military operations; so does author David Isenberg's *Shadow Force.*

To understand the conflict in the Balkans and the Clinton administration's response, I recommend *A Problem from Hell: America and the Age of Genocide* by Samantha Power. I also drew on reports by the US State Department and the Senate Foreign Relations Committee; President Bill Clinton's autobiography, *My Life;* and writings by Clinton administration officials Madeleine K. Albright and Nancy Soderberg.

Chapter 8: "One Hell of a Killing Machine"

There has been much good reporting on the drone warfare and other secret and privatized military operations in recent years. For bringing to light what the government would prefer to be essentially secret, credit is due Jane Mayer, James Risen, Mark Mazzetti, Greg Miller, Julie Tate, Nick Turse, Jeremy Scahill, and Eric Schmitt. The *Long War Journal* and New America Foundation have made it their mission to track each and every drone strike in Pakistan, and should be commended for it.

Thanks to David Corn for the "million years" quote from John McCain in 2008.

The reporting at the *Army Times* proved a great source throughout, but especially on the issues of the Guard and Reserves.

Chapter 9: An $8 Trillion Fungus Among Us

A number of official government and military reports on the nation's nuclear program, as well as congressional testimony of Air Force generals, helped in telling the recent (and not so recent) history of American nuclear weapons. The GAO's March 2009 report for a House subcommittee, entitled "NNSA and DOD Need to More Effectively Manage the Stockpile Life Extension Program," explains the Fogbank problem.

For the events surrounding the Minot-Barksdale *whoopsie* and the general readiness at Barksdale, I have relied in the main on the official reports commissioned by the Air Force and the Pentagon in the debacle's aftermath. Thank you to the pseudonymous "Nate Hale" for shaking loose the "Limited Nuclear Surety Inspection Report" that followed the September 2007 Air Combat Command inspection at Barksdale. Reporting by Joby Warrick and Walter Pincus in the *Washington Post* offered extra detail of the Minot-to-Barksdale mishap.

Jaya Tiwari and Cleve J. Gray have compiled a most useful index of nuclear near-disasters in their paper "U.S. Nuclear Weapons Accidents." For those particularly interested in the North Carolina incident, it's worth poking around the website Broken Arrow: Goldsboro, NC, The Truth Behind North Carolina's Brush with Disaster at www.ibiblio.org/bomb/index.html.

Readers might also enjoy *Nuclear Family Vacation: Travels in the World of Atomic Weaponry,* by Nathan Hodge and Sharon Weinberger; and *Bomb Scare: The History and Future of Nuclear Weapons,* by my friend Joseph Cirincione.

Epilogue: You Build It, You Own It

Although I have not used them as sources per se, readers interested in exploring the basic thesis here from different analytical and historical vantage points might find useful the writings of James Fallows (*National Defense*), Andrew Bacevich (*The New American Militarism, The Long War, The Limits of Power*), James Carroll (*House of War*), and Eugene Jarecki (*The American Way of War*).

Acknowledgments

I'm the slowest writer on earth. I make sloth look blurry with speed. First thanks therefore go to Crown and the very patient Rachel Klayman for letting this whole process take as long as it needed to.

Thanks to Mark Zwonitzer for expert research, assistance, and yet further calm, good-humored patience. With Mark: book; without Mark: no book. And thanks to Sierra Pettengill for appropriately ferocious fact checking.

If I ever write a sequel to this book that's just about the inadvertently hilarious policy and culture of nuclear weapons, it will be thanks to the early and very fun research I did on that topic with my friend Shelley Lewis.

Laurie Liss at Sterling Lord Literistic has been a stalwart pal as well as an extraordinarily effective noodge; I'm thankful also to the SLL office staff for letting me essentially take up room and board in their conference room on Bleecker Street for months at a time.

My boss at MSNBC, Phil Griffin, my executive producer, Bill Wolff, and the whole staff of *The Rachel Maddow Show* have been more than indulgent with the time, brainpower, and stress diversion this book entailed. Special thanks to Lauren Skowronski and Julia Nutter for making impossible logistics work as if by magic.

Thank you to Penny Simon at Crown for deftly ushering the book into the world in a way that I'd have no clue how to arrange on my own.

But mostly I am thankful to my beloved Susan, for letting this project and my obsession with these ideas take up so much space in our lives. Without family support, I never would have been able to do this.

And without the genuine inspiration I get from my generation of veterans, I never would have wanted to do this. Iraq and Afghanistan veterans are less than 1 percent of the US population. But they are a huge part of why I'm bullish on America's capacity to adapt, lead, and succeed in the twenty-first century.

Index

About the Author

Rachel Maddow has hosted the Emmy Award–winning *Rachel Maddow Show* on MSNBC since 2008. Before that, she was at Air America Radio for the duration of that underappreciated enterprise. She has a doctorate in politics from Oxford and a bachelor's degree in public policy from Stanford. She lives in rural western Massachusetts and New York City with her partner, artist Susan Mikula, and an enormous dog.